Guide to Growing
Beautiful
Flowers

Meredith® Books
Des Moines, Iowa

Miracle-Gro Guide to Growing Beautiful Flowers
Project Editor: Kate Carter Frederick
Editor: Denny Schrock
Contributing Writers: Janna Beckerman, John Pohly,
    Ray Rothenberger, Curtis Smith, Ellen Strother, Jon Traunfeld
Contributing Technical Reviewer: Ashton Ritchie
Photo Researcher: Harijs Priekulis
Copy Chief: Terri Fredrickson
Editorial Operations Manager: Karen Schirm
Edit and Design Production Coordinator: Mary Lee Gavin
Editorial and Design Assistants: Kathleen Stevens, Kairee Windsor
Marketing Product Managers: Aparna Pande, Isaac Petersen,
    Gina Rickert, Stephen Rogers, Brent Wiersma, Tyler Woods
Book Production Managers: Pam Kvitne,
    Marjorie J. Schenkelberg, Rick von Holdt, Mark Weaver
Photographers: Marty Baldwin, Scott Little, Blaine Moats,
    Dean Schoeppner, Jay Wilde
Contributing Production Designer and Stylists: Brad Ruppert,
    Sundie Ruppert, Karen Weir Jimerson
Contributing Copy Editors: Barbara Feller-Roth, Fran Gardner
Contributing Technical Proofreaders: Deb Brown, B. Rosie Lerner,
    Mary H. Meyer, Bob Polomski, Ann Marie VanDer Zanden,
    Douglas F. Welsh
Contributing Proofreaders: Mason Dolan, Alison Glascock,
    Juliet Jacobs
Contributing Map Illustrator: Jana Fothergill
Contributing Prop/Photo Stylist: Susan Strelecki
Indexer: Ellen Davenport

Additional Editorial Contributions from
Shelton Design Studios
Director: Ernie Shelton

Additional Editorial Contributions from
Art Rep Services
Director: Chip Nadeau
Illustrator: Dave Brandon

Meredith® Books
Executive Director, Editorial: Gregory H. Kayko
Executive Director, Design: Matt Strelecki
Executive Editor/Group Manager: Benjamin W. Allen
Senior Associate Design Director: Tom Wegner

Publisher and Editor in Chief: James D. Blume
Editorial Director: Linda Raglan Cunningham
Executive Director, Marketing: Jeffrey B. Myers
Executive Director, New Business Development: Todd M. Davis
Executive Director, Sales: Ken Zagor
Director, Operations: George A. Susral
Director, Production: Douglas M. Johnston
Business Director: Jim Leonard

Vice President and General Manager: Douglas J. Guendel

Meredith Publishing Group
President: Jack Griffin
Senior Vice President: Bob Mate

Meredith Corporation
Chairman and Chief Executive Officer: William T. Kerr
President and Chief Operating Officer: Stephen M. Lacy

In Memoriam: E.T. Meredith III (1933-2003)

All of us at Meredith® Books are dedicated to providing you with the
information and ideas you need to enhance your home and garden. We
welcome your comments and suggestions about this book. Write to us at:
    Meredith Gardening Books
    1716 Locust St.
    Des Moines, IA 50309–3023

If you would like to purchase any of our gardening, home improvement,
cooking, crafts, or home decorating and design books, check wherever
quality books are sold. Or visit us at: meredithbooks.com

Thanks to
Janet Anderson, Kathryn Anderson, Walt Blake, Wil Bruere, Joyce
DeWitt, Callie Dunbar, Khanh Hamilton, Wes Hunsberger, Rosemary
Kautzky, Cathy Long, Mary Irene Swartz,

Photographers
(Photographers credited may retain copyright ©
to the listed photographs.)
L = Left, R = Right, C = Center, B = Bottom, T = Top

Patricia Bruno/Positive Images: 63T, 88BL, 109BR, 119BL;
Karen Bussolini/Positive Images: 105BL; **David Cavagnaro:**
3BR, 30TL, 33B, 35T, 38T, 38BL, 39T, 43BL, 44TR, 45T, 46T, 46BL,
49BL, 50B, 51B, 52T, 55BL, 57T, 59BL, 60T, 62T, 62BL, 68T, 71T,
71BL, 72BL, 74T, 77T, 78T, 79T, 80B, 86BL, 90T, 92BL, 94BL, 97T,
100T, 100BL, 101BL, 105T, 110T, 110B, 113BL, 115BL, 118T, 120T,
123T, 124BL, 125BL, 126T, 127C, 132TR, 133BL, 135B, 137T, 137B;
Richard Day/Daybreak Imagery: 123B; **John Glover:** 3BL, 33T,
34T, 35TC, 47T, 50T, 52BL, 53BL, 56B, 58BL, 67T, 67BL, 70T, 74B,
75BL, 78BL, 79TC, 79B, 84BL, 85CL, 87BL, 98BL, 101T, 105TR,
108CL, 111BL, 117T, 119T, 119BR, 124T, 125T, 127T, 131T, 131B,
133B, 136BL; **Meredith Hebden/Positive Images:** 118BL;
Margaret Hensel/Positive Images: 70BL, 123BL; **Jerry Howard/
Positive Images:** 34TC, 61T, 95T; **Bill Johnson:** 77B; **Rosemary
Kautzky:** 69B, 76LC, 82BR, 88T, 103B, 104BL, 136T; **David
Liebman:** 92TR; **Lee Lockwood/Positive Images:** 35B; **Elvin
McDonald:** 23BR; **Jacob Mosser III/Positive Images:** 34BC; **Jerry
Pavia:** 33TC, 34B, 36T, 36BL, 37T, 39BL, 40BL, 41BL, 42T, 43T, 44T,
45B, 48BL, 51T, 55T, 57BL, 58T, 60B, 62B, 65T, 65B, 68B, 69T, 73T,
76T, 78TR, 82T, 85T, 90BR, 90BL, 91BL, 92T, 93BL, 96T, 96BL, 98T,
99B, 102B, 104T, 105B, 107T, 109T, 109BL, 115T, 116B, 117BL, 120B,
121T, 122T, 122BL, 128B, 129T, 130T, 132TL, 134BL, 137BL; **Diane
A. Pratt/Positive Images:** 66B, 102T; **Susan A. Roth:** 41TR; **Pam
Spaulding/Positive Images:** 32, 40T, 41T, 75T, 83T, 112T, 113T,
130BL; **Albert Squillace/Positive Images:** 33BC, 89BL, 134T;
Michael Thompson: 29B, 35BC, 42B, 44BL, 47TC, 48T, 49T, 53T,
56T, 59T, 61BL, 63BL, 64T, 64BL, 73BL, 80T, 81T, 81BL, 84T, 86T,
87T, 89C, 90BC, 94T, 97B, 99T, 106T, 106B, 107CL, 108T, 111T,
112BL, 114T, 114B, 116T, 121BL, 126BL, 128T, 128TR, 129B, 133T,
135T; **Ann Truelove/Unicorn Stock Photos:** 41B; **Martien
Vinesteijn Photography/Positive Images:** 82BL, 91T, 103T;
Rick Wetherbee: 72T

If you would like more information on other Miracle-Gro products,
call 888-295-6902 or visit us at: www.miraclegro.com

CONTENTS

Chapter 1
PREPARING TO PLANT

Great gardens start with great soil. Before you begin to dig, select the best site for your plants and the best plants for your site.

SITE SELECTION

Selecting specific planting sites and creating the best conditions for overall healthy plant growth entails thoughtful planning and preparation, but these steps will pay off handsomely in the long run. The success of a particular plant in a particular site will be determined by a host of factors, such as soil conditions, sun and wind exposure, space limitations, and microclimates (small areas where soil and climate differ from surrounding areas) affected usually by terrain.

Match Plants to the Site
As a general rule, flowering plants grow best in loose, friable soil that drains well and contains some organic matter. Know each of your plants' specific requirements.

If your soil is less than ideal, don't despair. There are plants for virtually any site, and most sites have room for improvement. Phlox, butterfly weed, and salvia require few nutrients and grow in poor soil, for example.

For dry sites, choose drought-tolerant plants, such as yarrow, yucca, and gaura. Improve the soil with loads of compost, composted manure, chopped leaves, and other organic matter. If your site is mostly shady, select plants that are adaptable to the conditions.

Where a sloping site prompts erosion, alter the terrain by forming terraces. Include ground covers in the plantings and mulch heavily to control erosion.

Identify microclimates in your landscape. Areas next to the house are warmer than outlying areas, for instance.

YOUR SOIL'S PROFILE

If you were to dig and remove a 2- to 3-foot-deep slice of your backyard, you would expose your soil's profile. The top 4 to 8 inches of the slice is topsoil—dark and fertile due to organic matter. Below the topsoil the profile changes gradually in color and texture depending on the soil's origin. Many gardeners find that their subsoil increases in clay content and stickiness with increasing depth. Subsoils heavy in clay may restrict the flow of water and air and the growth of plant roots. The rooting depth for most home garden plants rarely exceeds 4 feet.

Soil texture is an important aspect of the soil. It affects drainage, root growth, and plant stability. To test texture, squeeze a handful of lightly moistened soil. Any soil with good texture forms a ball that can be easily broken apart with your fingers. Very sandy soil will not form a ball. (It will dry out and leach nutrients rapidly.) Heavy, clay soil forms a sticky ball that does not break apart. (It tends to pack down and suffocate roots.)

When squeezed, a handful of heavy, poorly draining clay soil sticks together.

TROUBLESHOOTING SOIL PROBLEMS

The first step toward correcting a soil problem is identifying the specific cause. Gather soil samples and get soil tested.

Problem	What Can Be Done?
No topsoil The topsoil may have washed away or was removed during construction.	■ Purchase topsoil. (See page 6.) ■ Mix purchased topsoil with the existing topsoil. ■ Make raised beds and fill them with a mixture of purchased topsoil and compost.
Heavy, unmanageable clay soil	■ Loosen subsoil with a garden fork; work lots of organic matter into the top 12 inches of soil.
Compaction Driving machinery and vehicles on clay soils results in poor root growth, drowned roots, and root diseases. Hardpan is compacted soil impervious to water, air, and nutrients; it can occur at any depth and inhibits root growth.	■ Physically loosen the subsoil or break open the hardpan and add organic matter. ■ Plant in raised beds. ■ Plant a deep-rooted cover crop. ■ Plant a permanent, well-adapted ground cover.
Poor drainage To test drainage, dig a hole 12 inches deep and 8 inches in diameter. Fill it with water. Fill it again 12 hours later. All the water should drain out within 2 to 3 hours.	■ Grow plants adapted to wet soil. ■ Regrade the area to eliminate low spots. ■ Install drainage tile.
Erosion Rainwater can quickly wash away topsoil.	■ Install splash blocks or drainpipes under downspouts. ■ Plant bare soil with a cover crop, ground cover (from turf to trees), or mulch. ■ Terrace sloped ground that is cultivated.
Low fertility Many soils are naturally low in fertility.	■ Add organic matter: 3 to 4 cubic yards per 1,000 square feet (4 to 5 bushels per 100 square feet). ■ Feed according to product directions.
Extremely low or high pH Extreme pH can cause nutrient deficiency and nutrient toxicity.	■ Test soil and adjust pH according to the results.

To take a soil sample for testing, dig trowel-size samples from several places and thoroughly mix in a clean container.

Apply compost or thoroughly composted manure annually to planting beds to boost soil fertility.

Use a garden fork to dig the amendment into the top 12 inches of soil at the start or the end of the gardening season.

IMPROVING YOUR SOIL

After moving into a home in a new or an established neighborhood, gardeners are frequently disappointed to discover that the soil is causing flowering plants to struggle for survival. The soil may be full of clay or stones, too acidic or shallow, compacted, or lacking in organic matter.

With a little knowledge and a good bit of determination, you can use soil amendments to improve poor soil and make your landscape flourish. Soil amendments are materials that are mixed into the topsoil to promote healthy plant growth. Plant food is not usually classified as a soil amendment because its primary function is to supply nutrients. Soil amendments, such as lime, change the soil pH. Others, such as compost, supply nutrients that are most important as soil conditioners—bulky organic materials that improve soil structure. The addition of any organic matter, from composted manure to chopped leaves, leads to better air and water movement and root growth.

Most flowering plants perform best in soils high in organic matter. Enriched with organic amendments, soil becomes loose and easy to dig and plant in. It contains a large number of earthworms. You won't see a dramatic change the first year when you add soil amendments to a difficult soil, but over three to five years of regular incorporation, you will witness significant improvement in soil conditions and plant growth. Because organic matter is used up through oxidation, especially in warm climates and where soils are frequently tilled, organic matter should be added to the soil every year.

Add at least one inch of compost to beds each year.

TYPES OF SOIL AMENDMENTS

Coir is made from coconut fibers. It is used in commercial soil potting mixes to help prevent overwatering and underwatering. Coir improves the water-holding capacity of soil mixes and reduces the shrinkage that causes the soil to pull away from the sides of a container. Reduced shrinkage results in easier watering because water soaks into the root ball rather than running down the gap between the root ball and the pot.

Compost is made from decayed organic materials such as straw, grass clippings, newspaper, leaves, certain food wastes, spent plants, hay, chipped brush and trees, and farm manures. Compost holds 225 percent of its weight in water and, unlike peat moss, does not repel water when dry. Compost is not nutrient dense—it may contain only 1 percent nitrogen by weight—but it slowly releases a wide range of nutrients essential for plant growth. The pH of most compost is in the 6.6 to 7.2 range. Compost is the most important and frequently used soil amendment. It is easy to make at home and provides long-lasting benefits. Incorporate it into soils prior to planting, spread it over beds of perennials and annuals (topdressing), and use it to grow plants in containers.

Composted manure helps build good soil. Check with nearby farms and ask for manure that has been mixed with bedding material and allowed to compost for at least two months. Farm manures usually contain 1 percent or less of each of the three main nutrients found in plant foods—nitrogen, phosphorus, and potassium.

Gypsum is calcium sulfate. Gypsum can be applied to heavy clay soils to improve soil structure and add calcium and sulfur without raising the soil pH. It also ties up excess magnesium. Gypsum can help leach out sodium when mixed into the top few inches of soil with a high salt concentration from deicing materials. This helps prevent the burning of plant roots from excess salts.

Organic mulches, such as straw, newspaper, and grass clippings can be tilled into the soil at the end of the growing season. Others, such as shredded pine bark and hardwood chips, are not incorporated, but they act as soil amendments by slowly decomposing in place.

Peat moss is partially decomposed sphagnum moss mined from bogs. It absorbs 10 to 20 times its weight in water, but it repels water when it's dry. Peat moss contains little nutritive value. It is very acidic and is often mixed into beds prepared for acid-loving plants, such as blueberry, azalea, and rhododendron.

Sand can be used in small amounts to improve clay soils and create better growing conditions for certain types of plants, such as Mediterranean herbs and cacti. Only sharp builder's sand should be used. Avoid adding fine sand that causes clay to set up like concrete.

Sawdust that is well-aged and decayed can be added to soil. Fresh sawdust ties up nitrogen as it decomposes.

Topsoil can be purchased by the bag or in bulk. Quality varies widely. Inspect bulk topsoil prior to purchase and delivery and ask about its history: Where did it come from? Have tests been performed for pH and nutrient levels and for heavy metals such as lead and cadmium? Blended topsoil and leaf compost mixes are excellent for an instant raised-bed garden. Purchase the material by the cubic yard, if it is available in your area.

Water-absorbing polymers are sold as granules that can absorb 300 to 400 times their weight in water. As soil dries, stored water is released slowly back into it. Polymers are ideal for potted plants, but their cost-effectiveness is questionable for planting beds.

PLANT SELECTION

Resist the impulse to buy plants you don't need just because they are inexpensive or appealing. Your plant selection should follow the design that you created for your yard. There will always be opportunities to move, divide, and add plants. Consider the eventual, mature size of each plant. Squeezing in extra plants leads to overcrowding and frustration. Crowding causes stressful growing conditions that may contribute to insect and disease problems. Buy dwarf forms of desired plants when they are appropriate and available.

Always select plants adapted to your specific landscape and general region. Consult with local nurseries, gardening experts, and cooperative extension publications to determine a plant's pest susceptibility and invasiveness. If you live in an urban area, choose plants that can tolerate challenging site conditions such as compacted soil and air pollution.

Busy people often look for trouble-free plants to stock their landscape. Native plants are widely promoted as the key to a beautiful, low-maintenance garden. It's sensible to select plants that are indigenous to your region. However, many nonnative plants have become invasive and undesirable. It's a good idea to use native plants where appropriate, but don't exclude all nonnatives on principle. Native plants also need to be pruned, mulched, and watered to grow well.

WHAT TO LOOK FOR

All flowering annuals, vegetables, and herbs are grown and sold in some type of plastic or fiber container. The containers are a convenient way to purchase, transport, and plant nursery stock and herbaceous perennials.

Take your time when selecting plants for your garden. Bring a checklist to help remind you what species and cultivars will best fit into your plan. Gently remove the container to examine the root system.

Look for these characteristics of high-quality plants:
■ If a plant is pot bound and its root ball forms a tight mass with no soil between the roots, look for a better plant.
■ Plants are true to type; they have the correct leaf color, size, and shape. They also have the correct tag. (Mislabeling is not uncommon, especially with bedding plants and herb transplants.)
■ The root system is white to pale beige in color, and roots are growing throughout the container or root ball.
■ Top growth and root mass of container plants is balanced. Bedding plants and perennial transplants are generally as wide as they are tall.

■ The planting mix should not be matted at the edges or the bottom of the root ball.

WHAT ARE PLANT PLUGS?

Many nurseries and garden cetners offer sturdy starts—usually annuals—grown as plant plugs in multipacks. Marigolds, dusty miller, and similar seed-grown bedders are often available as one-inch-long miniplugs. Vegetatively propagated annuals and tropicals, such as coleus and marguerites, are grown from cuttings and appear in larger plugs.

Plugs reduce root trauma during transplanting. Popped out of their growth trays and transplanted into 4-inch pots, plugs soon develop into substantial plants. When transplanting, pinch off flowers and buds to force the plant's energy into root growth. Sacrificing those first flowers might be difficult, but you'll be rewarded with more blooms later.

Perennials come in many sizes. Here's an assortment:

(A) cell pack
(B) 3-inch pot
(C) 4-inch pot
(D) 6-inch pot
(E) 8-inch or 1-gallon pot
(F) 5-gallon tub
(G) rooted cutting
(H) division
(I) field-grown clump

Chapter 2
PLANTING BASICS

Planting is one of the most satisfying acts of gardening. Proper planting techniques have a profound impact on the beauty and productivity of the home landscape.

DIG IN

The best times to plant are when soil and environmental conditions are favorable for rapid root growth. Flowering plants are typically planted in spring when all danger of frost is past or in early fall. Spring-flowering bulbs are usually planted in fall before the ground freezes.

If you need to hold plants that are ready to go into the ground because you don't have time to plant them or the site is not yet prepared, keep the roots moist and cool. Keep bulbs cool and dry. Gradually introduce seedlings or plants grown in a greenhouse to outdoor life. Set them in a protected place, such as under a shrub in the yard, for a few days until they acclimate to the current conditions.

Before digging, set plants on the planting area and imagine how they will appear when they grow. Move the plants around, adjusting their spacing, based on their potential mature size. Adjust the arrangement until it pleases you.

An ideal marigold transplant displays a loose web of roots, a stocky stem, rich green foliage, and a perky bloom.

THE RIGHT PLANTING TOOLS

When you're ready to plant, select the best tool. Match the size of the tool—trowel, spade, or shovel—to the size of the planting holes needed. A trowel is best for planting seedlings or plugs from cell packs and up to 4-inch pots. Use a shovel or spade when making homes for plants in 6-inch pots and larger and for small bare-root plants. Once you unpot the plant and gently loosen the roots, spreading them in preparation for planting, you will probably need to make a bigger hole than you first thought.

PLANTING 1-2-3

Before planting—whenever possible—loosen soil to a depth of 12 inches and amend it with organic matter. If you're digging in between existing plantings, work carefully to avoid damaging nearby roots.

First, dig a hole as deep as the plant's container and 1 ½ to 3 times as wide, allowing for root growth.

Second, squeeze the container and gently tap it to remove the plant. Use your fingers to gently tease apart the roots. If the plant is tightly pot-bound, use a knife or trowel to cut into the root mass and loosen the roots. Spread the roots into the planting hole.

Third, spread amended soil around the root ball, filling the hole. Lightly press the soil around the plant to ensure good contact between roots and soil. Water thoroughly to settle the soil and moisten the root zone. If rain doesn't assist you in the process, water new plantings every few days until they're established.

Match the digging tool to the job. Use a trowel to make a small hole in a tight space, for instance.

PLANTING BULBS

Plant spring-flowering bulbs in fall and summer-flowering bulbs in spring. Find a sunny place in the yard or a roomy container and dig a hole that's three times the bulb's depth. For instance, plant a 2-inch-deep tulip bulb 6 inches deep; a 1-inch-deep grape hyacinth bulb goes 3 inches deep. Place groups of five to nine bulbs in planting holes to create natural-looking clumps rather than straight rows.

To create drifts of flowering bulbs in the lawn or garden that appear spontaneous, follow the steps shown below to naturalize bulbs. Some varieties of spring-flowering bulbs naturalize easily, blooming year after year and spreading on their own. Choose jonquils, species tulips, and other bulbs that are especially suited for naturalizing.

1

To naturalize bulbs, outline a planting area with an extension cord or hose and toss handfuls of bulbs onto the ground.

2

Using a trowel, slice through the turf along each bulb and open a pocket of sod. Tuck the bulb under the turf.

3

Gently tamp the sod in place over each bulb. After planting, water the entire area thoroughly.

STRATEGIES FOR GROUPING PLANTS

Some gardeners find it tempting to use color as the primary organizing principle when planning flower gardens. However, grouping plants by other criteria—such as mass, texture, or lines in the garden—is just as worthy of attention, for these subtleties contribute to the design's overall impact.

Mass refers to a plant's visual weight and bulk. Plant size, leaf color, and texture combine to give the effect of mass. For example, a large, dark-colored, bold-textured plant has more mass than a small, light green or bluish perennial with finely textured foliage. The mass of a plant is significant not just in relationship to other plant masses in the design, but also to open space.

When thinking about size, it's important to remember that a perennial may not grow to its expected full height the first year or two in a garden. Once established, the plant

Waves of colorful blooms roll across a perennial-packed garden from June through September. Repeated plantings include feverfew, coreopsis, Shasta daisy, and lily.

will not grow any taller but will continue to grow outward. When you plan a garden, keep in mind the perennial's mature spread—the width it can grow before needing to be divided—so that you allow enough space for it.

Mass similar flowers

Planting in drifts—grouping like flowers or planting several plants of one perennial species together—is a way to create mass. Drifts have more power than single blooms. For a natural effect, mass flowers in asymmetrical drifts flowing in and out of other flower groups. Use odd numbers of plants arranged densely in the middle and sparsely near the edges.

Use texture artfully

Skillfully combining textures enhances a garden's charm. Take both the flowers and the foliage into account. For perennials in particular, foliage is on view far longer than the flowers. To achieve a harmonious yet eye-catching look, combine coarse plants with plants of medium texture. At the same time, group medium-textured plants next to those with fine textures.

Include bedding plants

Annual all-stars are born to shine for one season only. The plants stand up and spread their colors under the hottest sun. The blooms keep coming until frost or seeds develop. Then the plants have finished their cycle, and you can add them to the compost pile. In the warmest climates, such as Southern coastal gardens, annuals can be planted in fall for blooms in winter and earliest spring, until the tropical heat does them in. Help bedding plants continue their show by shearing them to one-third of their size in mid- to late- summer. Feed the plants and watch them bloom with renewed vigor.

Every new gardening season brings a crop of new varieties. Plant breeders constantly strive to produce plants of outstanding vigor and nonstop blooms in fun new colors. that combine easily. Take advantage of the possibilities!

Read plant labels for recommended minimum and maximum spacing. Space closer together for faster effect and farther apart for economy.

PLANTING IN CONTAINERS

For the past decade, interest in all forms of container gardening has exploded. The quest for beautiful, colorful, and low-maintenance gardens has been matched by the introduction of innovative styles of containers and new dwarf cultivars of all types of plants. Even gardeners with large yards and extensive garden areas enjoy the beauty and intimacy of flowers in window boxes or containers on a deck or patio.

Containers provide versatility in gardening. Use them to create dramatic accents throughout the landscape; to make plants portable, shifting them from sun to shade or to fill empty spots in the garden; to add color and interest where nothing else will grow; and to lend an established look to a new garden.

Having a minilandscape plan for your container plantings will help make them successful. Decide what you'd like to grow and what size, type, and shape of containers will be needed. Will you need to move the containers once they are planted? If so, the containers should be light enough for one person to lift easily or have casters on the bottom for greater mobility. If you are placing containers directly on a wood, brick, or concrete surface, be aware that the containers may leave stains from plant food and organic compounds in the planting media that leach out of the drainage holes. Use pot feet to avoid this situation.

A combination of ornamental sweet potato vine, silvery helichrysum, magenta petunias, and yellow daisies makes a colorful accent.

Also, plan to empty annual containers at the end of the season, composting the spent plants and cleaning the pots before storing them. Protect potted perennials from damage caused by the freezing and thawing cycles in cold winter areas. Either transplant perennials to the garden in early fall or gather potted plants in a well-protected place until spring.

TYPES OF CONTAINERS & PLANTING MEDIA

Suitable containers range from elegant galvanized buckets and glazed terra-cotta to stone-look urns and half-barrel planters. Inexpensive plastic troughs may not add beauty to your balcony, but they are durable and inexpensive and can produce excellent results. Select from a wide array of sizes, shapes, and materials or make your own containers to suit the size and style of your outdoor areas.

Large containers become extremely heavy when filled with potting mix, water, and plants and can be difficult to move. Conversely, lightweight containers holding large plants may tip over in strong winds.

Garden soil is too variable, heavy, and weed-infested to be of practical use for container plants. Most gardeners choose from various types and brands of growing medium sold in retail garden centers. Some gardeners create their own potting mix, using a combination of store-bought and locally available ingredients.

Whether you make it or buy it, a good potting mix will:
- hold water and nutrients;
- be low in soluble salts and have a pH of 6.0–7.0;
- have adequate porosity, drain well, and allow strong root growth;
- be lightweight; and
- be free of weeds, diseases, insects, and contaminants.

Commercial potting mixes usually meet most of these requirements and are suitable for most types of containers and plants. Lightweight, soilless mixes contain three principal ingredients: peat moss, vermiculite (a mined mineral that holds water), and perlite (expanded volcanic rock that improves drainage). Manufacturers often add lime (because peat moss is acidic) and plant nutrients (because the main ingredients lack them).

Potting soil is a generic term for a wide range of products that differ greatly in content and quality. If you find one you like, stick with it. But you're likely to be more successful using commercial potting mixes. Enhance them by mixing in high-quality compost in a ratio of one-third compost to two-thirds potting mix. Used growing media from disease- and pest-free plants can be reused the following year. However, nutrients will be depleted, and the mix should be amended before planting. Feeding will be especially important for plants grown in a recycled medium.

Add planting media to pots, leaving enough headroom for watering.

Pots in full sun may need to be watered every day to keep plants healthy.

Chapter 3
POST-PLANTING CARE

Beautiful gardens depend on the proper amount of water and food to keep them in top shape.

SUPPLEMENTAL WATERING

In many regions it is possible to garden with only the water provided by natural precipitation. However, gardeners understand that plants sometimes need additional water to supplement rainfall. Even areas with sufficient total moisture may not have proper seasonal distribution for optimal plant growth. Landscapes adapted to frequent precipitation suffer in seasons when natural rainfall fails to arrive in sufficient quantities. Irrigation is needed to establish new plants in most landscapes. In arid regions, the need for irrigation is obvious. But the diversity and complexity of irrigation systems is commonly misunderstood—even where they are used widely.

WATERING NEW PLANTS

Supplying water to developing root systems is the single most important thing you can do for new plants. Flowering plants have relatively shallow root systems and usually require water weekly unless they are well established or drought tolerant.

Natural rainfall alone will probably not give your new plants adequate water at the right time. New plants require regular watering to promote root growth. Here are some guidelines to follow to determine when and how much to water:

Drip irrigation is an efficient method for watering the root zone of perennials.

■ Water all plants after planting. The amount depends on the type of soil, the size of the planting area, and the weather conditions at planting time.

■ Water plants growing in sandy soils more frequently. Soils high in clay absorb, release, and drain water slowly. Adding lots of organic matter to soils helps them hold more water for plant growth and drain away excess water.

■ Water before you notice wilting foliage. New plants require watering two to three times per week in spring if rainfall is lacking.

■ Water plants deeply and thoroughly. Dig down 2 to 4 inches with a trowel or finger to test for moisture.

■ Water in the morning if possible. Avoid wetting foliage if watering late in the day. Plants need time to dry off before nightfall to avoid disease.

■ Water spring-planted shrubs and trees throughout the growing season and into the fall. Roots actively grow in fall even though leaf growth has ceased.

HOW TO WATER

Once your plants are established, slow and deep watering is better than daily spritzing. Short bursts of water promote shallow rooting; deep watering promotes deep rooting. Plants with deep root systems are better able to withstand drought because their roots can search for moisture far into the ground.

Encourage moisture retention in the soil and reduce the need for watering by mulching and incorporating organic matter. A 3-inch layer of organic mulch slows evaporation and helps cool the soil on hot days. Increasing

A long-necked wand attached to a garden hose makes simple work of watering high-hanging baskets.

the content of organic matter in sandy or gravelly soil enhances its capacity to retain moisture.

Two simple items are handy for watering flower gardens: the watering wand and the soaker hose. Long-necked wands are excellent for reaching containers in out-of-the-way locations, as well as watering beds of delicate flowers and seedlings with a gentle yet efficient spray. Soaker hoses apply water gently and deeply. If you buy several and leave them in place for the entire season, you won't have to move them. Simply attach a garden hose to each, one by one, as you work elsewhere in the garden.

Bubblers keep foliage dry while watering a specific plant or series of plants using trenches to direct water where it's needed. Sprinklers, on the other hand, simulate rainfall by wetting the entire plant from above. The best time for overhead watering is in the morning, when sunlight gently dries the leaves.

Drip irrigation reduces water consumption—an especially welcome benefit in parts of the country where water is scarce and expensive. In a bed or container with drip irrigation, water slowly seeps through narrow emitters, giving nearby plants a deep, thorough soaking, with minimal evaporation.

Automatic irrigation systems are costly initially but save a lot of time and work over the years.

Place individual emitters next to the plants you want to water. Here an emitter is being placed in a container of pansies.

HOW MUCH TO WATER

Perennials need an average of 1 to 2 inches of water per week. How do you know if you apply that much?

To measure the output of a sprinkler, let it fill a rain gauge to the 1-inch mark, or use a straight-sided container, such as a coffee can. Filling it may take 15 minutes to six hours, depending on water pressure, hose length, sprinkler type, size of area, wind, and evaporation rate.

To measure the output of a drip or soaker line, check the soil 1 foot from an emitter or the far end of the hose. One inch of water wets clay soil 3 to 4 inches deep and sandy soil 18 inches deep. Dig down that far with a trowel. If the soil feels cool or moist, it has received 1 inch of water. It will take several hours to apply 1 inch of water through a drip system or soaker hose.

UNDERSTAND THE SITE

Every site has unique wet and dry areas. A bed catching overthrow from a neighbor's sprinklers won't need as much water as beds under rain-blocking eaves or next to brick walls, which wick away moisture. Check all beds regularly until you know which are the first and last to dry out. Use those as indicator beds to determine when it is time to water.

XERISCAPE PRINCIPLES

Wise gardeners also apply the concepts of Xeriscaping to their landscapes. The concept of Xeriscape was developed to conserve water in times of drought and in regions with limited availability of water by applying seven principles of good gardening practices to the landscape.

Plans or designs that incorporate proper irrigation zones into the landscape create zones for high water use that must be watered frequently, moderate water use that may be watered infrequently, and low water use that are irrigated only in times of drought. Irrigation zones for each system are included in the landscape. Limit high water use zones and place them where they provide the maximum benefit to the landscape. Trees and shrubs are among the plants in a moderate water use zone. Native plants and plants adapted to natural precipitation occupy the low water use zone.

Use of mulch conserves water and benefits plants in the landscape in a number of ways.

Proper preparation of soil allows better root growth as well as better absorption of water. Addition of organic matter where needed improves the soil's water-holding capacity and provides nutrients to plants.

Use of appropriate turf areas reduces labor and chemical applications when adaptable turfgrass varieties are chosen carefully and planted where water is available in the landscape.

Efficient irrigation maximizes water use efficiency and provides best conditions for plant growth in the landscape.

Selection of appropriate plants requires that plants be sited in the appropriate water use zone and that plants be climatically adapted.

Appropriate maintenance of plants assures that plants are maintained in a manner that maximizes their health, reducing the need for applications of water to compensate for poor plant care.

Group plants of similar water needs for the best plant performance and to avoid wasted water.

A soaker hose placed around hostas is an efficient way to keep moisture-loving plants watered.

WATER HARVEST

A final consideration in landscape irrigation is maximizing the efficiency of natural precipitation for the benefit of plants in the landscape. Use water harvesting methods to collect water falling on structures and paved areas and direct that water to parts of the landscape or into cisterns to hold the water for later use. Gutters, downspouts, and rain barrels help collect and direct rainfall. Otherwise, water falling on hard surfaces usually runs off your property and is unavailable for your plants to use. Water from rainfall is often of much higher quality, with lower mineral content, than water from wells. An additional benefit is that harvested water is free. The cost for harvested water is the cost of installation of the system to collect and direct water within the landscape. Water collected in cisterns can easily be distributed to the landscape through drip systems.

Use gutters and downspouts to collect rainwater and direct it to planting beds.

FEEDING

WHAT DO PLANTS NEED FOR OPTIMAL GROWTH?

Different plants have different feeding requirements, but most need some extra nutrients to stay healthy. Heavy-blooming, sun-loving annuals require more feeding than foliage plants grown in shade.

The three main elements of plant nutrition are nitrogen, phosphorus, and potassium, depicted in order as N-P-K on plant food labels. Nitrogen is necessary for healthy leaves, phosphorus for abundant flowers and fruiting, and potassium (potash) for sturdy roots. Plant food labels express the balance of these nutrients in numerical ratios. For nutrient absorption to occur, soil pH must be neutral (from 6.5 to 7.5) or slightly acidic (5.5 to 6). Some plant foods are designed to acidify the soil. To make soil more alkaline, apply lime according to package directions.

FEEDING SCHEDULE

The only nutrient a plant can use is one dissolved in water. Plant foods applied in solution, such as Miracle-Gro, are usable immediately. They will leach out of the root zone as rain and irrigation water move through soil. So use such products biweekly or monthly in small doses all season.

Many granular plant foods also dissolve readily, although at a slower pace than soluble foods. The garden may need two or three applications of these foods in a season.

Feeding plants in warm climates is as easy as applying one dose of time-release plant food each spring. Because sulfur-coated time-release foods do not reach their maximum release rate until soil temperatures reach 75°F, Osmocote or liquid plant foods are better choices for cool spring climates. To apply liquid plant foods, use a watering can or a hose fitted with a Y-connector and a short siphon hose leading into the pail.

Use houseplant fertilizer sticks to feed containers and hanging baskets that are difficult to reach. Replace sticks every other month.

DETERMINING NUTRIENT DEFICIENCIES

Soil testing gives you an idea of your soil's nutrient status and its pH. If soil is overly acid or alkaline, plants will not grow well. It is a waste of money and resources to apply nutrients that are already available in sufficient quantity. Excess nutrients pollute water supplies. Test the different areas of your landscape every four years.

Home soil test kits are available to gardeners, but they are not as accurate or complete as the analysis performed by a commercial or university soil-testing lab. Contact your local cooperative extension office for a list of approved labs in your state. A basic soil test is relatively inexpensive and measures levels of potassium, phosphorus, magnesium, sulfur, and calcium, as well as the soil pH. A lab issues recommendations for feeding and amending your soil.

TYPES OF PLANT FOODS

A wide range of plant food products are available to the home gardener. Plant foods come in a variety of forms: granules, powder, liquid, coated, and pelletized. Organic plant foods differ from manufactured plant foods in their chemical makeup, nutrient content, release rate of nutrients, and effect on soil structure and biology. However, the nutrients released from both types of plant foods and taken up by plant roots are identical.

Some examples of commercially available organic plant foods include rock phosphate (phosphorus), greensand (potassium), bone meal, fish emulsion, and seaweed extract. Blood meal, cottonseed meal, alfalfa meal, and composted chicken manure are examples of organic nitrogen sources. Compost and well-rotted manure improve soil structure and add various nutrients. Only 5 percent or so of the nitrogen in compost will be available to plant roots in a given year. This may increase for aged farm manure. The rest will be slowly released in subsequent years.

Specialty plant foods: Starter plant foods formulated for seedlings and transplants are high in phosphorus to foster root establishment. Some are ready to use; others should be mixed with water. Follow label directions and apply the solution at the base of each plant or spray it directly on foliage. You'll find plant foods formulated especially for acid-loving plants, roses, bulbs, and others.

The numbers on a label of plant food refer to the percentage of nitrogen, phosphorus, and potassium in the product.

Continuous feeding or instant feeding: Some plant foods can be absorbed immediately upon application. These are known as instant-feeding or highly soluble plant foods. They are useful when rapid results are desired. They come in liquid, powder, or crystal form and are applied to root zones or sprayed directly on foliage.

To reduce maintenance and cut down on the need for reapplications of plant food, inorganic continuous-feeding plant foods, such as Osmocote and sulfur-coated urea, make nutrients available in small amounts over an extended period. Either continuous-feeding or instant-feeding plant foods produce great results.

Label the sample with the name of the area from which the soil was taken.

Home soil testing kits provide rough estimates of soil pH and fertility needs.

Soil testing labs send a detailed report of soil test results.

FEEDING METHODS & EQUIPMENT

Good health in plants depends on a continuous supply of available nutrients from the soil or, in the case of container plants, the growing media. Nutrient needs vary from plant to plant, and the ability of the soil to supply those nutrients varies from site to site.

Once you've determined that you need to feed your plants and you've selected a food, calculate how much to apply, and determine when and how to apply it. Apply plant food to the root zone, the soil surface, or to plant foliage.

At planting or transplanting time, apply a quick-start solution according to package directions to help plants overcome transplant shock, take root, and thrive. Scatter granular food on soil around and between plants. Scratch it into the soil using a hand cultivator or similar tool.

Apply liquid foliar food to leaves once a month during the growing season using a plant sprayer. Attach a sprayer to a garden hose when spraying many plants. Bedding plants may require more frequent feeding.

FEEDING TIPS

Specialized formulations of plant food are available for plants such as African violets.

Pelletized plant foods release their nutrients over several weeks or months.

Sprinkle plant food beside growing plants as a side-dressing to boost growth.

■ Read and follow label directions on plant food products. Manufacturers provide recommendations for use that will give the best results for their product.
■ Use products with low risk of injury to plants. High-quality plant foods are unlikely to injure plants even if applied at rates greater than recommended levels.
■ When applying plant foods during hot, dry weather, water in the plant food, and keep plants actively growing by continuing to water regularly afterwards.
■ Mix plant foods into the top 4 to 6 inches of soil and apply water afterward, if rain is not forecasted.
■ Brush plant food granules off foliage when broadcasting granules in planting areas.
■ Feed trees and shrubs in the fall after leaf drop or during spring and summer when they are actively growing. In cold climates avoid feeding woody plants in late summer or early fall to prevent succulent late-season growth that doesn't harden off properly before winter.

Many potting mixes come with plant food in the mix to help get plants off to a quick start.

CONTINUOUS-FEED PLANT FOODS

Continuous-feed or time-release plant foods have become increasingly popular with gardeners. By selecting plant foods with a continuous release over two, three, or four months, you can match the food that you provide your plants with the length of your growing season. This is a convenient way to save time yet provide the nutrients plants need.

MULCHING

MULCH AS WEED CONTROL

These perennials were planted at the same time but mulched with different materials to demonstrate how a mulch can affect the growth rate. Those grown in high-carbon wood mulch (*top*) are smaller than those grown in leaf mold (*bottom*).

Mulching a weed-free bed keeps it looking neat and offers other benefits. It prevents rapid heating or cooling of the soil, thereby allowing steady root growth. It reduces water loss to evaporation. If an organic material is used as mulch, it becomes soil-enriching humus as it decomposes. In addition, a well-chosen mulch with a color and texture complementary to flowers makes a bed more attractive.

Choose from a range of mulches. Select one that is the color and texture you prefer, is readily available, and fits your garden budget. Also consider scent—some people like the aroma of ground cedar bark or cocoa hulls; others don't.

The best mulches for perennials are organic materials that last throughout the growing season. Mulches that decompose more rapidly, such as grass clippings, must be renewed more often as the mulch layer becomes thin and weed seeds begin to sprout. Those that decompose more slowly or not at all—rocks, large wood chunks, or fabric—may cause extra work for the gardener when dividing perennials, fertilizing, or weeding. They must be moved out of the way and put back later so that they do not mix with the soil as you work.

Do not overmulch. Two to 3 inches of wood chips or bark suffices. Materials that are quicker to break down, such as leaves, cocoa hulls, or compost, can be applied 3 to 4 inches thick.

If piled too deeply initially, grass clippings will rot to a slimy mess, then dry to a water-shedding, cardboardlike mat. Spread clippings no more than 2 inches deep at a time; they'll dry without matting. Once dry, you can put another layer on top of the first.

In extremely hot, humid climates, choose a coarse type of mulch, such as large bark chips, and use it sparingly. Denser mulches allow less air to reach soil and lead to plant injury if conditions become too warm and moist.

TYPES OF MULCH

■ **Newspaper:** All pages, except glossy paper, can be used. Most newspaper inks are soy based and contain no dangerous heavy metals. Overlap the newspaper sections and cover them with straw or grass clippings.

■ **Shredded bark or woodchip mulches:** These are used extensively around foundation plants; cedar or cypress last the longest. Freshen these mulches with a new thin layer each year. Avoid buying bulk mulch that is unseasoned, smells of alcohol, or is steaming and hot to the touch.

■ **Straw, grass clippings, shredded leaves, nut hulls:** These organic mulches decompose rapidly, adding organic matter to the soil.

■ **Black and red plastic:** This type of mulch is laid down on top of the soil and secured to the ground two or more weeks prior to planting. The soil under the plastic warms appreciably, making it popular for use in vegetable gardens where the mulch spurs rapid root growth and boosts yields of warm-weather crops.

■ **Woven landscape fabrics:** Lay these materials over a defined bed and secure the edges to the ground with landscape staples or soil. Cut holes into the fabrics, then plant through them.

Sierra red mulch and other color-enhanced mulches are designed to brighten a garden's appeal with all-season color.

Wood mulches colored a rich black help create a feeling of moist woodland that suits azaleas, wildflowers, and hardy ferns.

Some wood mulches, such as cedar or cypress, last longer than others.

Find cedar mulch in various forms, from shredded to chipped bark.

Attractive pine straw mulch works well in annual and perennial flower beds.

Gravel and crushed-stone mulches prove useful and appealing in the landscape.

PROPER MULCHING

Mulch in spring, after perennial plants have emerged and new plantings are complete. First, fertilize the garden, if needed. Water well or wait for a rain. Remove any weeds. Then spread a 2- to 3-inch layer of mulch between plants, keeping the material several inches away from plant stems. Mulch again in late fall (after the ground has frozen in cold climates or any time in warm climates) to help insulate plant root systems from extreme cold in winter. Mulch potted plants too. Their root systems are exposed to extreme cold.

Use compost as free, super-soil-building mulch. Pile it up to 4 inches on the garden every few months. You also can acquire free or low-cost mulch from local sources, such as pine straw in the Southeast, wood chips in the Northeast, and hazelnut shells in the Northwest.

MULCH MYTHS

Myth 1: Remove mulch in spring to allow soil to warm.

This is a misconception based on English practice. In cool, mild climates and areas far enough north that spring sun is at a low angle, removing the mulch may hasten warming. But in most of the United States, soil temperatures rise rapidly in spring, even under mulch.

Myth 2: Don't mulch in fall until the soil freezes.

No need to wait. Apply mulch anytime existing material is too thin to suppress weed germination. If you mulch heavily to protect crowns during winter, do so after freezing temperatures have stopped growth. Where voles are a problem, do wait until the soil freezes to stop them from taking up residence in the mulch and feeding on plant crowns over winter.

Myth 3: Salt-marsh hay is the best mulch for perennials.

Every region has a traditional, preferred, or most readily available mulch. Salt-marsh hay is no better than any of a dozen other regional mulches. Gardening books written by Northeastern gardeners in the mid-1900s popularized salt-marsh hay, and its reputation lives on.

Myth 4: Oak leaf and pine needle mulches are so acidic they kill plants.

Stop worrying. Almost all organic mulches affect soil pH as they break down. Oak and pine foliage are two that produce a slightly acidic reaction. They are not useful where soil is already very acidic and you want to raise the pH, but in slightly acidic to very alkaline soils they are excellent mulches. The notion that pine needles kill plants may be related to the barren earth often found under pines. This absence of vegetation usually has more to do with the lack of water and excess shade under a pine than the soil pH, which may be alkaline despite decades of needle fall. Oak leaves contain tannic acid, which is said to leach into standing water. Plant failure probably occurs because of poor drainage rather than low pH.

Myth 5: Mulch must be worked into the soil as it breaks down.

This is unnecessary. Once mulch is decomposed enough that it is no longer recognizable, allow it to mix into the soil during weeding or other garden work, but don't make a special effort to incorporate it. Soil organisms, such as earthworms, will do that for you with far greater effect and less trauma to plant roots.

Myth 6: If mulch is added every year, the soil level in a bed increases rapidly.

Two to 3 inches of mulch decompose to roughly ¼ inch of compost, which degrades further into humus and water-soluble nutrients. Plants take up the nutrients to incorporate into their tissues. You remove some of the remains of last year's mulch every time you remove plant matter in weeding, dividing, or general cleaning up. New mulch usually adds only enough material to replace what's lost in this cycle.

Myth 7: Mulch attracts termites.

Not true. Mulch does contribute to cool, moist, rich soil, which will sustain more life of all kinds than dry, worn-out soil. Such a variety and quantity of creatures is a sign of fertile soil and is usually self-regulating in that predator organisms in the soil will act to keep any pest populations in check. Wood chip mulches may provide food for termites; avoid direct contact with wooden foundations.

Myth 8: Weed barrier cloth hidden under bark is an excellent mulch for perennials.

Plastic and woven weed barriers do not completely curb weeds. Weeds can grow in decaying mulch on top of the barriers. Barrier cloths do not allow clumps of perennials to increase in size, cost more than mulch alone, and may reduce the amount of oxygen in the soil. Plastic mulches stop air movement into the soil, and weed barrier cloth, while air-permeable, reduces the activity of worms tunneling between the soil's surface and the subsoil, which indirectly decreases soil oxygen.

PROTECTING PLANTS

WINTER PROTECTION

Young perennial plants are especially susceptible to winter injury caused by ice-melting salts, extended freezing temperatures, alternating freezes and thaws, and browsing animals. Plants that are marginally hardy in your area are more prone to these problems.

Sometimes perennials appear to have survived winter and begin growing in early spring. But then, they suddenly take a turn for the worse and die. In other cases, they never awaken from their winter slumber. Either way, this is called "winter-kill."

You can minimize winter-kill and other winter-related problems by taking good care of your new plants. Avoid pruning or feeding in late summer; both practices stimulate late growth at a time when perennial plants are naturally becoming dormant. Water woody ornamentals throughout the fall and winter months if rainfall is inadequate.

Use straw to protect the crowns of tender perennials such as chrysanthemums.

DIGGING SUMMER BULBS

1

After canna foliage dies back in the fall, dig up the clump of rhizomes using a spading fork. Snip off the dead or dying foliage.

2

Gently shake off clinging soil and rinse off remaining soil. Set the rhizomes in a basket to air dry before storing them.

Unless you choose to treat summer-flowering bulbs as annuals and replant them each spring, dig the bulbs up in fall and store them indoors over the winter in cold climates. The bulbs, corms, or tubers of cannas, calla lilies, dahlias, and others should be dug carefully after the foliage of the plant dies. Remove any soil that clings to the bulbs. Place the clean, dry bulbs in a box filled with dry vermiculite. Cover the bulbs with vermiculite. Store the box in a cool, dry place until spring.

PROTECTING PLANTS FROM WILDLIFE

Many animals feed on and damage plants during the growing season and through the winter. The first step in preventing animals from damaging or destroying your flowering plants is to identify the culprit. Then evaluate how much damage is being done. Do a little research to understand more about their life cycle and habits before you attempt to circumvent them.

Deer feast on a variety of flowering plants, and they commonly wreak havoc even in city gardens. Fences—at least 8 feet tall—remain the best defense against deer.

Rabbits often work from the bottom toward the top of a plant. They may prefer to graze one side of a plant or the garden that is closer to shelter. Protect small or young plants from rabbits by placing a lightweight fabric row cover over the planting area. Surround larger plants or planting areas with half-inch mesh fencing.

Squirrels, ground squirrels, and chipmunks can be captured and relocated. Consult your county extension service for more suggestions about specific pests in your region.

1

Cut a length of chicken wire and bend it into a tube shape that will fit inside the diameter of the bulb planting hole.

2

Fit the wire tube into the planting hole, lining the sides and bottom of the hole.

3

Cover the bulbs with soil and a handful of stones. Lay a blanket of wire over them.

Chapter 4
GROOMING & TRAINING

Regular maintenance of plants helps them stay healthy and perform optimally. A little effort makes a big difference when you remove spent flowers and give plants support if they need it.

GROOMING

Grooming is a continual chore, but the more often it is done, the lighter the task becomes. Many gardeners enjoy the routine, taking advantage of the chance to inspect their plants.

Removing spent flowers (deadheading) and damaged or browning foliage keeps the garden pleasantly tidy and the gardener aware of its daily or weekly state and subtle changes. The process also eliminates old plant parts where some diseases can establish a foothold on otherwise healthy plants. It manipulates nature's floral insurance policy.

Buds on the stems or crowns of many plants can develop into flowers or flower stalks. Grooming stimulates these buds and ensures plentiful blooms. Many flowers, such as cosmos, zinnias, and dahlias, respond with profuse blooming, whether cut for a vase or, after their prime, for tidiness.

Use scissors, clippers, shears, or trimmers to remove spent blooms. Just aim to send a plant's ripening seedpods to the ground or the compost pile. Some quick-cut tools may leave a plant with more rough edges than pruners or scissors, but new growth soon covers up the cuts.

DEADHEADING

Most annuals experience increased flowering after deadheading. Perennials that bloom on leaf-bearing stems also keep producing flowers when deadheaded. Cutting back perennials, such as 'Dropmore' catmint and 'Moonbeam' coreopsis, promotes a second flush of flowers and a denser habit later in summer. Many perennials, including salvia, garden phlox, pincushion flower, and campanula, look tidier and fuller when you remove dead blossoms. Deadhead plants with basal foliage and leafless flower stems to clean them up and direct their energy into establishing vigorous roots. To deadhead plants with basal foliage, snip the flower stems at the bottom and compost the trimmings.

Leave interesting seed heads of plants in the garden. Some, such as purple coneflowers, are favored by birds; others add form and mass to the winter garden. Keep seed heads of ornamental grasses, money plant, 'Autumn Joy' sedum, and other garden plants with ornamental elements in your yard until early spring, when you can cut them down before they put on new growth. Remove annuals after they've been killed by frost, and cut back perennials whose forms will not persist through winter.

Pinks and many other blooming plants will produce more flowers if the old ones are removed after they fade.

TRELLISING

Trellising is a form of training in which a plant is fastened to a structure, giving it support or shape. Plants may be trained on a trellis to conserve space, increase light penetration to the plant's interior, display the plant and flowers in an interesting way, improve air circulation, reduce disease, ease harvesting, or give support to a weak trunk.

When a plant is trained to conform to a support, the trellis is usually two dimensional, having only height and width. A trellis can be as simple as a wooden stake or as intricate as interwoven latticework. In crowded gardens, a trellis can be mounted on a wall or in a place where a bushy plant doesn't suit the site.

When a plant has no clasping tendrils or twining shoots, attach it to the trellis using soft fasteners—strips of cloth or other flexible material. Secure the tie around the plant and trellis. The fastener must not be attached so tightly that it

crushes, bruises, or strangles the plant's growth. Fasteners that are loose when applied might be too tight within a few weeks as stems grow in diameter. Material that stretches is preferred to rigid fasteners, but even stretchy materials can become too tight.

Make sure the trellis is sturdy enough to hold up the plant and long-lasting enough that it doesn't rot or collapse while the plant is still growing. If the trellis will be anchored in the soil, the bottom of it should be made from a rot-resistant material, such as treated wood.

The usual approach is to plant a young plant at the base of the trellis, but an older one can be transplanted to a trellis after it has been carefully dug from its existing site. For best results, complete this transfer in early spring before the plant resumes growing. Or, transplant an established plant late in the season, first cutting it back by two-thirds.

Vines that cling by tendrils may need some assistance at first to clasp their supporting trellis.

Vines on a trellis can be used to frame a destination. Here sweet autumn clematis complements 'Annabelle' hydrangea.

STAKING

There are several reasons for staking plants. Plants with large, heavy blooms or particularly tall stems need staking to keep the flowers upright. Those with weak stems need staking to keep the stems from bending and breaking. Without support, plants such as baptisia, peonies, and asters tend to flop over.

Sometimes the garden setting creates the need for staking plants that are otherwise sturdy. You'll have to

Pinch stem tips once or more between spring and early summer. Pinched plants grow shorter but sturdier, and require less staking. Be aware that pinching delays flowering.

NO-STAKE SUPPORT

One alternative to using stakes is to grow sturdy plants next to unsteady ones. Plant stocky salvia on both sides of a tall, loose veronica, and let it lean on them, for example.

Another option to staking is to pinch plants, which promotes shorter stems and a bushier habit less likely to tumble. Pinching delays flowering, however.

The term pinch might mislead you—it can mean nipping off soft stem tips between thumb and forefinger, but more often it means cutting back stems with sharp shears. Many gardeners are familiar with pinching in relation to chrysanthemums but haven't realized how many other perennials can be clipped back several times between early May and their bloom time to achieve the same effect. The "Gallery of Flower Care" on pages 32–137 notes whether a plant is pinchable.

Tree trimmings are an abundant source of supports called "pea shrub" stakes. In early spring, insert the cut ends into the ground around the crown of the flowering plant, twiggy fingers up.

stake in windy locations and where the soil is too poor or too rich for the plant. Staking will correct plants that lean toward the light where sunlight is strongly one-directional, such as on the east or west side of a building.

Tall, large-flowered species, such as delphiniums, dahlias, and foxgloves, usually require staking. Others tend to flop only in certain circumstances, such as yarrow in a rich soil. Predicting whether a plant will fall may take a season's experience (with a plant) to learn whether it will need staking or will stand on its own.

Stake a plant in spring while it is still short. Stakes, cages, and other props might look awkward when first placed. If they do draw the eye, don't be concerned. Most flowering plants grow so quickly from midspring into early summer that they rapidly cloak the stakes with foliage.

Some annuals also need staking. When grown in ideal conditions with plenty of water, fertilizer, and sunlight, annuals develop lush growth that is soft and heavy because it contains a lot of moisture. Staking bolsters the soft stems and supports the lush foliage and flowers.

1 Cut off the tops of staking material below the expected mature height of the plant.

2 Crisscross twine between the stakes to form a support maze the plant will grow through.

STAKING TECHNIQUES

Staking flowering plants can be as simple as inserting a piece of bamboo in the soil next to a weak stem and tying the stem to the stake. When staking a plant, place the support close enough to the stems to hide among the foliage. When tying a stem to a stake, secure the tie to the support first, then make a loose loop around the stem. Avoid tying the stake and stem all in one loop. If the loop is tight enough to stay up, it can easily crush the stem.

Another simple method of staking flowers involves surrounding a plant with several stakes and loosely weaving string, twine, or a similar material between them. Green bamboo stakes and green or beige twine are less noticeable than more brightly colored materials. Place the stakes and string the twine before the

Place a wire support cage over false indigo. As the plant grows through the cage, it will be held upright.

plants get too large. As the plants grow up through the stake and twine maze, tuck stems and foliage inside it. The support system is not visible if done correctly, and the plant growth appears natural.

Save small branches from the annual pruning of trees and shrubs and use them as staking material. Push the base of a branch into the soil next to a plant. As long as the twiggy branches are shorter than the mature height of the plant, foliage hides the twigs.

When you grow a new perennial, stake the plant its first year if there is any doubt about its growth habit. If the plant is not staked and then grows and flops over, it may be too late to add a support without affecting the plant's appearance. Tall varieties of dahlias need to be staked when the tubers are planted. A stake pushed into the soil after the dahlias are planted can pierce a tuber and damage it.

A wire tomato cage makes an effective support for many bushy plants, especially those with large, heavy blooms, such as peonies. To keep the plant upright, place a cage over the young plant and tuck stems and foliage into the cage as the plant grows. Turn one tomato cage into two hoop-type supports by cutting the legs of the cage at the appropriate points, using heavy-duty wire cutters or a bolt cutter.

Stake dahlias at planting time. Staking later risks piercing a tuber.

Tall, spiked plants such as delphinium often need staking to prevent wind and rain from knocking them down.

When supporting lilies or other tall plants using branch ends, hide the twiggy trellises among the foliage.

Chapter 5
PROPAGATION

Propagation is one of the most rewarding aspects of gardening. Start new plants either by seed or vegetatively. Cutting, grafting, layering, or dividing increase your plant collection.

STARTING FROM SEED

To start growth from a seed, the appropriate temperature, moisture, and light are needed. Newly emerging roots and shoots must also have proper growing conditions. Follow the particular seed-sowing directions on seed packets for best results.

Some seeds germinate best when sown directly in the garden. For instance, you can sow annual poppies and pot marigolds outdoors in fall in warm-climate gardens and in early spring in cool areas. Tree mallow and love-in-a-mist prefer to be sown outdoors in early spring; nasturtium, cosmos, sunflower, and moss rose require waiting until after the last frost for outdoor sowing in warm soil.

Most perennials can also be started from seed. Get a jump on the growing season and sow seeds indoors in a soilless starting mix. Commercial seed-starting mixes are specially blended for optimum germination.

Seed packets give information on germination requirements, days to germinate, seed spacing, and other helpful hints.

GERMINATING SEEDS INDOORS

Good seeds may germinate poorly in a low-quality soil mix. Germinating seeds in a commercial soilless medium specially blended for this operation gives the best results. The mix will not contain weed seeds, insects, disease spores, or other germination-inhibiting elements that might be present in garden soil. Commercial mixes may also contain a wetting agent that promotes water absorption by the medium, as well as a dilute plant food that boosts the growth of newly germinated seeds.

Containers for growing plants should have drainage holes. Cell packs are ideal containers for growing young plants from seed until they are ready to set in the garden. If you sow seeds in plastic flats or other tray-type containers, plan to transplant the seedlings later to individual containers and allow them to grow to garden-ready size.

Expandable peat pellets provide a convenient option for sowing seeds. As both a container and a seed-starting medium, the waferlike pellets are ready to use after soaking in water. Place the peat pellets in a container of warm

water, making sure that the opening in the thin netting covering the pellet is facing up. Once the pellet has fully expanded, it is ready for planting.

Before filling flats, cell packs, or other containers with germinating mix, moisten it with warm water. Scoop seed-germinating mix into the cell pack or flat, scrape off any excess, and gently firm the mix.

Check the seed packet label and note any special germination requirements. Some seeds, such as yarrow, hollyhock, and alyssum, require light to germinate. Once the seeds are sown, they are not covered with germinating mix. Follow seed packet instructions for covering other seeds.

When planting a cell pack, use a pencil or chopstick to poke a hole in the germinating mix. Make the hole no deeper than the sowing depth specified on the seed packet. Place one or two seeds in the hole in each cell.

When using a flat or other large container, sow the seeds in rows. Mark shallow rows in the soil mix by pressing the edge of a ruler into the surface. For accurate seeding, use a device that dispenses seeds evenly.

As soon as seeds have been sown, label the container with the date the seed was sown and the plant name. Moisten the germinating mix thoroughly with warm water. Gently water with a trigger-type spray bottle or a sprinkling can. Alternatively, set the containers in a basin of shallow water, letting the germinating mix absorb water through the drain holes. Maintain uniform moisture throughout the process of germination. The germinating medium should feel damp but not wet or soggy.

To prevent evaporation, some commercial flats have a clear plastic top designed to fit perfectly over the flat, similar to a miniature greenhouse. Or make a cover from a bent coat hanger and a painter's lightweight plastic drop cloth.

Germination can be delayed or completely inhibited if the temperature of the medium is too low. Seed-starting containers placed in a sunny window may be warm enough during the day so a supplemental heat source is not needed. Where warm light is inadequate, bottom heat may be necessary for germination to occur. Waterproof propagation heat mats or heat cables are two types of heating devices. Place the germination containers on top of them. Some seeds do not require warmth to germinate. Again, the seed packet should indicate the conditions that will be most conducive for that plant.

1 Assemble necessary materials on a work area where spills can be easily cleaned.

2 Fill germination containers with seed-starting mix. Scrape off excess material with a trowel.

3 Use a seeding device for accurate seed placement.

4 Moisten the seeded medium to prompt germination.

CARING FOR SEEDLINGS

Whether planted indoors or out, in pots or flats, seedlings should be kept evenly moist. Adequate air circulation is important to control a seedling's worst enemy—a deadly fungal disease called damping-off. Clean pots, sterile soil mix, and good air circulation are essential to prevent it. Spacing germination containers several inches apart or installing a small oscillating fan helps to avert this problem.

When the seedlings develop two or three true leaves, transplant them into individual cell packs or 4-inch pots. Feed weekly with regular fertilizer at half strength. Prevent legginess by maintaining high light intensity. Pinch growing tips occasionally to promote bushiness.

Harden off the flower seedling when its roots fill its container, then plant it in the garden. If you choose to

transplant it to another pot, move it just one pot size at a time—from a 4-inch to a 5- or 6-inch container, and so on. Let the roots be your guide for how often to transplant: Some perennials may take two years to fill a gallon pot.

Zinnia seedlings started in a pot indoors will get the flowers off to a faster start than those sown directly in cold soil outdoors.

VEGETATIVE PROPAGATION

CUTTINGS

The most common ways to propagate flowering plants vegetatively include cutting, layering, and dividing. Some of the tools used to germinate seeds may also be used for vegetative propagation. Soilless germinating mix and cell packs or flats are also used in starting cuttings. You'll also need a sharp knife or a comparable tool, such as a box cutter or bypass pruners, to make cuttings. Sharp tool blades help avoid damaging plant tissue when cutting.

Take softwood cuttings from new shoots of many types of plants during the growing season. Coleus, begonia, geranium, plectranthus, and other herbaceous plants root easily from cuttings that will grow well outdoors or indoors.

Use a clean, sharp knife to take cuttings from these and other herbaceous plants. If a plant stem easily breaks without crushing or tearing, you may snap off a piece of the plant for propagating instead of cutting it with a knife.

New shoots of roses and many other plants make good terminal cuttings. Cut approximately 4 to 6 inches from the tip of the shoot. Remove the lower leaves from the cutting so they will not be buried in the rooting mix and rot. Dip the lower 2 inches of the cutting in rooting hormone, then place the cutting upright in a rooting or germination mix, such as Miracle-Gro Seed-Starting Mix, with the lower 2 inches inserted into the moist medium.

Take chrysanthemum cuttings in early summer before flower buds form.

Cut a scented geranium stem, remove its lower leaves and dip in rooting hormone.

Cuttings taken further down the plant, below the tip or terminal, are called stem cuttings. They are treated the same as terminal cuttings.

Cover propagation containers with clear plastic sheeting suspended from a framework that keeps the plastic from touching the cuttings. This cover lets light through to the cuttings and keeps the humidity high around them.

The new roots of cuttings are fragile and easily damaged. When checking the cuttings to see whether roots have formed after 4 to 6 weeks, gently tug on the cutting. If the cutting resists, roots have probably formed.

Transplant rooted cuttings to individual containers for growing until they are garden ready. Use a pencil to gently dig under the cutting and lift it out of the soilless medium. Gently place the roots in a container filled partially with potting mix. Cover the roots with potting mix; water.

DIVISION

Many perennials may be divided as a simple, reliable means of propagation. Division produces duplicates of the parent plant. Plants with multiple stems or shoots emerging from the soil are the best candidates for division.

Some perennials require division every few years to rejuvenate the plants or keep them in bounds. Flowers that benefit from division include aster, bleeding heart, chrysanthemum, coreopsis, daylily, hosta, iris, liriope, lily-of-the-valley, and yarrow.

Without regular division, some perennial plants' (bearded iris, for example) center portion dies, leaving an outer ring of growth. Divide the plant and remove the dead center; replant only the healthy parts.

Avoid dividing perennials when they are flowering. Divide spring-flowering plants in fall, and divide late-summer- or fall-flowering plants in spring.

1 Wash soil from the roots to allow easier separation and to see the root system.

2 Cut the root system into sections using a large knife, or pull the roots apart.

3 Plant divisions in holes spaced 18 inches apart.

4 Backfill around the plants with soil and water thoroughly.

DIVIDING PERENNIAL FAVORITES

1 In fall, carefully dig an overgrown clump of peonies.

2 Each peony division must include buds (eyes) from which new shoots will grow.

3 Place a section of the division with roots and at least three eyes in a prepared hole.

Daylilies grow in dense clumps. To divide them, first dig the clump. Then remove the soil from the roots using a strong stream of water from a garden hose. This makes it easier to separate the clump. Cut the plant into sections using a large knife or pull it apart.

To separate a very dense older clump of daylilies, insert two garden forks back-to-back into the root mass. Pull the tool handles in opposite directions to break apart the clump. After separating the larger plant into smaller units, trim each division to remove any dead plant parts. Replant the divisions, leaving room for them to grow.

Dahlias grow from bulbous roots called tubers. In cold climates, dahlias must be dug up and protected from freezing. After dahlia foliage has died in fall but before the ground freezes, carefully dig the plant and its tuberous roots from the soil. Avoid damaging the tubers. Gently shake the soil from the tubers, or remove it using a gentle spray of water. Snip off the plant's foliage.

Use a large, sharp knife to divide the plant into sections. For a new plant to grow from each division, the section must include a tuber and an eye (the bud from which new top growth will arise). Snip off any roots attached to the tuber. In cold climates, pack tubers in peat moss (to keep them from shriveling) and store in a cool location, such as a basement or heated garage.

Peonies have thick roots attached to a crown. Their division is similar to that of dahlias. In fall, dig and divide their cleaned crown and root system into sections using a large, sharp knife. Plan the cuts so each section includes several good roots and at least three buds. Remove any dead or damaged parts. Plant the peony divisions where they will not be disturbed for five to ten years. It is crucial to plant the bud or eye of each division one inch below soil level. When planted deeper, the peony will not bloom well if at all. In addition, peonies sometimes need

a year or two to recover from division before they resume booming.

Bearded irises have a growing point at the end of a stout rhizome. Over many years plants become crowded with dense masses of rhizomes. New growth forms at the outside of the clump and old and dead rhizomes fill the center. To reinvigorate older bearded iris, dig clumps of rhizomes from the ground and rinse them with a stream of water. Use pruning shears or a sharp knife to cut the rhizomes apart. Cut off the tops of the swordlike leaves attached to healthy rhizomes. Discard old rhizomes along with dead portions of the plant. Replant healthy rhizomes, laying them horizontally in the soil, with the top half of the rhizomes and their leafy tops visible above the soil surface.

1 To divide bearded iris, begin by digging the clump, using a spade or garden fork.

2 Wash soil from the roots and rhizomes so you can see their structure.

3 Using a sharp knife, separate the leaves and rhizomes from dead plant parts.

4 Replant healthy divisions in a triangular pattern.

Chapter 6
PROBLEMS WITH PLANTS

The health of your plants is in your hands. As you plot the garden, choose plants that are compatible with the conditions, and tend to the plants' needs. Prevent conditions that foster insect pests and diseases. In the process, discover ways to make your plants thrive.

PLANT HEALTH CARE

Plant health care is a holistic approach to gardening. It considers the garden as part of the whole landscape. A homeowner with a lawn, trees, shrubs, perennials, annuals, and a vegetable garden needs an effective garden plan that takes them all into consideration. A plan that focuses on only one or two problem plants does not address the best interests of the entire yard and garden. Instead, a garden plan should focus on fixing problems from previous years and preventing problems in the future. The best garden plan is a flexible one. Your goals should be adaptable to weather conditions and other variables.

PREVENTING PROBLEMS

There are five simple things you can do to maintain healthy plants during the growing season.

1. Maintain appropriate levels of plant food nutrients.
2. Supply plants with adequate moisture, especially during droughts, to protect them from stress. Pests and diseases tend to attack stressed or weak plants.
3. Mulch to conserve moisture and prevent weed growth.
4. Harvest fruits, vegetables, and flowers at timely intervals. Unremoved flowers result in seed formation instead of new flower production; they also serve as a site of infection.
5. Clean up the garden each fall. Remove spent annuals and any dead or diseased plant parts.

Healthy gardens consist of plants as well as bacteria, fungi, insects, and nematodes. Most of these organisms are benign and merely coexist with plants. Some of these organisms, such as fungi that form mycorrhizae, or nitrogen-fixing bacteria, are beneficial and are necessary for healthy plant growth. Other fungi and bacteria are essential for breaking down dead plant material into humus in the compost pile.

Beneficial insects and nematodes prey upon and parasitize pests in addition to having important roles in pollination. Although it may not seem like it to an embattled gardener, only a small percentage of insects actually cause damage, and only a few microorganisms are capable of causing disease.

When confronted with a plant problem, most gardeners assume that an insect or a disease is involved, then wonder what pesticide to spray. Most plant problems, however, are not due to disease-causing agents (pathogens) or insects but to environmental conditions and stresses. More often than not, these problems are caused by or due to actions taken—or not taken—by gardeners.

SCOUTING FOR PROBLEMS

1 Pick insects off infested plants. Wear gloves, if you prefer, to handle this task.

2 After removing insects from a plant, drop them into soapy water to kill them.

WEEDS

Weeds compete with more desirable plants in the garden. The pernicious ones vie for light, water, food, and space. Once plants are identified as weeds, they're usually removed easily without much thought. Identifying the plant and determining why it has invaded is the first step in weed management.

Traditional weed control consists primarily of hand pulling and mulching. When properly timed, this two-pronged approach is usually effective. Weeds are easiest to control when the seeds are germinating to prevent them from becoming established. They are most easily removed when the soil is moist, although not excessively wet. Once the weeds are established, control often requires hard work, herbicides, or both. For this reason, prevent weeds from going to seed.

After identifying the weeds, review your garden and lawn care practices. Carefully consider what adjustments are needed to maintain a healthy, weed-free garden.

INSECTS

Scouting for insects is more challenging than scouting for weeds. In a matter of days, insects can arrive, damage your plants, and then seemingly disappear. Monitoring your plants routinely will help you keep on top of the insect population and prevent infestations. Biweekly scouting of plants enables you to make some control choices before the damage reaches destructive levels. You can remove some pests physically from the plants by hand-picking them, by using a garden hose to wash them from the plants, or by spraying them with insecticidal soap or horticultural oil. These approaches are the least toxic way to control insect problems. For them to be effective, you must be vigilant to make sure the problem insect doesn't become established.

When scouting your yard or garden, include all plant groups (lawn, trees, shrubs, fruits, vegetables, annuals, and perennials), and inspect several plants within each group. Be sure to choose several plants at random. Inspect the tops and undersides of several leaves or leaflets per plant. Determine how much damage is acceptable to you. If damage is minimal, you may choose to hand-pick pests, avoiding the need for chemical control. If the infestation is severe, you may need to spray to prevent the problem from increasing or to reduce insect populations to a level that becomes manageable by hand picking.

Anyone who gardens will inevitably confront an insect infestation of some kind. Before reaching for a pesticide to spray, carefully examine the problem. Sometimes, it will take care of itself. Insects are susceptible to disease and predation too. Large populations of aphids are a food source for adult and immature beetles (ladybugs). These beetles are voracious. One beetle can eat several hundred aphids. Praying mantis prey upon smaller insects, as do spiders. Remember that your garden and yard are part of the larger environment. When spraying to control an insect pest problem, consider that you may unintentionally kill beneficial insects as well.

Aphids are a favorite food of lady beetles. Here an adult lady beetle is feasting on rose aphids.

DISEASES

Leaf spots, discoloration, and wilting are indications of plant distress. Early detection, accurate diagnosis, and understanding how pesticides and herbicides work are essential for plant disease management. By scouting regularly, you can quickly discover problems, correctly diagnose them, and prevent further spread of a pathogen before the disease reaches epidemic proportions.

The next step is accurately identifying the disease. Most disease diagnoses are not easily made in the home garden, so harvest a characteristic sample of the affected plant, wrap it in newspaper or paper towel (plastic causes samples to rot), and take it to the horticulture clinic of your cooperative extension service for identification.

DIAGNOSING PLANT DAMAGE

Diagnosing plant problems takes an investigative approach, like a criminologist working on a case. The key difference is that your victim and all the witnesses don't talk. You need to reconstruct the event and the factors that contributed to the problem. There can be numerous causes for any given symptom, not all of them related to insects or diseases. Soil nutrition and texture, weather conditions, quantity of light, and other environmental and cultural conditions influence the health of a plant. An accurate diagnosis helps ensure the success of your management strategy.

The chartreuse foliage of 'Sun Power' hosta could be mistaken for a nutrient deficiency, but it is normal coloration for this cultivar.

STEP ONE: KNOW YOUR HOST
Correctly identifying the affected plant is the first step to successful diagnosis. Using the plant's botanical (Latin) name is more helpful than using its common name.

STEP TWO: DETERMINE IF A PROBLEM EXISTS
Knowing what is normal and when problems occur allows you to recognize abnormalities. Keep in mind that many ornamentals have variegated leaves, brightly colored new growth, or double flowers.

A reliable reference book helps identify problems and solutions.

STEP THREE: DECREASE THE SUSPECT LIST
After identifying the host, look in books or log on to a website to research what insects and diseases affect that plant. When confronted with a garden problem, many beginning gardeners look at pictures of problems in gardening books and attempt to match the problem with the picture. Outstanding books, such as Ortho's *Home Gardener's Problem Solver,* have useful photos to aid you in your diagnosis. However it is easy to make a simple but incorrect, diagnosis instead of determining the cause of more complex problems. Like any skill, diagnosing plant problems requires practice. The more you garden, the more practice you will get.

STEP FOUR: DEVELOP AN INVESTIGATIVE APPROACH
Diagnose plant problems on the basis of symptoms and signs. Symptoms, such as wilting, leaf spotting, and discoloration, describe how a plant responds to damage. Signs, such as the webbing of insects, are the direct evidence of the organism causing the damage that creates the characteristic symptoms.

Wilting is a symptom with many possible underlying causes.

STEP FIVE: DETERMINE THE CAUSE OF THE PROBLEM
Plants require the appropriate light, temperature, humidity, nutrients, and water. Plants undergo stress when they receive too much or too little of these basic necessities. Stress predisposes plants to attack by insects and disease. Damage may be caused by these sources: environmental (weather or site), mechanical (foot traffic or wind), chemical (pesticides or herbicides), animals, insects, and diseases.

STEP SIX: DEFINE THE PROBLEM
Closely examine the entire plant and others around it. Know how normal appears so you can define what is abnormal about the plant. In defining the problem, determine exactly what is going on. For example, if the plant's leaves have insects on them, can you observe the insects actually causing damage? What kind of damage do you perceive? Do you see holes in the leaves; do the holes appear in patterns or randomly? Is there any discoloration of the plant parts or other symptoms?

Insecticidal sprays may be necessary to manage Japanese beetles.

STEP SEVEN: LOOK FOR PATTERNS

To find patterns, examine nearby plants to see if they have the same problem. Consider whether the problem is seasonal. Evergreens do lose their needles in fall and throughout the winter. Check to see whether the affected plants are all the same type. Pathogens are host specific; insects are less so. Are the affected plants in the same place or in different locations? Damage to a few species of plants or only to plants of the same species may indicate the presence of living factors.

STEP EIGHT: EXAMINE THE PROBLEM'S DEVELOPMENT

Living factors tend to multiply over time, resulting in a problem that spreads from one plant to the next. Note whether the problem is increasing on a single plant or multiple plants within a planting. This can indicate living factors. Many people mistakenly believe that a problem suddenly developed overnight. In most instances problems were already present at low levels, and environmental conditions changed to favor the growth of the living factor.

Symptoms that develop suddenly (within three days) or remain in a particular spot or on a particular plant are usually due to nonliving factors. They progress or get worse if they are not corrected.

STEP NINE: IDENTIFY THE SPECIFIC CAUSE

Uniform, unusual, distinct, or repeated patterns indicate damage caused by nonliving factors, including chemicals, nutrient disorders, mechanical damage, environmental factors, and animal damage. Insect damage is caused by chewing, piercing, or rasping. The presence of an insect is additional evidence that may support your diagnosis. Make sure that the damage you find is the type caused by the insect you suspect. Use a hand lens to identify the causal agents of plant disease. Pathogens include fungi, bacteria, viruses, nematodes, and even other plants.

STEP TEN: BE PATIENT

Experience with plant problem diagnosis is born of practice. There is no better teacher than to diagnose the plant problems outside your door. Know the host and its interactions with the factors that cause plant damage, both living and nonliving. Keep a balanced approach in managing problems rather than relying on any one strategy. Seek professional diagnostic help when in doubt.

Irregular holes chewed in leaves (above) are evidence of grasshopper feeding.

Use a live trap (below) to remove unwanted animal pests.

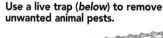

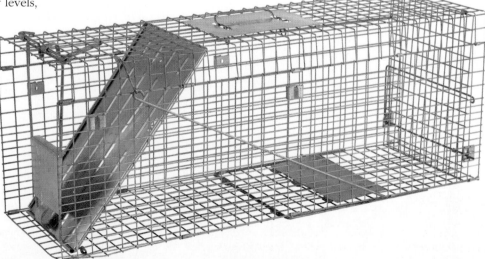

GALLERY OF
FLOWER
CARE

Flowering plants add beauty and delight to the landscape as the textures, colors, and fragrances intermingle. Each setting is unique and reflects the special characteristics and qualities of the people and the place.

Gloriosa Daisy, *Rudbeckia hirta* 'Toto'

Bloody cranesbill, *Geranium sanguineum*

Cushion spurge, *Euphorbia polychroma* (epithymoides)

Daylily, *Hemerocallis* 'Mardi Gras Parade'

COMMON NAME INDEX FLOWERS *continued*

**Goldenrod,
*Solidago***

**Grape hyacinth,
*Muscari botryoides***

Lupine, *Lupinus*

**Oriental poppy,
*Papaver orientale***

COMMON NAME	BOTANIC NAME	SEE PAGE
False sunflower	*Heliopsis helianthoides*	80
Fan flower	*Scaevola aemula*	122
Featherleaf rodgersia	*Rodgersia pinnata*	117
Flossflower	*Ageratum houstonianum*	38
Flowering kale	*Brassica oleracea*	52
Flowering tobacco	*Nicotiana alata*	104
Foxglove	*Digitalis purpurea*	71
French marigold	*Tagetes patula*	127
Fringed bleeding heart	*Dicentra eximia*	69
Fuchsia	*Fuchsia hybrids*	73
Garden phlox	*Phlox paniculata*	112
Gas plant	*Dictamnus albus*	70
Geranium	*Pelargonium ✕hortorum*	109
Germander	*Teucrium chamaedrys*	128
Giant kale	*Crambe cordifolia*	63
Giant onion	*Allium giganteum*	40
Giant taro	*Alocasia macrorrhiza*	40
Globe amaranth	*Gomphrena globosa*	77
Globe thistle	*Echinops ritro*	72
Gloriosa daisy	*Rudbeckia hirta*	118
Goatsbeard	*Aruncus dioicus*	45
Goldenrod	*Solidago hybrids*	126
Goldmoss stonecrop	*Sedum acre*	123
Gomphrena	*Gomphrena globosa*	77
Gooseneck loosestrife	*Lysimachia clethroides*	99
Grape hyacinth	*Muscari botryoides*	102
Grape-leaf anemone	*Anemone vitifolia*	42
Grass pink	*Dianthus plumarius*	69
Great white trillium	*Trillium grandiflorum*	131
Ground morning glory	*Convolvulus sabatius*	60
Hardy geranium	*Geranium sanguineum*	76
Heart-leaf bergenia	*Bergenia cordifolia*	51
Heart-leaf brunnera	*Brunnera macrophylla*	52
Helen's flower	*Helenium autumnale*	78
Heliopsis	*Heliopsis helianthoides*	80
Heliotrope	*Heliotropium arborescens*	81
Hellebore	*Helleborus orientalis*	81
Holly fern	*Cyrtomium falcatum*	65
Hollyhock	*Alcea rosea*	39
Hollyhock mallow	*Malva alcea 'Fastigiata'*	100
Hosta	*Hosta hybrids*	83
Houttuynia	*Houttuynia cordata*	85
Hyacinth	*Hyacinthus orientalis*	85
Hybrid bee delphinium	*Delphinium elatum*	67
Hybrid sage	*Salvia ✕superba*	120
Iceland poppy	*Papaver nudicaule*	108
Impatiens	*Impatiens walleriana*	87
Jack-in-the-pulpit	*Arisaema triphyllum*	44
Japanese anemone	*Anemone hupehensis japonica*	42

COMMON NAME	BOTANIC NAME	SEE PAGE
Japanese holly fern	*Cyrtomium falcatum 'Pictum'*	65
Japanese painted fern	*Athyrium nipponicum*	49
Japanese spurge	*Pachysandra terminalis*	107
Jonquil	*Narcissus jonquilla*	103
Lady's mantle	*Alchemilla mollis*	39
Lamb's-ears	*Stachys byzantina*	126
Lamium	*Lamium maculatum*	91
Lantana	*Lantana camara*	92
Large periwinkle	*Vinca major*	135
Larkspur	*Consolida hybrids*	59
Lavender	*Lavandula angustifolia*	93
Lavender cotton	*Santolina chamaecyparissus*	120
Leadwort	*Ceratostigma plumbaginoides*	57
Lemon thyme	*Thymus ✕citriodorus*	130
Lenten rose	*Helleborus orientalis*	81
Lily-of-the-valley	*Convallaria majalis*	60
Lobelia	*Lobelia cardinalis*	97
Lobelia	*Lobelia erinus*	97
Love-in-a-mist	*Nigella damascena*	105
Lungwort	*Pulmonaria saccharata*	117
Lupine	*Lupinus hybrids*	98
Many-flowered sunflower	*Helianthus ✕multiflorus*	79
Meadowsweet	*Filipendula rubra*	73
Mealy-cup sage	*Salvia farinacea*	119
Mexican heather	*Cuphea hyssopifolia*	65
Mexican hyssop	*Agastache cana*	37
Missouri primrose	*Oenothera macrocarpa*	105
Montbretia	*Crocosmia ✕crocosmiiflora*	63
Morning glory	*Convolvulus sabatius*	60
Morning glory	*Ipomoea tricolor*	88
Moss phlox	*Phlox subulata*	113
Moss rose	*Portulaca grandiflora*	115
Narrow-leaf blue-eyed grass	*Sisyrinchium angustifolium*	124
New England aster	*Aster novae-angliae*	47
New Guinea impatiens	*Impatiens hawkeri*	87
Nicotiana	*Nicotiana alata*	104
Obedient plant	*Physostegia virginiana*	114
Orange coneflower	*Rudbeckia fulgida*	118
Oriental poppy	*Papaver orientale*	108
Ornamental pepper	*Capsicum annuum*	55
Ostrich fern	*Matteuccia struthiopteris*	100
Oswego tea	*Monarda didyma*	101
Oxeye	*Heliopsis helianthoides*	80
Ozark sundrop	*Oenothera macrocarpa*	105
Pansy	*Viola ✕wittrockiana*	136
Pearly everlasting	*Anaphalis margaritacea*	41
Penstemon	*Penstemon barbatus*	110
Penstemon	*Penstemon digitalis*	110
Peony	*Paeonia officinalis*	107

COMMON NAME	BOTANIC NAME	SEE PAGE
Perennial salvia	Salvia ×superba	120
Periwinkle	Vinca minor	135
Perovskia	Perovskia atriplicifolia	111
Petunia	Petunia ×hybrida	112
Phlox	Phlox paniculata	112
Pigsqueak	Bergenia cordifolia	51
Pincushion flower	Scabiosa columbaria	122
Pink	Dianthus chinensis	68
Plumbago	Ceratostigma plumbaginoides	57
Plume poppy	Macleaya cordata	99
Polyanthus primrose	Primula ×polyantha	116
Portulaca	Portulaca grandiflora	115
Pot marigold	Calendula officinalis	53
Primrose	Primula ×polyantha	116
Pulmonaria	Pulmonaria saccharata	117
Purple coneflower	Echinacea purpurea	71
Purple hardy ice plant	Delosperma cooperi	66
Queen-of-the-prairie	Filipendula rubra	73
Red hot poker	Kniphofia uvaria	91
Rock soapwort	Saponaria ocymoides	121
Rodgersia	Rodgersia pinnata	117
Roger's flower	Rodgersia pinnata	117
Rose moss	Portulaca grandiflora	115
Rose-scented geranium	Pelargonium graveolens	109
Royal fern	Osmunda regalis	106
Russian sage	Perovskia atriplicifolia	111
Scabious	Scabiosa columbaria	122
Scaevola	Scaevola aemula	122
Scarlet sage	Salvia splendens	119
Sea pink	Armeria maritima	44
Sedum	Sedum acre	123
Sedum	Sedum 'Autumn Joy'	123
Shasta daisy	Leucanthemum ×superbum	93
Showy crocus	Crocus speciosus	64
Siberian bugloss	Brunnera macrophylla	52
Siberian iris	Iris sibirica	90
Siebold hosta	Hosta sieboldiana	84
Silver Mound artemisia	Artemisia schmidtiana 'Silver Mound'	45
Small Solomon's seal	Polygonatum biflorum	114
Smooth white penstemon	Penstemon digitalis	110
Snakeroot	Cimicifuga racemosa	58
Snapdragon	Antirrhinum majus	43
Sneezeweed	Helenium autumnale	78
Snowdrop	Galanthus nivalis	74
Snow-in-summer	Cerastium tomentosum	57
Soapwort	Saponaria ocymoides	121
Solomon's plume	Smilacena racemosa	125
Southern lupine	Thermopsis villosa	129
Southern maidenhair fern	Adiantum capillus-veneris	37

COMMON NAME	BOTANIC NAME	SEE PAGE
Spider flower	Cleome hassleriana	58
Spiderwort	Tradescantia virginiana	130
Spike gayfeather	Liatris spicata	94
Spike speedwell	Veronica spicata	134
Spotted deadnettle	Lamium maculatum	91
St. Johnswort	Hypericum calycinum	86
Strawflower	Helichrysum bracteatum	80
Sunflower	Helianthus annuus	79
Sunflower	Helianthus ×multiflorus	79
Sunflower heliopsis	Heliopsis helianthoides	80
Sweet alyssum	Lobularia maritima	98
Sweet flag	Acorus calamus 'Variegatus'	36
Sweet pea	Lathyrus odoratus	92
Sweet potato	Ipomoea batatas	88
Sweet violet	Viola odorata	136
Sweet William	Dianthus barbatus	68
Sweet woodruff	Galium odoratum	75
Tall cosmos	Cosmos bipinnatus	62
Threadleaf coreopsis	Coreopsis verticillata	61
Thrift	Armeria maritima	44
Tickseed	Coreopsis grandiflora	61
Toad lily	Tricyrtis hirta	131
Torch lily	Kniphofia uvaria	91
Touch-me-not	Impatiens walleriana	87
Tuberous begonia	Begonia Tuberhybrida hybrids	50
Tulip	Tulipa hybrids	132
Turk's-cap lily	Lilium superbum	95
Tussock bellflower	Campanula carpatica	54
Verbena	Verbena ×hybrida	133
Veronica	Veronica austriaca	133
Veronica	Veronica spicata	134
Vinca	Vinca major	135
Vinca	Vinca minor	135
Virginia bluebell	Mertensia virginica	101
Wall germander	Teucrium chamaedrys	128
Wavy hosta	Hosta undulata	84
Wax begonia	Begonia Semperflorens-Cultorum hybrids	50
White boltonia	Boltonia asteroides latisquama 'Snowbank'	51
White gaura	Gaura lindheimeri	75
Wild blue indigo	Baptisia australis	49
Willow amsonia	Amsonia tabernaemontana	41
Woodland forget-me-not	Myosotis sylvatica	102
Yarrow	Achillea 'Coronation Gold'	36
Yellow corydalis	Corydalis lutea	62
Yucca	Yucca filamentosa	137
Zinnia	Zinnia elegans	137
Zonal geranium	Pelargonium ×hortorum	109

Russian sage, *Perovskia atriplicifolia*

Siberian iris, *Iris sibirica* **'Silver Edge'**

Spike speedwell, *Veronica spicata* **'Red Fox'**

Tulip, *Tulipa* **'Kees Nelis'**

CHAPTER ⑦ GALLERY OF FLOWER CARE

CORONATION GOLD YARROW

Achillea 'Coronation Gold' *ah-KILL-ee-ah*

Coronation Gold yarrow, also known as yarrow, is a low-maintenance perennial with attractive golden-yellow flowers.

ZONES: 3–9
SIZE: 36"h × 18"w
TYPE: Perennial
FORM: Upright
TEXTURE: Medium
GROWTH: Fast
LIGHT: Full sun
MOISTURE: Medium to dry

SOIL: Fertile, well-drained
FEATURES: 3" blooms, silvery leaves
USES: Border, massing, butterflies
FLOWERS: ■
FALL COLOR: ■

SITING: Yarrow is heat tolerant and relatively drought tolerant and thrives in full sun. It prefers well-drained soil with moderate fertility and a pH of 5.5–6.6.

The 3"-diameter golden-yellow blooms and silvery foliage are good companions with 'David' garden phlox, 'The Fairy' rose, and purple coneflower.

CARE: Plant 18" apart in spring or fall. Feed with slow-release granular plant food at time of planting, or begin using water-soluble plant food 3 weeks after planting. Follow label directions for amount and frequency. Cease feeding 6–8 weeks prior to first frost date. Yarrow is drought tolerant but will perform better if it receives ample moisture during dry spells. Let the soil dry between waterings. Deadhead spent blooms to encourage reblooming. Blossoms may be cut and dried for arrangements; they hold their color best if harvested early in the bloom cycle. Apply 3" of vegetative mulch in summer and winter to reduce weed seed germination, retain soil moisture,

Remove faded flowers to stimulate new blooms.

and keep soil temperatures stable. Cut plants to the ground in late fall or leave erect for winter interest, then cut back in early spring.

PROPAGATION: In moderately fertile soil, plants may be divided every three years to maintain vigor. In rich soils, division is needed sooner to maintain vigor and control growth. Dig around the root clump and lift. Use a sharp spade to slice through the root system. The larger the portion, the larger the resulting plant during the first year. Smaller pieces may take 2–3 years to reach mature size and bloom. Reset only portions that contain both healthy roots and top shoots. Water deeply and apply 3" of vegetative mulch around, but not touching, the plants.

PESTS AND DISEASES: Plants are relatively pest free.

RELATED SPECIES: Common yarrow (*A. millefolium*) is vigorous and invasive. 'Fire King', 'Cerise Queen', and 'Red Beauty' add shades of red bloom to the garden. Moonshine yarrow (*A.* 'Moonshine') has the polite manners of 'Coronation Gold', but is slightly shorter and has a light yellow bloom.

SWEET FLAG

Acorus calamus 'Variegatus' *ah-KOR-uhs kal-AH-mus*

Sweet flag is an attractive addition to water's edge.

ZONES: 4–11
SIZE: 5'h × 24"w
TYPE: Perennial
FORM: Upright
TEXTURE: Medium
GROWTH: Fast
LIGHT: Full sun to part shade

MOISTURE: Moist to wet
SOIL: Sandy, well-drained
FEATURES: Foliage
USES: Water plant, naturalizing, container
FLOWERS: ■

SITING: Sweet flag thrives at the water's edge in full sun or partial shade. It prefers sandy loam with a pH of 5.5–7.0. It may be planted among bald cypress trees or as a companion to sweet flag iris.

CARE: Place at the edge of a pond or water feature in water up to 9" deep, or plant in moist soil that does not dry out. When placed close to water, do not apply plant foods or pesticides because they may leach into the water. In gardens feed at time of planting or begin using water-soluble plant food 3 weeks after planting. Follow label directions for amount and frequency. Cease feeding 6–8 weeks prior to first frost date. Cover surface roots with mulch. Cut back brown foliage in late winter before new growth appears.

PROPAGATION: Divide rhizomes in spring or fall by separating roots using a sharp spade. Reset healthy pieces, water deeply, and apply 3" of vegetative mulch around, but not touching, the plants.

PESTS AND DISEASES: Dislodge spider mites by frequently washing the leaves.

RELATED SPECIES: Grassy-leaved sweet flag (*A. gramineus*) is a smaller, 4–18" high semievergreen for Zones 8–9. 'Ogon' has yellow and cream leaves, 'Pusillus' has dark green leaves, and 'Variegatus' has variegated white and green leaves.

1 Divide rhizomes with a sharp spade.

2 Reset healthy roots, water deeply, and apply vegetative mulch around, but not touching, plants.

SOUTHERN MAIDENHAIR FERN
Adiantum capillus-veneris ad-ee-AN-tum kah-PIL-us-VEN-er-is

Southern maidenhair fern adds grace and beauty to the landscape.

ZONES: 8–10
SIZE: 12"h × 15"w
TYPE: Perennial
FORM: Upright arching
TEXTURE: Fine
GROWTH: Medium
LIGHT: Part shade

MOISTURE: Evenly moist
SOIL: Fertile, well-drained
FEATURES: Foliage
USES: Shade border, container, woodland

SITING: Southern maidenhair fern prefers light shade, good air circulation, and protection from direct afternoon sun and strong wind. It is evergreen down to 30°F. Attractive fronds are bright green on black stalks. Plants prefer high humidity and soil rich in organic matter, with a pH of 5.5–7.0. An attractive companion to this fern is white-leaved caladium.
CARE: Plant 15" apart in spring or fall. Feed with slow-release granular plant food at time of planting, or begin using water-soluble plant food 3 weeks after planting in spring. Follow label directions for amount and frequency. Cease feeding 6–8 weeks prior to first frost date. Apply 3" of vegetative mulch in summer and winter to protect roots from summer heat and winter cold. Mulch also reduces weed seed germination, holds moisture in the soil longer, and as it decomposes, adds organic matter to the soil, which increases fertility and plant health. Water deeply whenever the soil begins to dry out 2–3" below the surface to maintain uniform moisture. Brown fronds may be caused by dry soil, lack of organic matter, low humidity, too much water, too little water, or poor air circulation. Cut back after the first hard freeze.

Water slowly and deeply to thoroughly moisten the soil.

PROPAGATION: Divide rhizomes in spring by separating roots using a sharp spade. Reset healthy pieces, water deeply, and apply 3" of vegetative mulch around, but not touching, plants. In moderately fertile soil, plants may be divided every 3 years to maintain vigor.
PESTS AND DISEASES: These plants are basically pest free when their cultural preferences (soil, sun, moisture) are met. If the soil is too acidic, acid rot may occur.
RELATED SPECIES: Northern maidenhair fern (*A. pedatum*), grows larger, reaching nearly 2' tall, but retains the graceful habit of the Southern maidenhair fern.

MEXICAN HYSSOP
Agastache cana ah-guh-STAK-ee KAH-nah

Fragrant foliage and summer blooms are welcome additions in the landscape.

ZONES: 5–10
SIZE: 24–36"h × 18"w
TYPE: Perennial
FORM: Upright
TEXTURE: Medium
GROWTH: Medium
LIGHT: Full sun

MOISTURE: Medium
SOIL: Fertile, well-drained
FEATURES: Flowers, foliage
USES: Border, container
FLOWERS: ■ ■

SITING: Mexican hyssop prefers full sun and fertile, well-drained soil with a pH of 6.5–7.3. Loose spikes of deep pink to purple flowers appear in late summer and autumn. The oval blue-green leaves are fragrant. Place in odd-numbered groups in a border or informal cottage garden, or use in container plantings. Good companions include 'Taplow Blue' globe thistle, 'Fastigiata' hollyhock mallow, 'Icicle' spike speedwell, and white culver's root.
CARE: Plant 12–18" apart in spring or autumn. Feed with slow-release granular plant food in spring. Follow label directions for amount and frequency. Apply mulch to reduce weed seed germination, hold moisture in the soil, and as it decomposes, add organic matter to the soil, which increases fertility and plant health. Water deeply when the soil is dry. Deadhead spent blooms to encourage reblooming. Prune back in fall once frost withers the foliage.

PROPAGATION: Divide in spring. Dig around the root clump and lift. Use a sharp spade to slice through the root system. Reset only portions that contain healthy roots and top shoots. Water deeply and apply 3" of vegetative mulch around, but not touching, the plants.
PESTS AND DISEASES: Plants are relatively pest free when cultural requirements (sun, soil, planting depth, moisture) are met. Powdery mildew and rust may occur in dry weather.
RELATED SPECIES: Anise hyssop (*A. foeniculum*) reaches 3–5' high and bears spikes of blue flowers with violet bracts from midsummer into autumn. Anise-scented leaves are noticeably veined and whitish underneath. Plants reseed freely. Rock anise hyssop (*A. rupestris*) reaches 3–4' high and bears interesting orange flowers in summer. Gray-green leaves are licorice-scented.

FLOSSFLOWER
Ageratum houstonianum *a-jer-AY-tum hu-stow-nee-AY-num*

Flossflower produces tight mounds of non-stop color in summer. It is also known as ageratum.

ZONES: NA
SIZE: 6–24"h × 12"w
TYPE: Annual
FORM: Rounded or clumped
TEXTURE: Medium
GROWTH: Medium
LIGHT: Full sun to part shade

MOISTURE: Medium to high
SOIL: Fertile, well-drained
FEATURES: Flowers
USES: Bedding plant, container
FLOWERS: ■ ■ □

SITING: Ageratum tolerates full sun or partial shade; it prefers soil rich in organic matter with a pH of 5.5–7.0. It may be massed in the sunny border or planted in a rock garden or a container. Its striking blue blooms are complemented by the white blooms and/or silver foliage of 'Silver Carpet' lamb's-ears, white-flowering petunias, 'Icicle' spike speedwell, and 'Silver White' mealycup sage.

CARE: Plant 6–12" apart in spring after the last frost. Apply slow-release granular plant food at time of planting or begin using water-soluble plant food 3 weeks after planting. Follow label directions for amount and frequency. Water deeply

Plant ageratum 6–12" apart in staggered rows for best mass effect.

when the soil feels almost dry 2–3" below the surface. Apply 2–3" of organic mulch in summer to help retain soil moisture, minimize weed seed germination, and keep foliage clean. Mulch also adds organic matter to the soil as it decomposes. Deadhead spent blossoms to encourage reblooming. Remove the entire plant after frost and keep the ground covered with mulch to preserve the topsoil.

PROPAGATION: Sow seeds at 78–82°F under lights. Keep seeds evenly moist until germination, then allow seedlings to dry slightly between waterings. After germination, reduce the temperature to 60–65°F.

PESTS AND DISEASES: Plants are relatively pest free when grown in a favorable cultural environment; however, Southern blight and crown and root rots occur. During dry weather, powdery mildew and rust may be problems; during wet, cool weather, botrytis blight may occur.

RELATED SPECIES: Cultivars are largely mound-forming, compact plants bearing small flowers held above the foliage. 'Blue Danube' is 6" tall; 'Blue Horizon' is 18" tall and produces blooms suitable for cutting.

BUGLEWEED
Ajuga reptans *a-JOO-guh REP-tanz*

Bugleweed, also known as ajuga, is a low-maintenance ground cover in partial shade.

ZONES: 3–9
SIZE: 6"h × 15–24"w
TYPE: Perennial
FORM: Spreading
TEXTURE: Medium
GROWTH: Medium to fast
LIGHT: Partial shade

MOISTURE: Medium
SOIL: Medium-low fertility, well-drained
FEATURES: Foliage, flowers
USES: Ground cover
FLOWERS: ■ ■

SITING: Ajuga prefers partial shade, with good protection from afternoon sun and a pH of 5.5–7.4. Plants do not tolerate salt but can withstand moderate drought. The small, glossy leaves form an attractive evergreen ground cover that gets even better when spikes of gentian blue blooms appear in late spring and early summer. It is attractive planted in the rich soil under pine trees. Siebold hosta and lady's mantle are good companions.

CARE: Plant 12–24" apart in spring or fall. Apply slow-release granular plant food at time of planting or begin using water-soluble plant food 3 weeks after planting in spring. Follow label directions for amount and frequency. Cease feeding 6–8 weeks prior to first frost date. Apply 3" of vegetative mulch in summer and winter

Shear plants after they flower to stimulate compact foliar growth and improve the plants' appearance.

to reduce weed seed, protect the shallow-rooted stolons from excessive heat in summer and cold in winter, and improve soil texture and fertility as the mulch decomposes. Provide water during establishment and prolonged drought. If ajuga is planted among tree roots, deeply water during drought. Eliminate weeds prior to planting to avoid competition.

PROPAGATION: Divide plants in spring or fall when they become crowded, or take stem cuttings during the growing season. Plantlets that form along the stolons may be lifted with roots intact and reset. To divide plants, dig around the root clump and lift. Use a sharp spade to slice through the root system. Reset only portions that contain healthy roots and top shoots. Water deeply and apply 3" of vegetative mulch around, but not touching, the plants.

PESTS AND DISEASES: Plants are relatively pest free. Southern blight, crown rot, and fungal leaf spot are sometimes found.

RELATED SPECIES: Cultivars with attractive foliage include 'Burgundy Glow', with beautiful pink, silver, and green leaves, and 'Catlin's Giant', with larger glossy, deep bronze leaves.

HOLLYHOCK
Alcea rosea *al-SEE-uh ROZ-ee-uh*

Hollyhock blooms produce timeless beauty and nostalgia in the landscape.

ZONES: 3–9
SIZE: 5–8'h × 2'w
TYPE: Perennial
FORM: Upright
TEXTURE: Coarse foliage
GROWTH: Fast
LIGHT: Full sun

MOISTURE: High to medium
SOIL: Fertile, well-drained
FEATURES: Flowers, foliage
USES: Back of border, specimen
FLOWERS: ■ ■ ■ □ ■

SITING: Hollyhock prefers full sun and fertile, well-drained soil with a pH of 5.5–7.0. Foliage may be disfigured by disease and insect pests, so place it in the rear of the border. Plants require staking to remain erect, but a building or fence will support the plant as well. Good companions include 'The Fairy,' 'Alba-Meidiland,' and 'Iceberg' roses.

CARE: Plant 18–24" apart in spring or fall. Staking is usually required. Place stakes that are the same color as the stems alongside the stems and secure to the plant with green twine. Apply slow-release granular plant food at time of planting, or begin using water-soluble plant food 3 weeks after planting. Cease feeding 6–8 weeks prior to first frost date.

1 Collect hollyhock seeds before they spill to the ground.

2 Store seeds in an airtight container until ready to sow.

3 Sprinkle seeds over soilless media and lightly cover.

Deadhead spent blossoms to encourage reblooming, and remove diseased or disfigured foliage. Hollyhock is a short-lived perennial but may be treated as a biennial and cut back to 6" above the ground after blooming to extend its life span. Otherwise, cut to the ground in late fall, and remove all diseased foliage and stems from the planting area.

PROPAGATION: Sow seeds in soilless potting mix. Cover seeds lightly and provide a germination temperature of 72°F. Seeds will not produce true cultivars; the seedlings will vary.

PESTS AND DISEASES: Diseases include hollyhock rust, Southern blight, and bacterial and fungal leaf spot. Insect pests include flea beetles, Japanese beetles, aphids, and slugs.

RELATED SPECIES: 'Nigra' has single deep purplish-brown blossoms.

LADY'S MANTLE
Alchemilla mollis *al-kem-ILL-uh MAH-lis*

Lady's mantle is a low-maintenance perennial with superb flowers and foliage.

ZONES: 3–7
SIZE: 24"h × 24"w
TYPE: Perennial
FORM: Rounded
TEXTURE: Medium to fine
GROWTH: Medium
LIGHT: Full sun to part shade

MOISTURE: Medium
SOIL: Fertile, well-drained
FEATURES: Flowers, foliage
USES: Shade border, ground cover, container
FLOWERS: ■

SITING: Lady's mantle will thrive in full sun if the soil is fertile, but it prefers afternoon shade. It does not tolerate high humidity and prefers a pH of 5.5–7.0. Place it in the front of a border or at the edge of a container to fully enjoy the blooms and foliage. The tiny chartreuse blooms on wiry stems lace above silvery-green foliage intermittently from early summer into fall. Blooms may be used as fresh cut flowers or can be dried. Fan-shaped foliage is also a major attraction when dewdrops or water clings to it. Good companions include coral bells, astilbe, and 'The Rocket' ligularia.

CARE: Plant 18" apart in spring or fall. Apply slow-release granular plant food

Plant lady's mantle 18" apart in a triangular formation for best viewing effect.

at time of planting, or begin using water-soluble plant food 3 weeks after planting. Follow label directions for amount and frequency. Cease feeding 6–8 weeks prior to first frost date. Water deeply during establishment and anytime rainfall is low. Allow the soil to dry between waterings. Deadhead spent blossoms to encourage reblooming. Apply 3" inches of vegetative mulch in summer and winter to retain soil moisture, reduce weed seed germination, and stabilize soil temperatures. The decomposing mulch will add beneficial organic matter to the soil. Cut plants to the ground in late fall, or leave erect for winter interest and cut back in early spring.

PROPAGATION: In moderately fertile soil, plants may be divided every 3 years. Sever the root system with a sharp spade and reset portions with healthy roots and top shoots. Water deeply and apply 3" inches of vegetative mulch around, but not touching, the plants. Newly divided plants usually take a full year before they bloom on schedule.

PESTS AND DISEASES: Fourlined plant bug occasionally feeds on the foliage of lady's mantle.

GIANT ONION
Allium giganteum AL-ee-um jeye-GAN-tee-um

Purple flower balls of giant onion, also known as allium, add a touch of whimsy to the landscape.

ZONES: 4–8
SIZE: 3–5'h × 2'w
TYPE: Perennial bulb
FORM: Upright
TEXTURE: Coarse foliage, fine bloom
GROWTH: Fast to medium
LIGHT: Full sun

MOISTURE: Medium
SOIL: Fertile, well-drained
FEATURES: Flowers, foliage
USES: Border, specimen
FLOWERS: ■

SITING: Giant onion requires full sun, well-drained, fertile soil with a pH of 5.5–7.0. Sandy soils are fine as long as moisture is supplied during establishment and times of low rainfall. Avoid areas with high wind. Balls of purplish-pink blooms up to 4" across are held above the foliage in early summer. Place this plant in the middle or back of a perennial border, along a fence, or against a building. Blooms attract butterflies and are suitable for cutting. Companion plants include 'The Fairy' and 'Alba Meidiland' roses, and lady's mantle.

CARE: Plant bulbs 18–24" apart in fall. Mix bonemeal into the soil at planting time, and use slow-release granular plant food in spring. If planting in sandy soils, add organic matter to increase the soil's water-holding capacity and fertility. Let foliage die back naturally. The bulbs are relatively short-lived; replace or propagate to ensure a constant presence in the landscape.

PROPAGATION: Remove bulblets from the parent plant and reset. Dig down to the bulb and gently pull off the largest of the small bulbs that are attached to it. Cover the main bulb and plant the bulblets 18–24" away from other plants. Water deeply and apply 3" of mulch.

PESTS AND DISEASES: Fungal leaf spot may occur; wet conditions cause bulb rot.

RELATED SPECIES: Drumstick chives (*A. sphaerocephalum*) is similar to but smaller than *A. giganteum*. The leaves grow up to 14" long, and the plant grows 2–3' tall when in bloom. Chives (*A. schoenoprasum*) reaches 12–24" high, produces 1" balls of edible rosy-pink flowers, and has hollow dark green leaves.

1 Mix bonemeal into the soil at planting time and place bulbs 18–24" apart in fall.

2 Mark the spot so emerging foliage is easy to spot in spring.

ELEPHANT'S EAR
Alocasia macrorrhiza al-oh-KAY-zhee-uh mak-row-RYE-zuh

Elephant ear produces dramatic, exotic foliage. It is also known as giant taro.

ZONES: 8–10
SIZE: 12'h × 6'w
TYPE: Perennial
FORM: Upright clump-forming
TEXTURE: Medium to coarse
GROWTH: Medium
LIGHT: Full sun to partial shade

MOISTURE: Medium to high
SOIL: Fertile, well-drained
FEATURES: Exotic leaves
USES: Massing, specimen, container
FLOWERS: ■

SITING: Elephant's ear tolerates light shade or full sun in fertile, well-drained soil with a pH of 5.5–7.0. The exotic leaves deserve ample space and massing for best effect. The glossy green leaves are arrow shaped at their base, with contrasting pale green veins, on stalks up to 6' long. Each leaf blade is 3–4' long. Place these dramatic plants at the base of trees in a well-lit woodland setting, in containers, or as specimens in a tropical garden.

CARE: Plant in early spring. Feed with slow-release granular plant food at time of planting, or begin using water-soluble plant food in spring as foliage appears. Supply water during dry times to keep the soil moist but not soggy. Allow the soil to dry slightly between waterings. Apply 3" of vegetative mulch in summer and winter to help retain soil moisture. Cut back faded foliage in fall.

PROPAGATION: Divide rhizomes in spring or summer. Dig and lift the roots, cut away healthy sections of root that contain top shoots, and reset at the same depth 3–6' from other plants. Water deeply and apply 3" of vegetative mulch.

PESTS AND DISEASES: These plants are relatively pest free. Mealybugs and scale may be occasional problems but can be managed with insecticidal soap sprays or horticultural oil. Follow the label directions for recommended frequency.

RELATED SPECIES: 'Blackie' has almost black foliage. 'Violacea' has violet-tinged foliage. Giant caladium (*A. cuprea*) grows to 3' high and wide with glossy deep green and copper-hued leaves with reddish undersides. Kris plant (*A. sanderiana*) grows to 6' tall and wide and has deep green leaves with silver margins and silver veins. Wavy leaf edges add appeal.

In cooler climates dig rhizomes in fall, cut away soft spots, and store healthy roots in a cool, dry location until spring.

BLUE STAR
Amsonia tabernaemontana *am-SON-ee-uh tab-er-nay-mon-TAH-nuh*

Blue star, also known as willow amsonia, produces a multitude of periwinkle-blue blooms in late spring or early summer.

ZONES: 3–9
SIZE: 24–36"h × 18"w
TYPE: Perennial
FORM: Upright
TEXTURE: Fine to medium
GROWTH: Fast
LIGHT: Full sun to partial shade

MOISTURE: Low to high
SOIL: Fertile, well-drained, wet
FEATURES: Flowers, foliage
USES: Border, naturalizing, wetlands
FLOWERS: ■
FALL COLOR: ■

SITING: Blue star tolerates full sun or partial shade and a wide range of soil conditions, from wet to dry. It prefers low humidity and a pH of 6.5–7.5. Tiny star-shaped periwinkle-blue blooms appear in profusion during late spring, and the foliage is attractive all season long, even in autumn, when it turns from dark green to bright yellow. The blooms attract butterflies

Yellow fall foliage color is an added attraction to blue star.

and make good fresh cut flowers. Ornamental grasses make good garden companions for blue star.

CARE: Plant 18–24" apart in spring or fall. Feed with slow-release granular plant food at time of planting, or begin using water-soluble plant food 3 weeks after planting. Cease feeding 6–8 weeks prior to first frost date. This low-maintenance perennial is drought tolerant once established. All new transplants require ample and frequent moisture to grow. Cut plants to the ground in late fall, or leave erect for winter interest and cut back in early spring. Divide every 3 years or so to keep plants vigorous.

PROPAGATION: In moderately fertile soil plants may be divided every 3 years.

PESTS AND DISEASES: Plants are relatively pest free when their cultural preferences are met. Leaf spots and rust may occasionally occur.

RELATED SPECIES: Downy amsonia (*A. ciliata*) is slow growing and has threadlike leaves and panicles of blue blooms. Arkansas amsonia (*A. hubrectii*) grows to 4' wide and has panicles of sky blue blooms in late spring. Its foliage turns bright yellow in fall.

PEARLY EVERLASTING
Anaphalis margaritacea *a-NAF-uh-lis marg-uh-reet-AY-see-uh*

Silver foliage and white flowers of pearly everlasting add charm to the landscape.

ZONES: 4–8
SIZE: 24"h × 24"w
TYPE: Perennial
FORM: Upright clump-forming
TEXTURE: Medium
GROWTH: Fast to medium
LIGHT: Full sun

MOISTURE: Medium to low
SOIL: Average, well-drained
FEATURES: Foliage, flowers
USES: Border, container
FLOWERS: □

SITING: Pearly everlasting tolerates medium fertility and drought once established. The soil must be well-drained, not soggy, with a pH range of 5.5–7.0. The silver foliage and white blooms in late summer to early fall are the chief attraction. The blooms make excellent fresh cut or dried flowers. The silver foliage softens the effect of bright-blooming plants, such as red hot poker and 'Strawberry Fields' globe amaranth. The silvery foliage and pearly blooms are also suitable for moon or white gardens. Good companions for the white garden include 'Icicle' spike speedwell and 'Silver White' mealy-cup sage.

CARE: Plant 18–24" apart in spring or fall in average garden soil. In fertile soil the plant may become invasive and require

Harvest flowers for drying on a dry day during prime bloom cycle, before they begin to decline.

yearly division. Apply a slow-release granular plant food at time of planting. Deadhead spent blossoms to encourage reblooming. Cut plants to the ground in late fall, or leave erect for winter interest and cut back in early spring.

PROPAGATION: In moderately fertile soil, plants may be divided every 3 years; in fertile soil, more frequently. Sow seeds in fall or winter for flowering plants the following summer. Sow seeds in soil mix, leaving them exposed or only lightly covered. Water thoroughly and keep the mix moist but not soggy. Germination will occur in 4 to 8 days at 68–70°F (reduced to 55–58°F once plants are established). Seedlings will be ready for transplant 4–5 weeks after sowing. Take stem cuttings during the spring or summer. Remove the bottom leaves to expose nodes. Place the stems in water or soilless mix and keep moist until root growth starts.

PESTS AND DISEASES: Plants are susceptible to stem rot, rust, and Septoria leaf spot.

RELATED SPECIES: Var. *cinnamomea* is slightly smaller, with broader leaves and white or cinnamon-colored undersides.

JAPANESE ANEMONE
Anemone hupehensis var. japonica ah-NEHM-uh-nee hyoo-peh-HEN-sis juh-PON-ih-kuh

Pink flowers, bluegreen foliage, and seedpods of Japanese anemone add interest to the late-season landscape.

ZONES: 5–8
SIZE: 4–5'h × 2'w
TYPE: Perennial
FORM: Irregular or spreading
TEXTURE: Medium to coarse
GROWTH: Medium to fast

LIGHT: Sun to part shade
MOISTURE: High
SOIL: Fertile, well-drained, wet
FEATURES: Flowers, foliage
USES: Border
FLOWERS: ▨

SITING: Japanese anemone prefers full sun, or in hot areas, partial shade. The soil should be fertile and high in organic matter content with a pH range of 5.5–7.0. This plant performs best if sheltered from strong winds. The pale pink blooms appear in late summer and last into early fall. Blooms are semidouble, to 3½" across, with attractive prominent stamens. The appealing foliage is palmate, or lobed, with hairy undersides. Japanese anemone looks good in a border, preferably in groups or at the edge of an open woodland. Place this plant out of the reach of children, because the sap may cause skin irritation. The seedpods that remain after blooming are attractive. Good companions include Climbing rose 'Zephrine Drouhin,' sweet autumn clematis, and cardinal flower.

CARE: Plant 24" apart in spring or fall. Apply slow-release granular plant food at time of planting or begin using water-soluble plant food 3 weeks after planting. Cease feeding 6–8 weeks prior to the first frost date. Water regularly; this plant does not tolerate drought. Deadhead spent blossoms to encourage reblooming. Cut plants to the ground in late fall, or leave them erect for winter interest and cut back after frost withers the foliage.

PROPAGATION: Divide every 3 years or more frequently if the plant outgrows its space. Dig around the root clump and lift. Use a sharp spade to slice through the root system. Reset only portions that contain healthy roots and top shoots. Water and mulch all pieces.

PESTS AND DISEASES: Plants are relatively pest free. Aphids are occasional visitors and may be detected if their natural predator, the ladybug, suddenly appears. Exploding aphid populations can be temporarily managed with insecticidal soap. Be sure the label on the product mentions this plant and the specific insect.

RELATED SPECIES: Grecian windflower (*A. blanda*) grows 6" tall and wide and requires light, sandy soil and full sun. The deep blue, pink, or white blooms appear in late winter and early spring and are well suited for naturalizing. Snowdrop anemone (*A. sylvestris*) spreads rapidly, grows to 12" high and wide, and has fragrant single white blooms with yellow stamens in spring. It requires fertile, moist but well-drained soil and sun or partial shade.

GRAPE-LEAF ANEMONE
Anemone vitifolia ah-NEHM-uh-nee vit-ih-FOHL-ee-uh

White blooms with prominent yellow stamens and robust grape-leaved foliage are late-season stars in part shade.

ZONES: 5–8
SIZE: 36"h × 18–24"w
TYPE: Perennial
FORM: Rounded or clumped
TEXTURE: Medium to coarse
GROWTH: Medium
LIGHT: Part shade

MOISTURE: High
SOIL: Sandy, fertile, well-drained
FEATURES: Flowers, foliage
USES: Border, woodland, naturalizing
FLOWERS: □

SITING: Grape-leaf anemone prefers full sun or in hot areas partial shade. The soil should be fertile, high in organic matter, and well-drained with a pH of 5.5–7.0. This plant prefers bright shade, with shelter from the afternoon sun. Loose umbels of white blooms 1–3" across appear in late summer and last into early autumn. The flowers close at night and on cloudy days. The robust deep green foliage resembles grape leaves. Locate this plant away from romping children because the sap may cause skin irritation. Good garden companions include 'The Rocket' ligularia, 'Federsee' astilbe, 'Straussenfeder' astilbe, and cardinal flower.

CARE: Plant 18–24" apart in spring or fall. Apply slow-release granular plant food at time of planting or begin using water-soluble plant food 3 weeks after planting. Follow label directions for amount and frequency. Cease feeding 6–8 weeks prior to first frost date. Deadhead spent blossoms to encourage reblooming. Apply 3" of vegetative mulch in summer and winter to retain soil moisture and increase organic matter content. The soil should be moist, not soggy. When the soil feels dry or almost dry 2" below the surface, it is time to water deeply. If using an irrigation system, maintain infrequent deep waterings; avoid delivering a light sprinkle every day. Organic matter in the soil and mulch on the surface will help reduce watering frequency. Cut plants to the ground in late fall, or leave them erect for winter interest and cut back in early spring.

PROPAGATION: Divide in spring every 3 years, or more frequently if the plant outgrows its space. Dig around the root clump and lift. Use a sharp spade to slice through the root system. Reset only portions that contain healthy roots and top shoots. Water and mulch all pieces.

PESTS AND DISEASES: Nematodes (microscopic worms) are frequently a problem. Avoid cultivating around the roots; every nick or cut on the root is an easy entry point for nematodes. Caterpillars and slugs are also pests. *Bt (Bacillus thuringiensis)*, a microbial insecticide, controls caterpillars.

SNAPDRAGON
Antirrhinum majus *an-tih-RY-nuhm MAY-juhs*

Snapdragons offer cheerful color during the cooler months of the year.

ZONES: 6–9
SIZE: 9–72"h ×
6–24"w
TYPE: Perennial
FORM: Upright
TEXTURE: Medium
GROWTH: Medium
LIGHT: Full sun

MOISTURE: Dry to
moist
SOIL: Fertile, well-
drained
FEATURES: Flowers
USES: Bedding,
container
FLOWERS: □■■
■■

SITING: Snapdragons are fragrant, short-lived perennials that are usually grown as cool-season annuals. They extend the color palette for bedding plants into cooler temperatures in the South. Snapdragons attract butterflies and are excellent cut or dried flowers. They prefer fertile but well-drained soil with a pH of 5.5–7.0. They tolerate dry or moist soil.

CARE: Plant in spring in cooler climates or in early spring or fall in hotter areas. Apply slow-release granular plant food at the time of planting or begin using water-soluble plant food 3 weeks after planting. Water deeply whenever the soil begins to dry. Deadhead spent blossoms to

Remove faded flowers with sharp pruners to stimulate new growth and reblooming.

encourage reblooming. Remove plants after the first frost in cooler zones; leave plants in the ground in warmer climates and remove before the heat of summer.

PROPAGATION: Chill seeds for several days prior to sowing to improve germination. Sprinkle them over the soil mix and leave exposed to light. Germination should occur in 7–14 days at 70–75°F. Transplant 15–20 days after sowing, and reduce the temperature to 45–40°F.

PESTS AND DISEASES: Fungal leaf spot, aphids, beetles, spider mites, slugs, and caterpillars are all known pests of snapdragons. *Bt (Bacillus thuringiensis)* is effective against caterpillars. Spider mites and aphids can be managed by hosing them off the plants or by applying insecticidal soap or a chemical insecticide. Sprinkle diatomaceous earth or slug bait around the base of the plants to manage slugs. Beer baits are also useful for attracting slugs.

RELATED SPECIES: Tahiti Series cultivars are dwarf and rust resistant. Sonnet Series are intermediate plants that hold their color well in wet weather. 'Madame Butterfly' mixture is tall with double flowers.

COLUMBINE
Aquilegia McKenna Hybrids *a-kwih-LEE-juh*

Columbine's foliage and flowers add a light, airy quality to the landscape.

ZONES: 3–9
SIZE: 30"h × 24"w
TYPE: Perennial
FORM: Rounded or
clumped
TEXTURE: Fine
GROWTH: Medium
LIGHT: Full sun to
partial shade

MOISTURE: Dry to
moist
SOIL: Fertile, well-
drained
FEATURES: Flowers,
foliage
USES: Border,
woodland
FLOWERS: ■■■■

SITING: Columbine tolerates full sun or partial shade and fertile or average well-drained soil with a pH of 5.5–7.0. The plants are short lived. The blooms that appear from late spring into midsummer have spurs up to 4" long. Blooms are often two-toned and attract butterflies. Use columbine in woodland borders, for naturalizing, in rock gardens, and in containers. Good companions include hosta, lady's mantle, and Siberian bugloss.

CARE: Plant 18–24" apart in spring or fall in well-drained, fertile soil. In hotter areas provide afternoon shade. Apply slow-release plant food at the time of planting. Cease feeding 6–8 weeks prior to the first frost date. Deadhead spent blossoms to encourage reblooming. Water deeply

Deadhead faded flowers to reduce self-seeding and to prolong flowering.

whenever the soil is dry. After 2–3 years the base of this plant will become woody, and both bloom and foliage will begin to decline. Replace plants when this occurs. If blooms are not harvested, plants self-seed. Cut plants to the ground in late fall after frost withers the foliage.

PROPAGATION: Fresh seed will germinate in 10–20 days at 70–75°F. Stored seed may take up to 30 days to germinate. Seeds should be exposed to light, not covered with soil, during germination. If an exact replica of the parent plant is desired, divide the plant in spring. Transplants may take a full year to exhibit full healthy form, habit, and bloom schedule.

PESTS AND DISEASES: Leaf miners disfigure the leaves with "mining" lines left by feeding insects. Apply insecticide early in the season. Remove infested leaves.

RELATED SPECIES: Biedermeier Group hybrids reach 20" high by 12" wide. Bloom colors include white, pink, purple, and blue. The foliage is an attractive blue-green. Mrs. Scott-Elliot hybrids reach 36" high by 24" wide. Blooms occur from late spring to midsummer in a variety of shades. The foliage is medium green.

JACK-IN-THE-PULPIT
Arisaema triphyllum uh-RISS-uh-muh try-FILL-um

Jack-in-the-pulpit's unique purple-striped spathe (flowerlike leaf) adds wonder and delight to the woodland setting.

ZONES: 2–9
SIZE: 6–24"h × 6–12"w
TYPE: Perennial
FORM: Upright
TEXTURE: Medium
GROWTH: Slow
LIGHT: Full to partial shade

MOISTURE: High to medium
SOIL: Moist to wet
FEATURES: Foliage, spathe, fruit
USES: Woodlands, naturalizing
FLOWERS: ■■□
FALL COLOR: Red berries

SITING: Jack-in-the-pulpit is a striking native woodland plant that prefers full or partial shade. The soil should be fertile and moist but well-drained with a pH of 5.5–7.0. Cluster this plant in groups close to a woodland trail or bench to capture its subtle beauty. From spring to early summer, curious hooded spathes appear. They can be green or purple striped and 4–6" long. Large, showy clusters of red berries appear in fall and attract birds and wildlife, but are toxic when eaten by humans. Good companions include hosta, Siberian bugloss, and Bethlehem sage.

CARE: Plant 12–18" apart in spring or fall. Apply slow-release granular plant food at

Clusters of red berries appear in fall and attract wildlife.

the time of planting or begin using water-soluble plant food 3 weeks after planting. Follow label directions for amount and frequency. Cease feeding 6–8 weeks prior to the first frost date. Supply water whenever the soil begins to dry. Apply 3" of vegetative mulch in summer and winter to retain soil moisture and reduce weed seed germination. Mulch also adds beneficial organic matter to the soil as it decomposes. Jack-in-the-pulpit requires little care if sun, soil, and moisture preferences are met.

PROPAGATION: In spring, scoop away the soil to expose the tuberous root system. Gently snap or cut the offsets from the parent plant. Plant the offsets, water deeply, and apply 3" of mulch. Plants readily drop seed and self-sow unless foraging animals remove them.

PESTS AND DISEASES: Slugs and snails may damage foliage. Diseases include leaf blight, leaf spot, and rust. Discourage slugs and snails by sprinkling diatomaceous earth or slug bait around the plant. Good air circulation and adequate spacing will discourage disease infestations. Remove and discard diseased foliage.

SEA PINK
Armeria maritima ar-MARE-ee-uh mare-ih-TEYE-muh

Sea pink, also known as thrift, has mounds of pink blooms in spring and grassy foliage for the front of the border.

ZONES: 3–9
SIZE: 8"h × 12"w
TYPE: Perennial
FORM: Rounded
TEXTURE: Fine
GROWTH: Medium
LIGHT: Full sun
MOISTURE: Dry to medium

SOIL: Sandy to moderately fertile, well-drained
FEATURES: Flowers, foliage
USES: Border, rock, alpine
FLOWERS: ■

SITING: Sea pinks prefer full sun and sandy loam or moderately fertile soil with a pH of 5.5–7.0. The grasslike dark green clumps of foliage are attractive throughout the growing season. The 1" balls of deep pink blooms create a stunning show from late spring to summer and are excellent fresh cut flowers. Place at the edge of a border, in a rock garden or alpine garden, or in a container.

CARE: Plant 12" apart in spring or fall. Apply slow-release granular plant food at the time of planting or begin using water-soluble plant food 3 weeks after planting in spring. Follow label directions for amount and frequency. Cease feeding

Cut faded flowers and stalks away to stimulate reblooming.

6–8 weeks prior to the first frost date. This plant will withstand periods of drought but performs best if watered deeply during dry spells. Shear back the blossoms after blooming to stimulate reblooming. The foliage resembles clumps of grass and should be marked when not in bloom so it is not mistakenly "weeded" from the garden. Apply 3" of organic mulch in summer and winter to retain soil moisture and reduce weed seed germination. Mulch also adds beneficial organic matter to the soil as it decomposes. Cut plants to the ground in late fall.

PROPAGATION: To maintain vigor, divide every 3 years in fall or early spring. Dig around the root clump and lift. Use a sharp spade to slice through the root system. Reset only portions that contain healthy roots and top shoots, then water and mulch all the plants.

PESTS AND DISEASES: Sea pink is relatively pest free. Rust and root rot may occur if the soil is wet or heavy.

RELATED SPECIES: The cultivar 'Alba' has white blooms, 'Bloodstone' has dark red blooms, and 'Dusseldorf Pride' has rosy pink blooms.

SILVER MOUND ARTEMISIA
Artemisia schmidtiana 'Silver Mound' are-teh-MEEZ-ee-uh shmihd-tee-AY-nuh

Mounds of soft silver foliage add interest and charm to the landscape.

ZONES: 4–8
SIZE: 12"h × 18"w
TYPE: Perennial
FORM: Rounded mound
TEXTURE: Fine
GROWTH: Slow
LIGHT: Full sun

MOISTURE: Dry to medium
SOIL: Moderately fertile, well-drained
FEATURES: Foliage, flowers
USES: Border, container
FLOWERS: ■

SITING: 'Silver Mound' artemisia prefers full sun and well-drained, average or moderately fertile soil with a pH of 5.5–7.4. In hotter areas it will tolerate light afternoon shade. It has soft, fragrant silvery-green foliage that grows in a mound. Panicles of nonshowy yellow flowers appear in summer. 'Silver Mound' artemisia is well suited for the edge of sunny perennial borders, rock gardens, or spilling over the sides of a container. The silvery foliage is useful among bright-colored flowering plants. Companions that complement 'Silver Mound' artemisia include 'Coronation Gold,' Schwellenburg, and woolly yarrows.

CARE: Plant 15–18" apart in spring or fall. Apply slow-release granular plant food at the time of planting, or begin using water-soluble plant food 3 weeks after planting in spring. Cease feeding 6–8 weeks prior to the first frost date. Water deeply only when the soil is dry; this plant will not withstand constantly wet soil. Shear back heavily after bloom to restore the smooth-looking habit. If not sheared, the foliage may look untidy. Cut plants to the ground in late fall, or leave erect for winter interest and cut back in early spring.

PROPAGATION: In moderately fertile soil plants may be divided every 3 years, in spring or fall. Use a sharp spade to slice through the root system. Reset only portions that contain healthy roots and top shoots. Oftentimes the center of the plant does not produce top shoots and needs to be discarded.

PESTS AND DISEASES: Plants are relatively pest free when their cultural preferences are met.

RELATED SPECIES: 'Nana' closely resembles the species but is smaller, reaching only 3" high by 12" wide. Common wormwood (*A. absinthium*) is a woody perennial that reaches 3' high by 24" wide, and has silky silvery-gray leaves and a sprawling habit. Western mugwort (*A. ludoviciana*) has silvery-white leaves, reaches 4' high by 24" wide, and is often invasive. Western mugwort cultivars, 'Silver King' and 'Silver Queen,' are used in wreath making.

Shear back Silver Mound artemisia in mid-summer to retain a neat appearance.

GOATSBEARD
Aruncus dioicus ah-RUN-kuhs dy-OH-ik-uhs

Goatsbeard produces fernlike foliage and feathery flowers in bright shade.

ZONES: 3–7
SIZE: 6'h × 4'w
TYPE: Perennial
FORM: Upright clump-forming
TEXTURE: Fine to medium
GROWTH: Medium
LIGHT: Part shade

MOISTURE: Medium to high
SOIL: Fertile, moist, well-drained
FEATURES: Flowers, foliage
USES: Border, woodland
FLOWERS: ☐

SITING: Goatsbeard prefers shade in the afternoon and fertile, moist yet well-drained soil with a pH of 5.5–7.0. The panicles of white blooms appear from early to midsummer and occasionally arch with asymmetrical gracefulness. The attractive fernlike leaves can reach up to 3' long. The foliage and blooms are light and airy—you can see through this plant—so it looks best when planted in groups in borders. Good companions include Siebold hosta, Siberian bugloss, snakeroot, and 'Fanal' astilbe.

CARE: Plant 3–4' apart in spring or fall. Apply slow-release granular plant food at time of planting, or begin using water-soluble plant food 3 weeks after planting in spring. Cease feeding 6–8 weeks prior to the first frost date. If the plant is located on the bank of a natural body of water, avoid chemical plant foods; they can leach into the water. Instead, mix compost into the soil and apply 3" of vegetative mulch in summer and winter to retain soil moisture and to reduce weed seed germination. Water deeply whenever the soil begins to dry. Deadhead spent blossoms to encourage reblooming. Cut plants to the ground in late fall, or leave erect until frost damages the structure.

PROPAGATION: In moderately fertile soil divide plants in early spring or fall every 2–3 years to maintain vigor. Older rootstocks do not divide as easily because they become woody. Dig around the root clump and lift. Use a sharp spade to slice through the root system. Reset only portions that contain healthy roots and top shoots, then water and mulch. Goatsbeard seed yields good stock. Sow fresh seed (stored seeds have a greatly reduced germination rate) and lightly cover with soilless mix. Seeds germinate in 15–25 days at 70°F. Seedlings are slow growing and may take 50–70 days before they are ready for transplanting.

PESTS AND DISEASES: Plants are relatively pest free when their cultural preferences (sun, soil, moisture) are met.

RELATED SPECIES: 'Kneiffii' is slightly smaller than the species, reaching 4' high by 18" wide, with finely cut leaves and cream-colored blooms on arching stems. 'Kneiffii' must be propagated by division.

CANADIAN WILD GINGER
Asarum canadense *Ah-SARE-uhm kan-uh-DEHNS*

Canadian wild ginger is a superb ground cover for shade. It has heart-shaped leaves and hidden bell-shaped flowers.

ZONES: 2–8
SIZE: 6"h × 6"w
TYPE: Perennial
FORM: Spreading
TEXTURE: Medium
GROWTH: Slow
LIGHT: Full to partial shade

MOISTURE: Medium
SOIL: Fertile, moist, well-drained
FEATURES: Foliage, flowers
USES: Ground cover
FLOWERS: ■

SITING: Canadian wild ginger prefers shade and fertile, well-drained soil with a pH of 5.5–7.0. The main attraction of this native plant is the heart-shaped leaves. Curious bell-shaped brownish-purple flowers appear in early spring and are well hidden by the foliage. This plant is at home in shade borders or woodland gardens or under irrigated trees. Good companions include hosta, astilbe, Siberian bugloss, and Japanese painted fern.

CARE: Plant 6–12" apart in spring or fall. Apply slow-release granular plant food at time of planting, or begin using water-soluble plant food 3 weeks after planting in spring. Cease feeding 6–8 weeks prior to first frost date. Water deeply whenever the

Plant Canadian wild ginger on shady slopes to add beauty as well as stabilize the soil.

soil begins to dry out; let the soil dry slightly between waterings. Apply 3" of vegetative mulch in summer and winter to retain soil moisture and reduce weed seed germination. Plants are deciduous and will die back to the ground each winter.

PROPAGATION: Plants rarely require division. When desired, divide plants in early spring. Dig around the root clump and lift. Use a sharp spade to slice through the root system. Reset portions that contain healthy roots and top shoots, then water and mulch.

PESTS AND DISEASES: Slugs and snails are common pests. Diatomaceous earth, a powderlike substance made from fossils, or slug bait may be sprinkled over the soil around the plant. As a soft-bodied pest slides across the powder, tiny sharp fossil points pierce the outer coat, causing dehydration. Replace diatomaceous earth frequently, especially after heavy rains.

RELATED SPECIES: European wild ginger (*A. europaeum*) has darker, intensely glossy, heart-shaped leaves and reaches 3" high by 12" wide. The leaves are more striking than those of Canadian wild ginger and form an attractive ground cover.

BUTTERFLY MILKWEED
Asclepias tuberosa *Ah-SKLEEP-ee-us too-ber-OH-suh*

Butterfly weed's brilliant orange blooms attract butterflies and are followed by attractive seedpods.

ZONES: 4–9
SIZE: 36"h × 12"w
TYPE: Perennial
FORM: Upright
TEXTURE: Fine to medium
GROWTH: Medium
LIGHT: Full sun

MOISTURE: Dry to moist
SOIL: Sandy loam or clay, well-drained
FEATURES: Flowers, foliage, fruit
USES: Border, naturalizing
FLOWERS: ■

SITING: Butterfly milkweed prefers full sun and fertile, well-drained soil but tolerates a variety of soil textures, from sandy to clay. It prefers a pH of 5.5–7.0. This plant looks good in groups in perennial borders, in rock gardens or containers, or naturalized in sunny spots. The blooms range from orange to yellow to red from midsummer into early fall. Flowers attract butterflies. Stems exude a milky sap that may cause skin irritation. Good companions include 'Coronation Gold' yarrow, 'David' garden phlox, and 'Goldsturm' black-eyed Susan.

CARE: Plant 12" apart in spring or fall. Plants resent transplanting, so obtain container-grown stock. Apply slow-release granular plant food at time of planting

Spray butterfly milkweed with a strong stream of water to dislodge aphids and other pests.

or begin using water-soluble plant food 3 weeks after planting. Cease feeding 6–8 weeks prior to first frost date. Butterfly milkweed tolerates drought but performs better if it receives deep but infrequent waterings during dry spells. Deadhead spent flower stalks to encourage repeat blooming. Cut plants to the ground in late fall or leave erect for winter interest until frost collapses the stems. Seedpods are attractive and cling to the stems in winter. This plant is late to emerge in spring.

PROPAGATION: Sprinkle fresh seed over soil mix and either cover lightly or leave uncovered and exposed to light. Germination occurs in 21–28 days at 70–75°F. Transplant 35–55 days after sowing seed. If seed is not fresh, refrigerate moist seeds for 2 weeks, then sow seed as described above.

PESTS AND DISEASES: Caterpillars eat the foliage, but it is probably best to live with the damage because the pests may be butterfly larvae. Aphids are also common, but attracting or introducing lady beetles can be an environmentally friendly and effective management tool.

NEW ENGLAND ASTER

Aster novae-angliae *AS-stir noh-vee-ANG-lee-ee*

New England aster's daisylike flowers offer late-summer and autumn interest.

ZONES: 4–8
SIZE: 5'h × 2'w
TYPE: Perennial
FORM: Upright
TEXTURE: Fine to medium
GROWTH: Medium
LIGHT: Full sun

MOISTURE: Dry to moist
SOIL: Fertile, moist
FEATURES: Flowers
USES: Border, wetlands
FLOWERS: ■ ■ ■ □

SITING: New England aster prefers full sun and fertile, moist soil with a pH of 5.5–7.0. The daisylike light violet blooms have a yellow center and appear in late summer to midautumn. The foliage is abundant; the 5"-long leaves are medium green and lance-shaped. Lower leaves often drop during the summer. New England aster may require staking to remain upright and should be placed where the foliage can be supported either by stakes or other plants. This plant looks good in the back of borders, in cottage gardens, in wetland areas, or, if cut back to promote compact growth, in containers. The blooms attract butterflies and are excellent fresh-cut flowers. Good garden companions include 'Snowbank' boltonia, purple-flowered Russian sage, and rosemary.

CARE: Plant New England aster between 18 and 24" apart in spring or fall. Apply slow-release granular plant food at time of planting or begin using water-soluble plant food 3 weeks after planting in spring. Follow label directions for amount and frequency. Cease feeding 6–8 weeks prior to first frost date. If planting in a wetland, avoid plant foods or chemical pesticides to prevent chemicals from leaching into bodies of water. This plant tolerates dry soil once established but performs better in moist soils. Water deeply when the soil begins to dry out. Cut back at 6–12" and again in early to midsummer to promote compact growth. Apply 3" of vegetative mulch in summer and winter to retain soil moisture and reduce weed seed germination. Mulch also adds beneficial organic matter to the soil as it decomposes.

Cut back in late fall and dispose of diseased foliage.

PROPAGATION: Divide every 2 years in spring or fall to maintain vigor and control growth. Dig around the root clump and lift. Use a sharp spade to slice through the root system. Reset portions that contain healthy roots and top shoots, then water and mulch. Discard any pieces that do not contain both healthy roots and top shoots.

PESTS AND DISEASES: Numerous insects and diseases frequent asters. Root rot is possible if the soil is too wet, and powdery mildew is likely if the soil and air are too dry. Fungal leafspot is common. Regular fungicidal treatments are needed unless the plant is at the rear of the border where the foliage is not readily visible.

RELATED SPECIES: Alpine aster (*A. alpinus*) has violet blooms with a deep yellow center in early and midsummer; the plants reach 10" high and 18" wide. They prefer moderately fertile, well-drained soil and full sun. Frikart's aster (*A. frikartii*) bears deep violet blooms with an orange center in late summer and early fall. It reaches 30" high and 15" wide and prefers full sun and well-drained, not wet, soil. New York aster (*A. novi-belgii*) reaches 4' high and 3' wide. Blooms are violet blue and appear from late summer into fall. The plant needs dividing every other year to maintain vigor and stem rampant growth. Cut back at 6" and again by one-half in early summer to create bushy, compact plants.

Frikart's aster blooms earlier in the summer than does New England aster. 'Monch' is a popular cultivar.

Asters that are not cut back often require staking and may appear leggy.

Cut back aster once or twice during the growing season to promote compact growth.

HYBRID ASTILBE
Astilbe ×arendsii *Ah-STIL-bee ah-REND-zee-eye*

Astilbes, also known as false spirea, are low-maintenance plants for moist sites in part or full shade.

ZONES: 4–8
SIZE: 1½–4'h × 2'w
TYPE: Perennial
FORM: Upright
TEXTURE: Medium
GROWTH: Medium
LIGHT: Partial to full shade

MOISTURE: Medium to high
SOIL: Fertile, well-drained
FEATURES: Flowers, foliage
USES: Border, woodland
FLOWERS: ■ ■ ■ □

SITING: Astilbe prefers moist yet well-drained soil with a pH of 5.5–7.0. It prefers partial to full shade and requires shelter from the afternoon sun. It has plumes of blooms in colors ranging from purple to rose to white. The blooms attract butterflies and dry to a faded, muted color. The fernlike foliage is handsome and low maintenance. Place groups of astilbe in shade borders, woodland gardens, in wetlands, or in containers. Good companions include hosta, heuchera hybrids, and snakeroot.

CARE: Plant astilbe 18"–2' apart in spring or fall. Apply slow-release plant food, such as Miracle-Gro Shake 'n Feed All Purpose, at time of planting or begin using water-soluble plant food, such as Miracle-Gro Water Soluble All Purpose, 3 weeks after planting in spring. Follow label directions for amount and frequency. Cease feeding 6–8 weeks prior to first frost date.
If planting in a wetland, avoid plant foods and pesticides. Astilbe will not tolerate soil that dries out in summer. Water deeply whenever the soil begins to dry. Apply 3" of vegetative mulch in summer and winter to retain soil moisture and reduce weed seed germination. Mulch also adds beneficial organic matter to the soil as it decomposes. Cut back after frost collapses the foliage.

PROPAGATION: Divide in spring or fall every 3 years to maintain vigor and control growth. Dig around the rhizomes and lift. Use a sharp spade to slice through the root system. Reset portions that contain healthy roots and top shoots, then water and mulch. Discard any pieces that do not contain both healthy roots and top shoots. Cut plants to the ground in late fall or leave erect for winter interest (the dried blooms are attractive) and cut back in early spring.

PESTS AND DISEASES: Plants are relatively pest free when their cultural preferences (sun, soil, moisture) are met.

RELATED SPECIES: 'Amethyst' reaches 36" high and 24" wide and has lilac-pink blooms in early summer; 'Bressingham Beauty' is 36" high and 24" wide, with bright pink blooms in midsummer; and 'Cattleya' grows to 36" high and 36" wide, with reddish-pink blooms in midsummer. Chinese astilbe (*A. chinensis*) grows to 24" high and wide with pink blooms in late summer. *A. c.* var. *davidii* has appealing bronze-tinged leaves and bears purplish-pink blooms. It grows in sun or shade, is drought tolerant, and reaches 6" high and 24" wide. *A. c.* var. *pumila* reaches 12" high and wide and has purple flowers.

RAISED BEDS

Most annuals and perennials perform best in soil that contains organic matter and drains well. An easy way to enhance drainage and add organic matter is to create raised beds or berms. Raised beds usually have constructed sides that hold soil, while berms are freestanding beds.
■ Select the place and the plants for the bed.
■ Draw the landscape bed on paper or outline it on the ground using hoses to create the shape and landscape paint to mark the perimeter.
■ Till the area.
■ Add 6–12" of good garden soil and compost and mix thoroughly with existing soil.
■ Install the edges for raised beds. These are commonly made of timbers, blocks, or stone. Shape the berm so the top is relatively flat and the sides gently slope to the ground.
■ Set plants in place, apply 3" of vegetative mulch around, but not touching, plants, and water deeply.

You can create a freestanding raised bed from cedar lumber and garden soil directly on top of existing sod.

Benefits of raised beds and berms
■ Promote water drainage.
■ Allow for importation of improved soils.
■ Raise plants higher in the landscape for better viewing.
■ Protect plants from mechanical injury.
■ Protect soil from compaction due to foot and vehicle traffic.
■ Warm soil earlier in the spring.

Showy plumes of color are held above attractive fernlike foliage.

Water astilbes deeply and let soil dry between waterings.

JAPANESE PAINTED FERN
Athyrium nipponicum 'Pictum' *Ah-THEE-ree-uhm nip-PON-ih-kum*

Japanese painted fern's fronds are beautiful silver-gray and green with red midveins.

ZONES: 4–8
SIZE: 12"h × 12"w
TYPE: Perennial
FORM: Irregular
TEXTURE: Fine
GROWTH: Medium
LIGHT: Partial shade
MOISTURE: Medium to high
SOIL: Fertile, well-drained
FEATURES: Leaves
USES: Border, woodland, container

SITING: Japanese painted fern prefers partial shade with shelter from the afternoon sun, and fertile, well-drained soil with a pH of 5.5–7.0. The beauty of this plant is the silver-gray and green fronds with reddish midveins. It looks good in shade borders, woodland gardens, or containers. Companions include 'Mrs. Moon' Bethlehem sage, lady's mantle, heuchera hybrids, and astilbe.

CARE: Plant Japanese painted fern 12–18" apart in spring or fall in fertile soil high in organic matter. After planting, water deeply and add 3" of mulch around, but not touching, the plant. Apply slow-

Mix organic matter thoroughly into existing soil prior to planting to increase fertility.

release granular plant food at time of planting, or begin using water-soluble plant food 3 weeks after planting. Cease feeding 6–8 weeks prior to first frost date. Water deeply whenever the soil becomes dry. Cut back this deciduous fern in fall, or leave erect for late-season viewing and cut back after frost collapses the foliage.

PROPAGATION: Divide in spring or fall every 3 years. Dig around the root clump and lift. Use a sharp spade to slice through the root system. Reset portions that contain healthy roots and top shoots, then water and mulch. Discard any pieces that do not contain both healthy roots and top shoots.

PESTS AND DISEASES: Plants are relatively pest free when their cultural preferences are met. Snails and slugs may pose problems. Brown leaves can indicate too much or too little moisture, too much sunlight, or low soil fertility.

RELATED SPECIES: The larger lady fern (*A. felix-femina*) has light green fronds and reaches 4' high and 2' wide. Numerous choice cultivars include 'Acrocladon' (12" high and wide), 'Frizelliae' (8" high and 12" wide), and 'Verononiae' (3' high and wide).

FALSE BLUE INDIGO
Baptisia australis *bap-TEES-ee-uh aw-STRAL-is*

False blue indigo is also known as wild blue indigo or baptisia.

ZONES: 3–9
SIZE: 5'h × 2'w
TYPE: Perennial
FORM: Upright
TEXTURE: Medium to fine
GROWTH: Medium
LIGHT: Full sun to partial shade
MOISTURE: Dry to medium
SOIL: Fertile, sandy, well-drained
FEATURES: Flowers, foliage, seedpods
USES: Border, container
FLOWERS: ■

SITING: Baptisia prefers full sun and well-drained soil, preferably sandy yet fertile, with a pH of 5.5–7.0. The full-season appeal of false blue indigo starts with the deeply divided leaves, moves into the tiny

Remove seedpods before seeds mature and self-sow in the landscape.

deep blue blooms that cover the plant in early summer, and ends with the pealike green seedpods that eventually turn black. It is well suited for borders, containers, or wild gardens. The pods are used in flower arrangements, and the flowers are used fresh cut or dried. Good companions for the sunny border include 'Goldsturm' black-eyed Susan, 'Snowbank' boltonia, and purple coneflower.

CARE: Plant 24" apart in spring or fall. Apply slow-release granular plant food at time of planting, or begin using water-soluble plant food 3 weeks after planting. Cease feeding 6–8 weeks prior to first frost date. False blue indigo tolerates drought but performs better with deep but infrequent waterings during dry spells. Apply 3" of vegetative mulch in summer and winter to retain soil moisture and reduce weed seed germination. This plant self-sows prolifically. Deadheading after bloom will thwart the proliferation but eliminate the attractive black seedpods.

PROPAGATION: Divide in fall or early spring. Dig around the root clump and lift. Use a sharp spade to slice through the root system. Because false blue indigo has a taproot, it is difficult to move, and may take several years to recover from division.

PESTS AND DISEASES: Plants are relatively pest free when their cultural preferences are met. Powdery mildew and fungal leaf spot may occur. Fungicides may be applied, or light infestations (less than 15 percent damage to foliage) can be tolerated in the landscape.

WAX BEGONIA

Begonia Semperflorens-Cultorum hybrids *Beh-GOHN-yah sem-per-FLOR-enz-kuhl-TOR-uhm*

Wax begonias are attractive, durable, and versatile in the container or landscape.

ZONES: NA
SIZE: 8–24"h × 8"w
TYPE: Annual
FORM: Rounded
TEXTURE: Medium
GROWTH: Medium
LIGHT: Full sun to part shade

MOISTURE: Medium to high
SOIL: Fertile, well-drained
FEATURES: Flowers, foliage
USES: Bedding, container
FLOWERS: ■■□

SITING: Wax begonia prefers full sun or partial shade and well-drained, fertile soil with a pH of 5.5–7.0. Tiny single or double flowers in red, pink, or white cover this plant all summer long. The stems are succulent, and the green or bronze leaves have a rounded outline. The bronze-leaved plants are better adapted to full sun. This prolific bloomer is useful as a bedding plant, massed as a flowering ground cover, or in containers.

CARE: Plant 6–12" apart in spring after last frost in cooler climates. In frost free zones, grow as a perennial. Apply slow-release granular plant food at time of planting, or begin using water-soluble plant food 3 weeks after planting. Follow label directions for amount and frequency. Water deeply whenever the soil starts to dry. Apply 3" of vegetative mulch to retain soil moisture and reduce weed seed germination. Mulch also adds beneficial organic matter to the soil as it decomposes. Plants are considered self-cleaning and do not need to be deadheaded. Remove plants before or after the first hard freeze.

PROPAGATION: Highest germination rates occur when seed is sprinkled evenly over the soil mix and temperatures are 78–80°F. Germination occurs in 14–21 days; plants are ready for transplanting 45–50 days after sowing, when the temperature can be reduced to 60°F. In frost free areas wax begonia may be treated as a perennial and divided every spring to maintain vigor.

PESTS AND DISEASES: Wax begonia is susceptible to mealybugs, mites, thrips, powdery mildew, stem rot, and nematodes. Providing preferred cultural conditions will minimize pest infestations, though not eliminate them. Insecticidal soaps may be used to manage the insects, and fungicides may be used to manage the diseases.

1 Fill a window box with Miracle-Gro potting mix.

2 Place plants in the window box and gently firm mix around roots.

3 Apply water to thoroughly moisten the mix.

TUBEROUS BEGONIA

Begonia Tuberhybrida hybrids *Beh-GOHN-yah too-ber-HY-brid-uh*

Tuberous begonias have lush leaves and blossoms in a variety of rich colors.

ZONES: 9–10
SIZE: 6–12"h × w
TYPE: Perennial
FORM: Rounded
TEXTURE: Medium
GROWTH: Medium
LIGHT: Partial shade
MOISTURE: Medium to high

SOIL: Fertile, well-drained
FEATURES: Flowers, foliage
USES: Bedding, container
FLOWERS: □■■ ■■

SITING: Tuberous begonia prefers fertile, well-drained soil with a pH of 5.5–7.0 and shelter from the afternoon sun. Bright blooms up to 5" wide appear all summer long in shades of pink, red, rose, orange, or white. Stems are succulent and leaves are pointed and glossy. Tuberous begonia can be successfully used as a bedding plant, in containers, or as a houseplant.

CARE: Plant tuberous begonia 12" apart in late spring or early summer after the last frost. Apply slow-release plant food, such as Miracle-Gro Shake 'n Feed All Purpose, at time of planting or begin using water-soluble plant food, such as Miracle-Gro Water Soluble All Purpose, 3 weeks after planting. Follow label directions for amount and frequency. Water deeply whenever the soil begins to dry. Apply 3" of vegetative mulch to retain soil moisture. Plants grow from tubers that do not overwinter successfully outdoors. Lift tubers in fall, before the first hard freeze,

and let dry. Dust with fungicide and store in a cool (41–45°F), dry place. In spring replant tubers, hollow side up.

PROPAGATION: Sow seed on top of soilless potting mix exposed to light, and provide temperatures of 70–72°F for up to 30 days. Transplant 45–50 days after sowing. Begonias in the Nonstop, Clip, and Musical Series require 12-hour days from October to March to germinate. This is achieved by leaving lights on for 4 hours after sunset. After the day-length requirement is satisfied, follow regular germination procedures outlined above.

PESTS AND DISEASES: Tuberous begonia is susceptible to mealybugs, mites, thrips, powdery mildew, stem rot, and nematodes. Providing ideal cultural conditions will minimize pest infestations, though not eliminate them. Use insecticidal soaps or beneficial/predatory insects to manage the insects, and spray fungicides to manage the diseases.

HEART-LEAF BERGENIA
Bergenia cordifolia ber-JEEN-ee-uh kord-ih-FOL-ee-uh

Heart-leaf bergenia's evergreen leaves and rose-colored blossoms are main attractions. It is also known as pigsqueak.

ZONES: 3–8
SIZE: 24"h × 36"w
TYPE: Perennial
FORM: Rounded
TEXTURE: Medium
GROWTH: Medium
LIGHT: Partial shade to full sun
MOISTURE: Low to high

SOIL: Fertile, well-drained
FEATURES: Flowers, foliage
USES: Border, woodland
FLOWERS: ■
FALL COLOR: ■

SITING: Heart-leaf bergenia prefers afternoon shade and fertile, well-drained soil high in organic matter with a pH of 5.5–7.0. The heart-shape leaves reach 12" long, and the blooms range from pale to deep pink and appear in late winter or early spring. In the border this evergreen plant offers long-season foliage color; the leaves often assume more reddish hues with cold weather. Good companions include snakeroot, European ginger, and dwarf Chinese astilbe.

CARE: Plant 24–36" apart in spring or fall. Pigsqueak tolerates poor soil but performs best in fertile, humus-rich soil. To increase organic matter in the soil, add 1–2" of composted material and till in to a depth of 12–15". After planting, water deeply and add 3" of mulch around, but not touching, the plant. Apply slow-release granular plant food at time of planting, or begin using water-soluble plant food 3 weeks after planting in spring. Follow label directions for amount and frequency. Cease feeding 6–8 weeks prior to first frost date. Water deeply whenever the soil begins to dry out, being sure to allow the soil to dry between waterings. Cut back whenever the foliage becomes leggy. Reapply mulch whenever necessary to maintain 3" in summer and winter. Mulch also adds beneficial organic matter to the soil as it decomposes. Leave erect for winter interest unless frost collapses the foliage. Heart-leaf bergenia performs best in cool weather. It dislikes the heat of summer.

PROPAGATION: Divide rhizomes in early spring or fall when clumps become crowded. Dig around the root clump and lift. Use a sharp spade to slice through the root system. Reset portions that contain healthy roots and top shoots, then water and mulch. Discard any pieces that do not contain both healthy roots and top shoots.

PESTS AND DISEASES: Plants are relatively pest free when their cultural preferences are met, although slugs and snails may feast on bergenia leaves. Brown leaves can mean too much or too little moisture, too much sun, or poor soil.

RELATED SPECIES: The cultivar 'Purpurea' has thick deep red leaves and pinkish-purple flowers. 'Perfecta' is taller than the species with rosy-red flowers and purplish leaves. 'Redstart' has red flowers in late spring, and 'Rotblum' bears red flowers and has red-tinged leaves in winter.

WHITE BOLTONIA
Boltonia asteroides latisquama 'Snowbank' bohl-TOHN-ee-ah a-ster-OY-deez lat-is-KWA-muh

'Snowbank' white boltonia is a low-maintenance perennial with white daisylike blooms late in the season.

ZONES: 4–9
SIZE: 5'h × 3'w
TYPE: Perennial
FORM: Upright
TEXTURE: Medium
GROWTH: Medium
LIGHT: Full sun
MOISTURE: Medium to high

SOIL: Moderately fertile, moist, well-drained
FEATURES: Flowers, foliage
USES: Border, wetlands
FLOWERS: □ ■ ■

SITING: White boltonia prefers full sun, though it tolerates light shade in the afternoon in hot climates. The soil should be moderately fertile and moist yet well-drained, with a pH of 5.5–7.0. This plant can also grow in a wetland or moist area. Clusters of tiny, daisylike white blooms appear in late summer into early fall. White boltonia is a good choice because its habit is sturdy and upright, it does not need staking like other boltonias, and it is not invasive. Give this plant plenty of room in borders for mid- to late-season color and low-maintenance foliage. Flowers attract butterflies and are excellent fresh-cut. Good companions include Russian sage, bluebeard, aster, and rosemary.

CARE: Plant 36" apart in early spring or fall. Apply slow-release granular plant food at the time of planting, or begin using water-soluble plant food 3 weeks after planting in spring. Follow label directions for amount and frequency. Cease feeding 6–8 weeks prior to first frost date. Water deeply when the soil dries. Apply 3" of vegetative mulch in summer and winter to help retain soil moisture. Cut back in fall or leave erect for late-season viewing and cut back in early spring.

PROPAGATION: Divide in fall or early spring. Dig around the root clump and lift. Use a sharp spade to slice through the root system. Reset portions that contain healthy roots and top shoots, then water and mulch. Discard any pieces that do not contain both healthy roots and top shoots. Plants started from seed will not come true to type.

PESTS AND DISEASES: Plants are relatively pest free when their cultural preferences (sun, soil, moisture) are met. Moderate soil fertility helps create strong, robust foliage that is not as easily penetrated by pests. Plants grown in too-fertile soil often have more succulent leaves and are more easily invaded by pests. Powdery mildew and fungal leaf spot may occur. Fungicides may be applied, or light infestations (less than 15 percent damage to foliage) can be tolerated in the landscape.

RELATED SPECIES: 'Pink Beauty' is a cultivar with pink ray florets. Siberian boltonia (*B. incisa*) is only 2–3' tall, and bears lilac purple flowers.

FLOWERING KALE

Brassica oleracea BRASS-ik-uh ob-ler-A-see-uh

Ornamental kale adds striking color and texture to the landscape or container.

ZONES: NA
SIZE: 12–18"h × 12–18"w
TYPE: Annual
FORM: Rounded
TEXTURE: Coarse
GROWTH: Medium
LIGHT: Full sun to partial shade

MOISTURE: Medium to high
SOIL: Fertile, well-drained
FEATURES: Foliage
USES: Bedding, container

SITING: Ornamental kale prefers cool temperatures, full sun, and fertile, well-drained soil. Like cabbage and broccoli, it prefers a limed soil (pH of 5.5–7.5). The ornamental leaves are rosettes of green, pink, purple, or white. The ruffled edges on the leaves add texture to any planting. Use ornamental kale as a cool-season bedding or container plant. Companions for the container include ornamental grasses, asters, and rose-colored pansies.

CARE: Plant 12–18" apart in late summer or early spring. Apply slow-release granular plant food at time of planting. Water deeply whenever the soil is dry. Apply 3" of vegetative mulch to help retain soil moisture and keep soil temperatures from fluctuating. Remove older leaves that discolor or are damaged. When flowers appear or when temperatures near 68–70°F, remove and replace with heat-tolerant bedding plants.

PROPAGATION: Sprinkle seeds over the seed starting mix, cover lightly, and thoroughly moisten. Seeds germinate in 7–14 days at 68°F. Transplant when several true leaves develop, and reduce the temperature to 55–58°F.

PESTS AND DISEASES: Pests include aphids, cabbage white butterfly, and flea beetles. Diseases include downy and powdery mildew.

RELATED SPECIES: Cultivars include 'Osaka' (to 12" tall, with blue-green leaves and pink or red centers), Peacock Series (red or white leaves and feathery foliage), and Sparrow Series (dwarf plants with red or white ruffled leaves).

Plant ornamental kale in early autumn to provide color.

Plant ornamental kale in containers using Miracle-Gro potting mix.

HEART-LEAF BRUNNERA

Brunnera macrophylla BRUH-ner-uh mak-ro-FY-luh

Heart-leaf brunnera, also known as Siberian bugloss, produces clouds of sky blue blossoms in spring.

ZONES: 3–7
SIZE: 18"h × 24"w
TYPE: Perennial
FORM: Rounded
TEXTURE: Medium
GROWTH: Medium
LIGHT: Full to partial shade

MOISTURE: Medium
SOIL: Moderately fertile, well-drained
FEATURES: Leaves, flowers
USES: Border, woodland
FLOWERS: ■

SITING: Light to deep shade suit heart-leaf brunnera. The soil should be moderately fertile to ensure low maintenance. The hairy, heart-shaped deep green leaves grow 2–8" long and form an attractive mound. Clusters of sky blue blooms appear in mid- to late spring and contrast beautifully with the deep green foliage. Plant brunnera in groups in a large shade border, or use singly as a specimen in a smaller space. Good companions include Bethlehem sage, Siebold hosta, astilbe, snakeroot, and Japanese painted fern.

Deadhead variegated brunnera before seeds fall to the ground to prevent nonvariegated seedlings from springing up.

CARE: Plant 24–36" apart in spring or fall. Apply slow-release granular plant food at time of planting or begin using water-soluble plant food 3 weeks after planting in spring. Cease feeding 6–8 weeks prior to first frost date. Water deeply whenever the soil begins to dry out; let the soil dry between waterings. Apply 3" of vegetative mulch in summer and winter to help retain soil moisture. The plant will lightly self-seed, but the seedlings will not be identical to the parent plant. Cut back in fall.

PROPAGATION: Divide in fall or early spring every 3 years. Dig around the root clump and lift. Use a sharp spade to slice through the root system. Reset portions that contain healthy roots and top shoots, then water and mulch. Discard any pieces that do not contain both healthy roots and top shoots.

PESTS AND DISEASES: Plants are relatively pest free when their cultural preferences (sun, soil, moisture) are met.

RELATED SPECIES: 'Dawson's White' ('Variegata') has attractive creamy white coloring along the leaf margins. 'Hadspen Cream' has narrow white leaf margins. Leaves of 'Langtree' have silver speckles.

CALADIUM
Caladium bicolor ka-LAY-dee-uhm BY-kuhl-ur

Caladium's graceful leaves and exotic colors are appealing in the shade.

ZONES: 8–11
SIZE: 24"h × 24"w
TYPE: Perennial
FORM: Irregular
TEXTURE: Medium
GROWTH: Fast
LIGHT: Full to partial shade

MOISTURE: Medium to high
SOIL: Fertile, well-drained
FEATURES: Leaves
USES: Bedding, border, container

SITING: Caladium prefers fertile, well-drained, acidic soil with a pH of 5.5–7.0, and full to part shade. The 12"-long arrowhead-shaped leaves come in pink, white, green, or red variegation. The large leaves can be damaged by excessive wind.

CARE: Plant 24" apart in late spring after the last frost. Caladium needs warm weather to grow well. Apply slow-release granular plant food at time of planting or begin using water-soluble plant food 3 weeks after planting in spring. Cease feeding 6–8 weeks prior to first frost date. Brown leaf edges may be the result of too much sun or improper watering. Lift tubers before a hard freeze and store in a cool (60–65°F), dry place during the winter.
PROPAGATION: Divide tubers in spring. Cut portions that include an "eye," or bud.

Dust with fungicide, then plant, water, and mulch.
PESTS AND DISEASES: Diseases include tuber rot, Southern blight, and bacterial and fungal leaf spots. Pests include root-knot nematodes, slugs, and snails.
RELATED SPECIES: 'Little Miss Muffet' is 12" tall and has green leaves with red veins and speckles. 'Pink Beauty' has red veins and pink-speckled margins, and 'White Queen' has white leaves with red veins and green margins. 'Florida Beauty' and 'Florida Carnival' are sun tolerant.

1 Cut back the leaves before lifting the tubers for winter storage.

2 Lift tubers and brush off soil before storing them.

3 Cover tubers with dry peat moss and store in a dry, cool location until spring.

POT MARIGOLD
Calendula officinalis kuh-LEN-dyoo-luh uh-fish-ih-NAL-iss

Pot marigold produces bright yellow or orange flowers during cooler summer temperatures.

ZONES: NA
SIZE: 12–30"h × 12–18"w
TYPE: Annual
FORM: Upright
TEXTURE: Medium
GROWTH: Fast
LIGHT: Full sun

MOISTURE: Medium to high
SOIL: Moderately fertile, well-drained
FEATURES: Flowers, foliage
USES: Bedding, border, container
FLOWERS: ■ ■

SITING: Calendula prefers full sun and moderately fertile soil with a pH of 5.5–7.0. The bright orange, yellow, gold, or cream blooms provide long-season color from

summer into fall. In hot climates use calendula as a cool-season annual. Place groups in the front of borders, in containers, or as bedding plants covering a large area. Pot marigold makes an excellent fresh-cut flower. Container companions include 'Brilliant' and 'Autumn Joy' sedums, cockscomb, and white-flower 'Miss Wilmott' pincushion flower.
CARE: Plant 12" apart in late spring or early summer after the last frost. Apply slow-release plant food, such as Miracle-Gro Shake 'n Feed All Purpose, at time of planting. Water deeply when the soil is dry. Deadhead the blooms to encourage reblooming. Remove the plants just prior to or after the first frost.
PROPAGATION: Sprinkle seeds over the soil mix and cover lightly. Thoroughly moisten and keep moist but not soggy. Germination will occur in 10–14 days at 70°F. After transplanting, reduce the temperature to 55°F.

PESTS AND DISEASES: Diseases include aster yellows, powdery mildew, and fungal leaf spots. Slugs feed on the foliage.
RELATED SPECIES: Cultivars include 'Art Shades' (24" tall with orange and cream flowers), 'Fiesta Giant' (a dwarf that reaches 12" tall and has double flowers in light orange and yellow), 'Indian Prince' (dark orange flowers with a reddish tint), and Pacific Beauty Series (double flowers that include interesting bicolors with a mahogany-colored center).

1 Harvest flowers just as they open for use in salads.

2 Sprinkle flower petals over salad for a festive look.

CARPATHIAN HAREBELL

Campanula carpatica *kam-PAN-yew-luh kar-PAT-ih-kuh*

Carpathian harebell, also known as Carpathian bellflower or tussock bellflower, produces bell-shaped blooms.

ZONES: 2–7
SIZE: 12"h × 12–24"w
TYPE: Perennial
FORM: Mound
TEXTURE: Fine
GROWTH: Medium
LIGHT: Partial shade to full sun

MOISTURE: Medium
SOIL: Moist, well-drained
FEATURES: Flowers, foliage
USES: Border, rock garden, container
FLOWERS: ■■□

SITING: Carpathian harebell prefers full sun or partial shade and well-drained, moderately fertile soil with a pH of 5.5–7.0. The upturned, bell-shaped blooms appear in shades of blue, violet, and white during the summer. Group plants in a border or rock garden, or use in containers. Good companions include bloody cranesbill and 'Elizabeth' campanula.

CARE: Plant 12–24" apart in spring or fall. Apply slow-release granular plant food at time of planting or begin using water-soluble plant food 3 weeks after planting in spring. Water deeply when the soil is dry. Apply 3" of mulch in summer to retain soil moisture. Blooms rarely require deadheading. Cut back in late fall.

PROPAGATION: Divide every 3 years in August or September, or in early spring when the plant is dormant. Sprinkle seeds lightly over soil mix and lightly cover. Germination occurs in 14–21 days at 70°F. Transplant 20–30 days after sowing.

PESTS AND DISEASES: Plants are relatively pest free. Slugs and snails may feed on the leaves, and Southern blight may be a problem on foliage.

RELATED SPECIES: Cultivars of note include 'Blue Clips,' 'White Clips,' 'Bressingham White,' and 'Jewel'.

1 Divide roots with a sharp spade or trowel.

2 Replant healthy roots in fertile soil, apply mulch, and water deeply.

CANNA

Canna ×*generalis* *KAN-uh jen-er-AL-is*

Canna has exotic foliage and vibrant-colored blooms. This is 'Black Knight'.

ZONES: 7–11
SIZE: 3–9'h × 2'w
TYPE: Perennial
FORM: Upright
TEXTURE: Coarse
GROWTH: Fast
LIGHT: Full sun
MOISTURE: Medium to high

SOIL: Fertile, moist, well-drained
FEATURES: Flowers, foliage
USES: Border, container
FLOWERS: ■■■■

SITING: Canna prefers full sun and deep, fertile soil that does not dry out or stay wet with a pH of 5.5–7.4. The foliage is bananalike. Flowers appear in terminal spikes for long-season color. Tuck canna into the back of a perennial border to soften its presence. Use daylilies 'Stella de Oro' and 'Hyperion' to edge a canna planting.

CARE: Plant canna 18–24" apart after the last frost and the soil is warm. Apply slow-release granular plant food at time of planting or begin using water-soluble plant food 3 weeks after planting. When the soil feels dry 2" below the surface, water deeply. Blooms require deadheading to maintain a good appearance. In cold climates after frost has caused the stems to turn black, remove the stems and leaves and store rhizomes in barely moist peat moss in a cool, frost-free location.

PROPAGATION: Divide stored rhizomes in spring. Cut the rhizome into sections and replant pieces that have a prominent eye, or bud.

PESTS AND DISEASES: Slugs, snails, spider mites, and caterpillars may feed on canna. Diseases include bacterial blight, rust, and fungal leaf spot.

RELATED SPECIES: 'Black Knight' bears deep red blooms. 'Wyoming' has bronze-colored leaves and orange flowers.

1 Cut back frosted foliage.

2 Dig rhizomes with a fork and shake off soil.

3 Store labelled rhizomes in a cool location.

ORNAMENTAL PEPPER

Capsicum annuum KAP-sih-kuhm AN-yew-uhm

Ornamental pepper's fruits are bright, colorful and extremely hot to the taste.

ZONES: 10–11
SIZE: 12–24"h × 20"w
TYPE: Annual
FORM: Upright
TEXTURE: Medium
GROWTH: Medium

LIGHT: Full sun
MOISTURE: Medium
SOIL: Fertile, moist
FEATURES: Fruit
USES: Edging, container, border
FLOWERS: ☐ ■

SITING: Ornamental pepper is a short-lived perennial commonly grown as an annual. It prefers full sun and fertile, moist soil with ample organic matter and a pH of 5.5–7.0. The ornamental fruits appear in midsummer and last until frost. Shiny black, red, yellow, cream, or purple fruits grow 1–6" long. Tiny, star- or bell-shaped white or yellow flowers form in the leaf axils. Plant this pepper in groups for best effect. It may be used to edge a small garden or container. Select companions that have comparable bold color or act as a subtle foil and background to the peppers. Bold companions include gladiolus and dahlia. Subtle companions include rosemary, blue oat grass, and 'Gracillimus' maiden grass.

CARE: Plant 12–18" apart in spring after the last frost. Ornamental pepper performs best in fertile soil high in organic matter. To increase organic matter in the soil, add 1–2" of composted material (food and leaf waste, animal manure more than 1 year old, mushroom compost, peat moss, or bagged humus) to the planting bed and till in to a depth of 12". After planting, water deeply and add 3" of mulch around, but not touching, the plants. Apply slow-release plant food, such as Miracle-Gro Shake 'n Feed All Purpose, at time of planting or begin using water-soluble plant food, such as Miracle-Gro Water Soluble All Purpose, 3 weeks after planting in spring. Follow label directions for amount and frequency. Ornamental pepper prefers even moisture, so water deeply when the soil is almost dry. Cut back the growing tips of young plants to promote branching. Remove plants after or right before the first frost. Cover the bare soil with 3" of mulch to protect the topsoil over the winter.

PROPAGATION: Sprinkle seeds over the soil mix and cover. Thoroughly moisten and keep moist, not soggy, until seeds germinate. Germination occurs in 10 days at 70°F. Transplant 21–26 days after sowing and reduce the temperature to 62°F.

PESTS AND DISEASES: Diseases include anthracnose and wilt diseases, southern blight, and fruit rot.

CUPID'S DART

Catananche caerulea kat-uh-NAN-kee suh-ROO-lee-uh

The lilac-colored flowers of Cupid's dart attract butterflies and may be used fresh cut or dried. It is also know as blue succory.

ZONES: 4–8
SIZE: 24–36"h × 12"w
TYPE: Perennial
FORM: Upright
TEXTURE: Medium
GROWTH: Medium
LIGHT: Full sun

MOISTURE: Medium
SOIL: Moderately fertile, well-drained
FEATURES: Flowers, foliage
USES: Border, container
FLOWERS: ■ ■ ☐

SITING: Cupid's dart prefers full sun and moderately fertile, well-drained soil with a pH of 5.5–7.0. Striking lilac-blue flowers with a darker center appear from midsummer until autumn. Grasslike leaves are hairy and silvery. Flowers attract bees and butterflies and are excellent fresh cut or dried. Good companions include purple fountain grass, rosemary, and thyme.

CARE: Plant 8–12" apart in spring or fall. Apply slow-release plant food, such as Miracle-Gro Shake 'n Feed All Purpose, in spring or begin using water-soluble plant food, such as Miracle-Gro Water Soluble All Purpose, 3 weeks after planting. Follow label directions for amount and frequency. Apply 3" of vegetative mulch in summer and winter to reduce weed germination, hold moisture in the soil, and as it decomposes, add organic matter to the soil. Water deeply when the soil is dry. Deadhead spent blooms to encourage reblooming. Divide annually in spring to extend the life of these short-lived plants. Prune back in fall once frost collapses the foliage.

PROPAGATION: Divide in spring. Dig around the rhizomes and lift. Use a sharp spade to slice through the root system. Reset portions that contain healthy roots and top shoots. Discard any pieces that do not contain both healthy roots and top shoots. Water deeply and apply 3" of vegetative mulch around, but not touching, the plants.

PESTS AND DISEASES: Plants are relatively pest free when cultural requirements (sun, soil, planting depth, moisture) are met. Powdery mildew is an occasional pest.

RELATED SPECIES: 'Alba' bears white flowers, 'Bicolor' has white flowers with a deep blue center, 'Blue Giant' bears cornflower-blue flowers on silvery foliage, 'Major' has deep lavender flowers, and 'Perry's White' has white blooms.

Deadhead Cupid's dart as flowers fade to stimulate rebloom throughout the summer.

COCKSCOMB
Celosia argentea sel-OH-see-uh ar-JEN-tee-uh

Cockscomb flowers add vibrant color and texture to the landscape.

ZONES: NA
SIZE: 24"h × 18"w
TYPE: Annual
FORM: Upright
TEXTURE: Medium
GROWTH: Medium
LIGHT: Full sun
MOISTURE: Medium
SOIL: Fertile, well-drained, moist
FEATURES: Flowers
USES: Bedding, container
FLOWERS: ■■■■

SITING: Cockscomb prefers full sun and fertile, well-drained soil with a pH of 5.5–7.0. Plants are technically perennials but are commonly grown as annuals. The Plumosa cultivars produce feathery flowers; Cristata cultivars bear blooms that resemble a rooster's comb, and last all summer. They are useful as bedding plants, in a border, or in containers. The orange, yellow, and red colors are perfect for a hot patio or pool area. Blooms may be dried or used as fresh-cut flowers. Companions include dahlia, gladiolus, 'David' garden phlox, and goldenrod.

CARE: Plant 12–18" apart, depending on the cultivar. Apply slow-release granular plant food at time of planting, or begin using water-soluble plant food 3 weeks after planting in spring. Follow label directions for amount and frequency. Cockscomb prefers even moisture, so water deeply as soon as the soil is almost dry. Apply mulch to help retain soil moisture. Remove plants after or right before the first frost. Cover the bare soil with 3" of mulch to protect the topsoil over the winter.

PROPAGATION: Sprinkle seeds over the soil mix and cover. Thoroughly moisten and keep moist, not soggy, until seeds germinate. Germination occurs in 10 days at 75°F. Transplant 10–15 days after sowing, and reduce the temperature to 65–68°F.

Harvest cockscomb for drying while it is in peak bloom.

PESTS AND DISEASES: Fungal leaf spot, root and stem rot, and spider mites are occasional problems.

RELATED SPECIES: Plumosa cultivars include 'Apricot Brandy' (20" high with apricot-colored blooms), 'Fairy Fountains' (16" high, with pastel shades of pink, salmon, and yellow), Kimono Series (8" high, with large flowers of bright yellow, rose red, cream, and salmon pink), and 'New Look' (18" high with rich red blooms and bronze-tinged foliage). Cristata cultivars include Big Chief Mix (3' high with 6"-wide yellow, pink, and red flowers), Jewel Box Mix (8" high with bright yellow, red, salmon, and pink flowers, occasionally several colors on one flower), and Kurume Series (4' high bearing a wide range of bright colors including bicolors).

To dry the flowers, hang them upside down in a dry location out of direct sunlight .

CORNFLOWER
Centaurea cyanus sen-TOR-ee-uh sy-AN-us

Cornflower, also known as bachelor's buttons, has blue flowers that are excellent fresh cut or dried.

ZONES: NA
SIZE: 12–30"h × 6"w
TYPE: Annual
FORM: Upright
TEXTURE: Medium
GROWTH: Fast
LIGHT: Full sun
MOISTURE: Medium
SOIL: Well-drained
FEATURES: Flowers, foliage
USES: Border, container, naturalizing
FLOWERS: ■■□

SITING: Cornflower prefers full sun and well-drained soil with moderate fertility and a pH of 5.5–7.5. The 1" blue blooms appear from late spring to midsummer. Plants are prolific self-seeders, so informal areas, especially cottage gardens, are ideal sites. Mass plants in a mixed border for early-season color. Cornflower blooms are excellent as fresh-cut or dried flowers. Companions include 'Strawberry Fields' globe amaranth, 'The Fairy' rose, and 'Horizon Red Halo' petunia.

CARE: Plant 6" apart in spring after the last frost. Apply slow-release plant food, such as Miracle-Gro Shake 'n Feed All Purpose, at time of planting or begin using water-soluble plant food, such as Miracle-Gro Water Soluble All Purpose, 3 weeks after planting in spring. Follow label directions for amount and frequency. Cornflower is relatively drought tolerant, so let the soil dry between waterings. Apply 3" of vegetative mulch to help retain soil moisture and add organic matter to the soil as it decomposes. If seedlings are not desired, deadhead blooms early on. Remove plants after or right before the first frost. Cover the bare soil with 3" of mulch to protect the topsoil over the winter.

PROPAGATION: Cornflower is easy to direct seed into the garden. Sprinkle seeds over the soil mix and lightly cover. Thoroughly moisten and keep moist, not soggy, until seeds germinate. Germination occurs in 7–14 days at 65–70°F. Transplant 20–25 days after sowing, and reduce the temperature to 50–55°F.

PESTS AND DISEASES: Downy and powdery mildew, crown rot, and rust may occur.

RELATED SPECIES: Perennial (Zones 3–8) mountain bluet (*C. montana*) has blue flowers on plants 18–24" tall.

SNOW-IN-SUMMER
Cerastium tomentosum *seh-RAS-tee-uhm toh-men-TOH-suhm*

Snow-in-summer performs well in hot, dry places. Its name derives from its snowy white summer blooms.

ZONES: 3–7
SIZE: 6–8"h × 12"w
TYPE: Perennial
FORM: Spreading
TEXTURE: Medium to fine
GROWTH: Fast
LIGHT: Full sun
MOISTURE: Medium to low

SOIL: Low to moderately fertile, sandy
FEATURES: Flowers, foliage
USES: Naturalizing, ground cover, container
FLOWERS: □

SITING: Snow-in-summer prefers full sun and well-drained, sandy soil with moderate to low fertility and a pH of 5.5–7.0. This plant may be invasive, so select a location where it has room to grow, or confine it to a container. The woolly silver-gray foliage is attractive all season, and many star-shaped white flowers appear in late spring and summer. Plants are well suited for difficult hot, dry locations such as containers on pool patios, along hot walls, between stepping-stones, or as a ground cover on a steep slope.

CARE: Plant 1–2' apart in early spring or fall. Apply slow-release granular plant food at time of planting. It is relatively drought tolerant, so let the soil dry between waterings. Apply 3" of vegetative mulch to help retain soil moisture and add organic matter to the soil as it decomposes. To encourage a tidy appearance, cut the plants back after flowering. Cut back again in fall after frost has collapsed the foliage.

PROPAGATION: Divide the fibrous roots in spring or fall. Dig around the root clump and lift. Use a sharp spade to slice through the root system. Reset portions that contain healthy roots and top shoots, then water and mulch. Discard any pieces that do not contain both healthy roots and top shoots. Sprinkle seeds over the soil mix and leave exposed to light. Thoroughly moisten and keep moist, not soggy, until seeds germinate. Germination occurs in 7–14 days at 65°F. Transplant 15–25 days after sowing, and reduce the temperature to 50°F.

PESTS AND DISEASES: Plants are relatively pest free when their cultural preferences are met. Root rot may occur if planted in wet soil.

RELATED SPECIES: 'Silver Carpet' and 'Yo-yo' are more compact than the species. Taurus chickweed (*C. biebersteinii*) grows 6–12" tall and bears ¾" white flowers. It is hardy in Zones 3–7.

LEADWORT
Ceratostigma plumbaginoides *ser-ah-toh-STIG-muh plum-ba-jih-NOY-deez*

Leadwort provides attractive late-season blooms. It is also known as plumbago.

ZONES: 5–9
SIZE: 18"h × 12"w
TYPE: Perennial
FORM: Spreading
TEXTURE: Medium
GROWTH: Fast
LIGHT: Part shade to full sun
MOISTURE: Medium to low

SOIL: Moderately fertile
FEATURES: Foliage, flowers
USES: Ground cover, border, container
FLOWERS: ■
FALL COLOR: ■ ■

SITING: Leadwort prefers full sun or afternoon shade and moderately fertile, well-drained soil with a pH of 5.5–7.5. The foliage boasts red stems and bright green leaves that turn bronzy red in autumn. Pinwheellike bright blue flowers appear in late summer and last into fall.

Use in containers or as a ground cover in the rock garden or shrub border.

CARE: Plant 12" apart in spring or fall. Apply slow-release granular plant food at time of planting. Leadwort is relatively drought tolerant; let the soil dry between waterings. Apply 3" of vegetative mulch to help retain soil moisture and add organic matter to the soil as it decomposes. Cut back in late fall or leave erect for late-season viewing and cut back in early spring before growth begins.

PROPAGATION: Divide in early spring. Dig around the clump and lift. Use a sharp spade to slice through the root system. Reset portions that contain healthy roots and top shoots, then water and mulch. Discard any pieces that do not contain both healthy roots and top shoots. Root softwood cuttings in spring. Remove the bottom leaves from cuttings, exposing the nodes. Each cutting should have two or three nodes exposed and one pair of leaves. Insert the cutting in moist soil mix. Nodes should be below soil level and leaves above. Keep the soil mix moist but not soggy until roots form. Ideal temperatures are 65–70°F for the soil mix and 55–60°F for the air. High humidity hastens growth.

PESTS AND DISEASES: Plants are relatively pest free when their cultural preferences are met.

Mark leadwort's location in the garden because it emerges late in spring.

SNAKEROOT
Cimicifuga racemosa sim-ih-sib-FEW-guh ray-seb-MOH-sub

Cimicifuga racemosa adds stately grace to the shade border. It is also known as cohosh, black cohosh, or bugbane.

ZONES: 3–8
SIZE: 4–7'h × 2'w
TYPE: Perennial
FORM: Upright
TEXTURE: Medium
GROWTH: Medium
LIGHT: Partial shade
MOISTURE: Medium to high

SOIL: Fertile, moist, well-drained
FEATURES: Flowers, foliage
USES: Border, woodland, container
FLOWERS: ☐

SITING: Snakeroot prefers afternoon shade and fertile, moist, well-drained soil with a pH of 5.5–7.0. It is a choice addition to the shade border with deep green toothed leaves and slender, curving racemes of creamy white blooms in midsummer. Place odd-numbered groups in the middle or rear of a border or use as a tall focal point in a container planting. Plants are also suited to a woodland garden. Good companions include astilbe, fingerleaf rodgersia, 'The Rocket' ligularia, and Siebold hosta.

CARE: Plant 18–24" apart in spring or fall in soil containing ample organic matter. To increase organic matter in the soil, add

Plants receiving one-sided light may lean and require staking to compensate.

1–2" of composted material and till in to a depth of 15–18". After planting, water deeply and add 3" of mulch around, but not touching, the plants. Apply slow-release granular plant food at time of planting. Water deeply whenever the soil is dry, allowing the soil to dry between waterings. Reapply mulch whenever necessary to maintain 3" in summer and winter. Mulch also adds beneficial organic matter to the soil as it decomposes. Leave plants standing in fall until they no longer look attractive, then cut back.

PROPAGATION: Snakeroot recovers slowly from division. If you decide to split clumps, divide them in spring or fall. Dig around the root clump and lift. Use a sharp spade to slice through the root system. Reset portions that contain healthy roots and top shoots, then water and mulch.

PESTS AND DISEASES: Plants are relatively pest free when their cultural preferences for sun, soil, and moisture are met.

RELATED SPECIES: Autumn snakeroot (*C. simplex* 'Brunette') has dark brown foliage with a purple tint, purple stems, and creamy white blooms with a pinkish-purple tinge.

SPIDER FLOWER
Cleome hassleriana klee-OH-mee hass-lair-ee-AY-nuh

Spider flowers offer a profusion of pink and purple blooms in summer.

ZONES: NA
SIZE: 5'h × 18"w
TYPE: Annual
FORM: Upright
TEXTURE: Medium
GROWTH: Fast
LIGHT: Full sun
MOISTURE: Low to medium

SOIL: Fertile, sandy, well-drained
FEATURES: Flowers, foliage
USES: Naturalizing, border, container
FLOWERS: ■■☐

SITING: Spider flower prefers full sun and fertile, sandy, well-drained soil with a pH of 5.5–7.0. This robust annual has an abundance of spidery fragrant pink, white, and purple flowers in summer. Plants self-sow freely, so place where weeding them is feasible or there is room for them to naturalize or colonize. The spines on the base of the leaf stalk warrant wearing gloves and long sleeves when working nearby. In South Carolina, spider flower is a common highway planting, testimony to its ruggedness. Plant near a white picket

Remove unwanted self-sown spider flower seedlings. They can become weedy.

fence for old-fashioned nostalgia, in a cottage garden, or in containers. Good companions include 'David' garden phlox, and 'Carefree Wonder,' 'Bonica,' and 'Iceberg' roses.

CARE: Plant 18" apart in spring after the last frost. Apply slow-release granular plant food at time of planting. Allow the soil to dry between waterings. Apply 3" of vegetative mulch to help retain soil moisture and add organic matter to the soil as it decomposes. Plants readily self-seed. Be prepared to remove volunteer seedlings the following year. Remove plants after or right before the first frost.

PROPAGATION: Sprinkle seeds over the soil mix and cover lightly. Thoroughly moisten and keep moist but not soggy until seeds germinate. Germination occurs in 10–12 days with a daytime temperature of 80°F and a nighttime temperature of 70°F. Transplant 21–25 days after sowing and reduce the temperature to 70–75°F.

PESTS AND DISEASES: Aphids are common pests. Diseases include fungal leaf spot, rust, and powdery mildew.

RELATED SPECIES: Sparkler Series is more compact than most cultivars.

AUTUMN CROCUS
Colchicum autumnale KOHL-chih-kuhm aw-tuhm-NAL-ee

Clusters of autumn crocus flowers are welcome additions to the late-season landscape.

ZONES: 5–9
SIZE: 4–6"h × 4"w
TYPE: Perennial
FORM: Upright
TEXTURE: Fine to medium
GROWTH: Medium
LIGHT: Partial shade to full sun

MOISTURE: Medium to high
SOIL: Deep, fertile, well-drained
FEATURES: Flowers
USES: Naturalizing, border, container
FLOWERS: ■■□

SITING: Autumn crocus prefers full sun or partial shade and deep, fertile, well-drained soil, with a pH of 5.5–7.0. It is among the earliest of the *Colchicums* to flower in fall, bearing as many as six flowers 6" high. Foliage appears after flowering. Autumn crocus looks best grown in groups among trees and shrubs, naturalized at the edge of the woodlands, or placed in containers. All parts of the plant are toxic.

CARE: Plant corms 6" apart in partial shade or full sun in late summer. Apply slow-release granular plant food at time of planting. Water during dry spells. Apply 3" of vegetative mulch to help retain soil moisture and add organic matter to the soil as it decomposes. Allow leaves to die back naturally; cutting foliage prematurely weakens the corm.

PROPAGATION: Divide or separate corms while plants are dormant in summer. Small corms, called cormels, produced at the base of the parent corm can be snapped or cut off and replanted.

PESTS AND DISEASES: Slugs are common pests on autumn crocus.

RELATED SPECIES: 'Alboplenum' has double white flowers, and 'Pleniflorum' has double pink-lilac flowers.

1 Healthy corms will feel firm to the touch.

2 Place corms, wide side down, tip up, 6" apart in a large hole.

3 Cover corms with soil and water deeply.

LARKSPUR
Consolida hybrids kohn-sah-LEE-dah

Larkspur flowers are classic additions to cottage gardens and English perennial borders.

ZONES: NA
SIZE: 12–36"h × 6–14"w
TYPE: Annual
FORM: Upright
TEXTURE: Medium
GROWTH: Fast
LIGHT: Full sun
MOISTURE: Medium

SOIL: Fertile, well-drained
FEATURES: Flowers, foliage
USES: Border, naturalizing, container
FLOWERS: ■■■□

SITING: Larkspur prefers full sun and fertile, well-drained soil with a pH of 5.5–7.5. Showy, delphiniumlike flowers appear in summer. The feathery bright green foliage is an added attraction. Grow in large groups and mixed colors for an old-fashioned cottage garden effect.

CARE: Plant larkspur 6-12" apart, depending on the cultivar, in late spring after frost has passed. Apply slow-release plant food, such as Miracle-Gro Shake 'n Feed All Purpose, at time of planting, or begin using water-soluble plant food, such as Miracle-Gro Water Soluble All Purpose,

Deadhead larkspur before seed pods mature to prevent self-seeding.

3 weeks after planting. Follow label directions for amount and frequency. Water deeply whenever the soil is dry. Apply 3" of vegetative mulch to help retain soil moisture and add organic matter to the soil as it decomposes. Remove plant just prior to or right after first frost.

PROPAGATION: Plants self-sow in the garden. To sow seed indoors, chill the seeds for 7 days at 35°F. Sprinkle seeds over the soil mix and cover. Thoroughly moisten and keep moist, not soggy, until seeds germinate. Germination occurs in 10–20 days at 55–65°F. Transplant 28–35 days after sowing and reduce the temperature to 50–55°F.

PESTS AND DISEASES: Slugs, snails, and powdery mildew are problems.

RELATED SPECIES: The cultivar 'Blue Bell' has sky blue flowers, 'Blue Spire' has deep blue flowers that hint of purple, 'Brilliant Rose' flowers are deep pink, 'Dazzler' flowers are scarlet, and 'Exquisite Rose' flowers are bright pink. Plants in the Imperial Series are tall, some reaching 3', with spurred double flowers in mauve, pink, blue, and white.

LILY-OF-THE-VALLEY
Convallaria majalis kahn-vuh-LAIR-ee-uh mah-JA-liss

Lily-of-the-valley produces fragrant nodding flowers in spring.

ZONES: 2–7
SIZE: 9"h × 12"w
TYPE: Perennial
FORM: Upright
TEXTURE: Medium
GROWTH: Medium
LIGHT: Full to partial shade

MOISTURE: Low to medium
SOIL: Fertile, moist
FEATURES: Flowers, foliage, fruit
USES: Ground cover, woodland
FLOWERS: □ ■

SITING: Lily-of-the-valley prefers partial or full shade and fertile, loose soil with a pH of 5.5–7.0. Lance-shape to elliptic basal leaves are bright green and attractive all season long. Brilliant tiny, bell-shaped fragrant white blooms appear on arching stems in spring. As a ground cover, lily-of-the-valley is indispensable. It is one of the few plants that can successfully compete with tree roots. Plant in groups for best effect.

CARE: Plant 12" apart in spring or fall in humus soil high in organic matter. To increase organic matter in the soil, add 1–2" of composted material and till in. After planting, water deeply and add 3" of mulch around, but not touching, the plants. Apply slow-release granular plant food at time of planting. Water deeply whenever the soil is dry, allowing the soil to dry between waterings. Reapply mulch whenever necessary to maintain 3" in summer and winter. Plants rarely need to be cut back in fall. If you would like to cut the back, place your lawn mower on its highest setting and mow them off.

PROPAGATION: Divide in spring or fall. Dig around the rhizomes and lift. Use a sharp spade to slice through the root system. Reset portions that contain healthy roots and top shoots, then water and mulch. Discard any pieces that do not contain both healthy root and top shoots.

PESTS AND DISEASES: Diseases that affect lily-of-the-valley include white mold, gray mold, and anthracnose. Provide good air circulation to minimize diseases.

RELATED SPECIES: 'Albostriata' has cream-striped leaves, 'Aureovariegata' has yellow-striped leaves, and var. *rosea* has pale pink flowers. No other species exist in the genus.

1 In spring or fall lift roots for dividing.

2 Separate roots so each section contains healthy top growth.

3 Reset plants in a new location.

4 Apply mulch and water deeply.

GROUND MORNING GLORY
Convolvulus sabatius kon-VULV-yew-luhs sub-BA-tee-uhs

Ground morning glory climbs along sunny slopes and banks.

ZONES: 8–9
SIZE: 6"h × 20"w
TYPE: Perennial
FORM: Spreading
TEXTURE: Medium
GROWTH: Fast
LIGHT: Full sun
MOISTURE: Low

SOIL: Low fertility, well-drained
FEATURES: Flowers
USES: Container, ground cover, walls
FLOWERS: ■

SITING: Ground morning glory prefers full sun and poor, well-drained soil with a pH of 5.5–7.0. It has trailing stems, evergreen leaves, and clusters of funnel-shaped lavender-blue blooms from summer to early fall. Grow in containers, along walls, or as a ground cover on a sunny bank. Shelter from wind.

CARE: Plant 12–18" apart in late spring after the last frost. Apply slow-release granular plant food at time of planting, or begin using water-soluble plant food 3 weeks after planting in spring. Follow label directions for amount and frequency. Let the soil dry between waterings. Apply 3" of vegetative mulch to help retain soil moisture and add organic matter to the soil as it decomposes. Cut plants back if more compactness is desired. Remove plants in fall after frost has collapsed the foliage in zones where it will not survive the winter.

PROPAGATION: Sow seed in spring and provide 55–65°F temperatures.

PESTS AND DISEASES: Rust may be a problem.

TICKSEED
Coreopsis grandiflora kor-ee-OP-sis grand-ih-FLOR-uh

Tickseed, also known as coreopsis, produces bright golden yellow summer color. Some cultivars have red centers.

ZONES: 4–9
SIZE: 18–36" × 24"w
TYPE: Perennial
FORM: Upright
TEXTURE: Medium to fine
GROWTH: Medium
LIGHT: Full sun

MOISTURE: Medium
SOIL: Fertile, well-drained
FEATURES: Flowers, foliage
USES: Border, container
FLOWERS: ■

SITING: Tickseed prefers full sun and fertile, well-drained soil with a pH of 5.5–7.0. Flowers with a deep yellow center and scalloped tips appear from late spring to late summer and are ideal for cutting. Plant in odd-numbered groups in a perennial border or place in containers. Companions include purple coneflower, 'Snowbank' white boltonia, 'David' garden phlox, and torch lily.

Deadhead flowers to stimulate reblooming.

CARE: Plant 18–24" apart in spring or fall. Apply slow-release granular plant food at time of planting. Water deeply only when the soil is dry. Apply 3" of vegetative mulch to help retain soil moisture and add organic matter to the soil as it decomposes. Deadhead to stimulate flowering. Cut back in fall after frost has collapsed the foliage.

PROPAGATION: Tickseed is a short-lived perennial that self-seeds. Start new plants from seed, save some of the self-sown seedlings for transplanting or divide existing plants in spring or early fall. Reset portions that contain healthy roots and top shoots, then water and mulch.

PESTS AND DISEASES: Slugs and snails are pests. Diseases include botrytis flower blight, aster yellows, and powdery and downy mildew.

RELATED SPECIES: The cultivar 'Badengold' (36" high) has golden-yellow flowers with an orange center, and 'Early Sunrise' (18" high) has semidouble yellow flowers with an orange tint near the center.

THREADLEAF COREOPSIS
Coreopsis verticillata kor-ee-OP-sis ver-tiss-ih-LAHT-uh

Threadleaf coreopsis is a low-maintenance long season bloomer.

ZONES: 4–9
SIZE: 24–36"h × 24"w
TYPE: Perennial
FORM: Upright
TEXTURE: Fine
GROWTH: Medium
LIGHT: Full sun

MOISTURE: Medium
SOIL: Fertile, well-drained
FEATURES: Flowers, foliage
USES: Border, container
FLOWERS: ■

SITING: Threadleaf coreopsis prefers full sun and fertile, well-drained soil with a pH of 5.5–7.0. Plants tolerate humidity and heat. The fine-textured, threadlike foliage is attractive throughout the growing season. Small yellow flowers appear in early summer and bloom through fall. Place in the front of a perennial border, or add to a mixed container planting. Good companions include 'Coronation Gold' achillea, 'Goldsturm' black-eyed Susan, pink coreopsis, 'Stargazer' lily, and 'Stafford,' 'Red Rum,' 'Scarlet Orbit,' and 'Red Joy' daylilies.

CARE: Plant 18" apart in spring or fall. Apply slow-release granular plant food at time of planting. Water deeply whenever the soil is dry; allow the soil to dry between waterings. Apply 3" of mulch and reapply whenever necessary to maintain 3" in summer and winter. Flowers are considered self-cleaning and do not need to be deadheaded. Leave plants standing in fall until frost collapses them, then cut back. Plants may be slow to appear in spring.

Use a sharp spade to slice through roots of threadleaf coreopsis during division.

PROPAGATION: Divide in spring or early fall. Dig around the root clump and lift. Use a sharp spade to slice through the root system. Reset portions that contain healthy roots and top shoots.

PESTS AND DISEASES: Except for rabbits, plants are relatively pest free when their cultural preferences are met.

RELATED SPECIES: *C. verticillata* 'Zagreb' has golden-yellow flowers. 'Moonbeam', a superior cultivar, grows 18" high and wide and has threadleaf foliage and pale yellow blooms from summer through autumn. Pink coreopsis (*C. rosea*) has pink blooms on and off all summer into fall, fine texture, and a neat habit.

YELLOW CORYDALIS
Corydalis lutea kor-IH-duh-lis LOO-tee-uh

Yellow corydalis boasts attractive yellow tubular flowers and mounding blue-green foliage for the shade.

ZONES: 4–8
SIZE: 15"h × 12"w
TYPE: Perennial
FORM: Rounded
TEXTURE: Fine
GROWTH: Medium
LIGHT: Full sun to partial shade

MOISTURE: Medium
SOIL: Fertile, well-drained
FEATURES: Flowers, foliage
USES: Woodland, border, rock garden
FLOWERS: ■

SITING: Yellow corydalis tolerates full sun or partial shade and prefers fertile, well-drained soil with a pH of 5.5–7.0. Fernlike leaves form mounds that are attractive throughout the growing season. Tiny, tubular yellow flowers appear from late spring into early fall. Place yellow corydalis among rocks, in a perennial border, at the edge of a woodland, or in containers. Good companions include 'Alba' fringeleaf bleeding heart, 'Moonbeam' threadleaf coreopsis, 'Rubra' Japanese blood grass, and 'White Swirl' Siberian iris.

CARE: Plant 12" apart in spring or fall. Apply slow-release granular plant food at time of planting. Water deeply when the soil is dry. Plants will self-seed but will not be invasive. After frost cut back collapsed foliage.

1 Dig self-sown seedlings of yellow corydalis.

PROPAGATION: Divide in spring or early fall. Dig around the root clump and lift. Use a sharp spade to slice through the root system. Reset portions that contain healthy roots and top shoots.

PESTS AND DISEASES: Plants are relatively pest free when their cultural preferences are met. Rusts and downy mildew occasionally occur.

RELATED SPECIES: *C. flexuosa* (Zones 6–8; 12" high) has neon-blue tubular blooms from late spring to summer and prefers partial shade. 'Blue Panda' (8" high) has bright blue flowers.

2 Relocate seedlings to other areas of the shade garden.

TALL COSMOS
Cosmos bipinnatus KAHZ-mohs beye-pin-A-tuss

A mass planting of tall cosmos creates a sea of red and pink on feathery foliage.

ZONES: NA
SIZE: 5'h × 18"w
TYPE: Annual
FORM: Upright
TEXTURE: Fine
GROWTH: Fast
LIGHT: Full sun
MOISTURE: Dry to moist

SOIL: Well-drained
FEATURES: Flowers, foliage
USES: Border, naturalizing, container
FLOWERS: □ ■ ■

SITING: Tall cosmos prefers full sun and moderately fertile, well-drained soil with a pH range of 5.5–7.0. Attractive, single, 3" flowers are red, pink, or white with a yellow center; they appear in summer and attract butterflies. Foliage is feathery bright green. Plants are heat and drought tolerant. Good companions include 'The Fairy' and 'Iceberg' roses and 'David' garden phlox.

CARE: Plant 12–18" apart in late spring. Apply slow-release granular plant food at time of planting, or begin using water-soluble plant food 3 weeks after planting. Water deeply when the soil is dry. If naturalizing, water new transplants until they are actively growing. Remove plants after the first frost.

PROPAGATION: Plants self-sow in the garden. To sow seed indoors, sprinkle

Cosmos sulphureus cultivars are tall with gold or reddish-orange flowers.

seeds over the soil mix and cover. Thoroughly moisten and keep moist, not soggy, until seeds germinate. Germination occurs in 5–7 days at 70°F. Transplant 11–15 days after sowing, and reduce the temperature to 65°F.

PESTS AND DISEASES: Aphids are a common pest; powdery mildew and Rhizoctonia stem rot are known diseases.

RELATED SPECIES: 'Picotee' reaches 30" tall and has white flowers with a dark crimson margin, 'Seashells' grows 3' tall and has curiously rolled red, pink, or white flowers, 'Sonata Series' are 12" tall with white, red, or pink flowers, and 'Sonata White' reaches 18" tall with clear white blooms that contrast well with the feathery bright green foliage. Sulphur cosmos (*C. sulphureus*) has orange, reddish, or reddish-yellow flowers and reaches 6' tall and 18" wide. Klondike Series 'Sunny Gold' is dwarf, reaches 16" high, and has semidouble yellow flowers. Klondike Series 'Sunny Orange-Red' reaches 12" high and has reddish-orange flowers. Plants in the Ladybird Series grow 12" high and bear semidouble yellow, red, or orange flowers.

GIANT KALE
Crambe cordifolia KRAM-bee kord-ih-FOH-lee-uh

Giant kale may reach 8' high.

ZONES: 4–8
SIZE: 8'h × 5'w
TYPE: Perennial
FORM: Mound
TEXTURE: Coarse foliage, fine bloom
GROWTH: Fast
LIGHT: Full sun

MOISTURE: Medium
SOIL: Fertile, deep, well-drained
FEATURES: Foliage, flowers
USES: Accent, container
FLOWERS: □

SITING: Giant kale prefers full sun and deep, fertile, well-drained soil but tolerates poor soil. It prefers a pH of 5.5–7.5. Select a site that has shelter from strong winds. The plant has huge (to 15" wide) crinkled deep green leaves that die down in mid- to late summer. The plant is stately, and in full bloom is spectacular with clouds of tiny white flowers covering the top of the plant from late spring to midsummer. Place in a large space, along a stream bank, in the center of a border, or in a container. Neighboring plants should be able to cover the space left after foliage dies back in summer. Good garden companions include 'Goldsturm' black-eyed Susan, 'Autumn Joy' sedum, Kansas gayfeather, and 'Kobold' blazing star.

CARE: Plant 3–5' apart in spring or fall. Apply slow-release granular plant food at time of planting, or begin using water-soluble plant food 3 weeks after planting in spring. Cease feeding 4–6 weeks prior to first frost date. Water deeply when the soil is dry. Apply 3" of vegetative mulch in summer and winter to help retain soil moisture and add organic matter to the soil as it decomposes.

PROPAGATION: Divide in early spring. Dig around the root clump and lift. Use a sharp spade to slice through the root system. Reset portions that contain healthy roots and top shoots, then water and mulch. Discard any pieces that do not contain both healthy roots and top shoots.

PESTS AND DISEASES: Plants are relatively pest free when their cultural preferences (sun, soil, moisture) are met.

RELATED SPECIES: Sea kale *(C. maritima)* has blue-green leaves and white flowers and grows 3' high and 2' wide.

CROCOSMIA
Crocosmia ×crocosmiiflora kroh-KOZ-mee-ah kroh-koz-mee-ih-FLO-rah

Crocosmia, also called montbretia, bears nodding yellow or orange flowers and has swordlike leaves.

ZONES: 6–9
SIZE: 2–3'h × 1'w
TYPE: Perennial
FORM: Upright
TEXTURE: Medium
GROWTH: Fast
LIGHT: Sun to partial shade

MOISTURE: Medium
SOIL: Moderately fertile, well-drained
FEATURES: Flowers, foliage
USES: Border, container
FLOWERS: ■ ■

SITING: Crocosmia tolerates full sun or partial shade and prefers moderately fertile, well-drained soil with a pH of 5.5–7.0. The nodding yellow or red-orange flowers are funnel-shaped and appear along the length of the arching stems during the summer. Blooms are excellent cut flowers. Leaves are swordlike and pale green. Place odd-numbered groups in the border or in containers for best effect. Companions include 'Morning Light' maiden grass, Siberian iris, and threadleaf coreopsis.

CARE: Plant corms 3" deep and 6" apart in spring in humus-rich soil. Apply slow-release granular plant food at time of planting. Water deeply whenever the soil is dry. Apply 3" of vegetative mulch in summer and winter to help retain soil moisture and add organic matter to the soil as it decomposes. After frost, cut back foliage. In cooler locations lift corms in fall after flowering but before the first hard frost. Remove offsets (cormels), dead roots, and stems. Store firm, healthy corms and cormels in a dry, warm place (60–70°F) until spring.

PROPAGATION: Divide in spring or fall. Unearth the corm and separate offsets that form around its base. Replant healthy, firm corms 6" apart in moderately fertile, well-drained soil, then water and mulch.

PESTS AND DISEASES: Spider mites are common pests. Dislodge with a stream of water, or use a pesticide to manage troublesome infestations.

RELATED SPECIES: 'Emily McKenzie' has orange flowers; 'Golden Fleece' has yellow blooms. *C. masoniorum* is hardy in Zones 6–9 and bears red-orange flowers on plants 3' tall. Intergeneric hybrids 'Bressingham Blaze', 'Emberglow', and 'Lucifer' have outstanding red-orange blooms on plants 3' tall.

Clip faded flower stalks of crocosmia to keep the plants tidy.

SHOWY CROCUS
Crocus speciosus KRO-kuhs spee-see-O-suhs

Showy crocus, also known as fall crocus, is fall-blooming and durable.

ZONES: 3–8
SIZE: 4–6"h × 6"w
TYPE: Perennial
FORM: Clump
TEXTURE: Medium
GROWTH: Medium
LIGHT: Full sun
MOISTURE: Medium to low
SOIL: Moderately fertile, well-drained
FEATURES: Flowers, foliage
USES: Naturalizing, container
FLOWERS: ■□

SITING: Showy crocus prefers full sun and very well-drained, moderately fertile soil with a pH of 5.5–7.0. It is one of the earliest fall crocus to emerge. Violet-blue blooms with darker blue veins appear in fall before the leaves. The styles in the center of the flower are bright orange and contrast nicely with the flower petal color. The leaves are broad, lance shaped, and dark green. Plants are drought tolerant, low maintenance, and durable. Plant in drifts in the lawn, scatter about the base of trees and shrubs in borders, or place in mixed container plantings for late season color.

CARE: Plant corms 2–3" deep and 6" apart in spring. Apply slow-release granular plant food at time of planting. Apply 3" of vegetative mulch in summer and winter to help retain soil moisture and add organic matter to the soil as it decomposes.

PROPAGATION: Unearth the corm and separate offsets that form around its base. Replant healthy, firm corms and cormels 6" apart in moderately fertile, well-drained soil, then water and mulch.

PESTS AND DISEASE: Plants are relatively pest free when their cultural preferences are met. Squirrels and mice may feed on the corms.

RELATED SPECIES: The cultivar 'Aitchisonii' has large pale lilac flowers with darker feathered veins, 'Albus' has pure white flowers, 'Cassiope' has large pale blue blooms with a yellow throat, 'Pollux' has large light mauve flowers with a pearly-silver exterior, and 'Oxonian' has indigo-blue blooms.

DUTCH CROCUS
Crocus vernus vernus KRO-kuhs VER-nubs VER-nubs

Dutch crocus blooms in spring.

ZONES: 3–8
SIZE: 4–6"h × 6"w
TYPE: Perennial
FORM: Clump
TEXTURE: Foliage fine, flower medium
GROWTH: Medium
LIGHT: Full sun
MOISTURE: Medium to low
SOIL: Moderately fertile, well-drained
FEATURES: Flowers, foliage
USES: Naturalizing, container
FLOWERS: □■■■

SITING: Dutch crocus prefers full sun and very well drained, moderately fertile soil with a pH of 5.5–7.0. Goblet-shaped purple, lavender, yellow or white blooms appear from spring to early summer. The leaves are lance shaped and often have a silver stripe down the center. Plants are drought tolerant, low maintenance, and durable. Plant in drifts in lawns, scatter about the base of trees and shrubs in borders, or place in mixed container plantings for early-season color.

CARE: Plant corms 2–3" deep and 6" apart in autumn. Apply slow-release granular plant food at time of planting. Apply 3" of vegetative mulch in summer and winter to help retain soil moisture and add organic matter to the soil as it decomposes.

PROPAGATION: Unearth the corm and separate offsets that form around its base. Replant healthy, firm corms and cormels 6" apart in moderately fertile, well-drained soil, then water and mulch.

PESTS AND DISEASES: Plants are relatively pest free when their cultural preferences (sun, soil, moisture) are met. Squirrels and mice may feed on the corms.

RELATED SPECIES: The cultivar 'Early Perfection' has blue blooms with dark edges, 'Jeanne d'Arc' has white flowers with a dark purple base and light purple feathering, 'Kathleen Parlow' has white blooms with a purple base, 'King of the Striped' has light-and-dark-purple-striped flowers, and 'Pickwick' has white-, light-, and dark-lilac-striped flowers with a darker lilac-purple base.

1 Naturalize crocus by tossing corms on the lawn to create varied spacing.

2 Plant the corms 2–3" deep wherever they land on the lawn.

MEXICAN HEATHER
Cuphea hyssopifolia KOO-fee-uh hiss-ahp-IF-uh-luh

Mexican heather forms small but attractive pinkish-purple blooms in the landscape.

ZONES: 8–10
SIZE: 12–24"h ×
8–32"w
TYPE: Woody
perennial
FORM: Upright
TEXTURE: Medium
GROWTH: Medium
LIGHT: Full sun to
partial shade

MOISTURE: High
SOIL: Moderately
fertile, well-drained
FEATURES: Flowers,
foliage
USES: Border,
container, massing
FLOWERS: ■■□

SITING: Mexican heather prefers ample and frequent moisture and plant food, full sun or partial shade, and moderately fertile, well-drained soil with a pH of 5.5–7.5. Tiny pink, pinkish purple, or white flowers appear from summer into autumn. Woody stems and tiny, pointed dark green leaves create attractive foliage. Plants may be massed in the garden, used in the front of the border in odd-numbered groupings, or placed in mixed planting containers. Companions for full sun include rosemary, lavender cotton, vinca, and violet-colored pansies in autumn. Companions for part shade with complementary foliage include

Pinch back tips to encourage bushy growth.

McKenna hybrids columbine, fringeleaf bleeding heart, and wax begonia.
CARE: Plant 12–18" apart in late spring. Apply slow-release plant food, such as Miracle-Gro Shake 'n Feed All Purpose, at time of planting or begin using water-soluble plant food, such as Miracle-Gro Water Soluble All Purpose, 3 weeks after planting. Water deeply when the soil is dry. Apply 3" of vegetative mulch in summer to help retain soil moisture and add beneficial organic matter to the soil as it decomposes. Cut back tips in the growing season to encourage bushy growth. To rejuvenate, cut back woody stems in spring. In cooler climates treat as an annual and remove after the first frost.
PROPAGATION: Sow seeds at 55–60°F in early spring. Keep moist until seeds germinate, then allow soil to dry out slightly between waterings.
PESTS AND DISEASES: Whiteflies and aphids are occasional insect pests. Diseases include powdery mildew, fungal leaf spot, and root rot.

JAPANESE HOLLY FERN
Cyrtomium falcatum ser-TOH-mee-uhm fal-KAY-tuhm

Japanese holly fern has shiny dark evergreen fronds.

ZONES: 6–10
SIZE: 24"h × 36"w
TYPE: Perennial
FORM: Irregular
TEXTURE: Medium
GROWTH: Slow
LIGHT: Full to partial
shade

MOISTURE: High
SOIL: Fertile, moist,
well-drained
FEATURES: Leaves
USES: Border,
woodland, container

SITING: Holly fern prefers full shade or partial shade with shelter from the afternoon sun and fertile, well-drained soil with a pH of 5.5–7.0. The shiny, leathery deep green fronds are evergreen and are coveted for floral arrangements. This fern does not tolerate extreme cold and benefits from shelter from direct sun and extreme wind and cold. Place in shade borders, woodland gardens, or in containers. Companions include European wild ginger, astilbe, toad lily, and false Solomon's seal.
CARE: Plant 15–18" apart in spring or fall in fertile soil high in organic matter. If in doubt take a professional soil test to determine the percentage of organic matter in the soil. To increase organic matter, add 1–2" of composted food and leaf waste, composted animal manure, mushroom compost, peat moss, or bagged humus to the planting bed and till in to a depth of 12–15". After planting, water deeply and add 3" of mulch around, but not touching, the plants. Mulch helps retain soil moisture. Apply slow-release plant food, such as Miracle-Gro Shake 'n Feed All Purpose, at time of planting or begin using water-soluble plant food, such as Miracle-Gro Water Soluble All Purpose, 3 weeks after planting in spring. Follow label directions for amount and frequency. Cease feeding 4–6 weeks prior to first frost date. Water deeply whenever the soil is dry; let the soil dry slightly between waterings. Leave this evergreen fern erect for winter viewing and cut back brown fronds in spring. In marginally hardy areas cover the crown with 3–6" of straw in winter.
PROPAGATION: Divide every 3 years in spring or fall. Dig around the rhizomes and lift. Use a sharp spade to slice through the root system. Reset portions that contain healthy roots and top shoots, then water and mulch. Discard any pieces that do not contain both healthy roots and top shoots.
PESTS AND DISEASES: Plants are relatively pest free when their cultural preferences (sun, soil, moisture) are met. Snails and slugs may pose problems. Brown leaves can indicate cold damage, too much or too little moisture, too much sun, or low soil fertility. Leaf spot occasionally plagues holly fern.
RELATED SPECIES: 'Cristatum' has twisted pinnae (leaflet) tips, and 'Rochfordianum' has coarsely-toothed margins.

DAHLIA
Dahlia hybrids *DAHL-yuh*

Dahlias come in a variety of sizes and a broad array of flower colors.

ZONES: 9–11
SIZE: 1–6'h × 1–3'w
TYPE: Perennial
FORM: Upright
TEXTURE: Medium
GROWTH: Medium
LIGHT: Full sun
MOISTURE: High

SOIL: Fertile, well-drained
FEATURES: Flowers, foliage
USES: Border, massing, container
FLOWERS: ■ ■ ■ ■ ■ □

SITING: Dahlias prefer full sun and fertile, humus-rich, well-drained soil with a pH of 5.5–7.0. Flowers range from 2" to more than 10" across. Dahlias are considered the backbone of the late-season border, though in many parts of the country the care they require reduces their appeal. The bright-color blooms appear from midsummer to first frost. Plant tall dahlias in groups at the back of the border. Bedding dahlias are low growing and often treated as annuals, flowering from midsummer into autumn.

They are useful in containers or in massed plantings. Dahlia blooms attract butterflies and are superb fresh-cut flowers.

CARE: Plant 12–36" apart in late spring. Apply slow-release granular plant food at time of planting or begin using water-soluble plant food 3 weeks after planting. Dahlias are heavy feeders, so pay attention to soil pH and fertility. Water deeply when the soil is dry. Tall cultivars may require staking. Install stakes early in the season to avoid impaling growing tubers later on. In cool climates lift tubers when foliage has been damaged by a light frost, but before a severe frost. Dust off the soil and let dry. Store tubers in a box or breathable container in vermiculite or dry sand and place in a cool well-ventilated, frost free place. Check periodically for fungal infection. Dispose of diseased tubers or cut away infected areas, dust again with

fungicide, and replace in the container. Plant tubers outdoors in spring.

PROPAGATION: For bedding plants sprinkle seeds over the soil mix and cover. Thoroughly moisten and keep moist, not soggy, until seeds germinate. Germination occurs in 5–10 days at 60–65°F. Transplant 11–15 days after sowing and reduce the temperature to 55–60°F. Harden off and plant outdoors after all danger of frost has passed. Divide the tuberous roots in early spring after shoots have begun to grow by cutting them into sections that contain an actively growing bud or shoot. Replant pieces, then water and mulch.

PESTS AND DISEASES: Pests include aphids, stem borers, spider mites, caterpillars, plant hoppers, thrips, slugs, and snails. Diseases include powdery mildew, smut, dahlia mosaic viruses, fungal leaf spot, soft rot, crown gall, and tomato spotted wilt virus.

1

After the first light frost damages the foliage, dig the tubers for storage.

2

Remove stems from the tuberous roots and brush away soil before storing.

PURPLE HARDY ICE PLANT
Delosperma cooperi *del-oh-SPERM-uh KOOP-er-eye*

Purple hardy ice plant is a low-maintenance perennial.

ZONES: 6–10
SIZE: 4–8"h × 24"w
TYPE: Perennial
FORM: Mound
TEXTURE: Medium
GROWTH: Fast
LIGHT: Full sun
MOISTURE: Medium to low

SOIL: Moderately fertile, well-drained
FEATURES: Flowers, foliage
USES: Border, container, ground cover
FLOWERS: ■

SITING: Purple hardy ice plant prefers full sun and moderately fertile, well-drained soil with a pH of 5.5–7.0. A multitude of 1–2" daisylike glossy purple flowers appear in mid- to late summer. The appealing leaves are succulent, cylindrical, and bright green. Plants are top performers in the Low-Maintenance Perennial Plant Field Trials at Clemson University's Sandhill Research and Education Center in South Carolina, testimony to their heat tolerance and pest resistance. Place in odd-numbered groups in the front of borders or in containers. Good companions include 'Moonbeam' threadleaf coreopsis, 'Red Fox' spike speedwell, and 'Blue Spruce' sedum.

CARE: Plant 18–24" apart in spring or fall. Apply slow-release granular plant food at time of planting. Cease feeding 4–6 weeks prior to first frost date. Water deeply when the soil is dry. Even though the plants are low maintenance and drought tolerant,

they perform better if watered during dry spells. Apply 3" of vegetative mulch in summer to help retain soil moisture and add organic matter to the soil as it decomposes. Cut back the foliage after frost damage.

PROPAGATION: Sow seeds at 75–80°F or take stem cuttings in spring or summer.

PESTS AND DISEASES: Plants are relatively pest free when their cultural preferences are met. Mealybugs and aphids are occasional pests.

RELATED SPECIES: Orange-yellow hardy ice plant (*D. nubigerum*) grows 2" tall and spreads. The 1" orange-yellow blooms appear in summer. Plants have attractive succulent foliage and are cold hardy in Zones 6–9.

HYBRID BEE DELPHINIUM
Delphinium elatum *del-FIHN-ee-uhm ay-LAYT-uhm*

Hybrid bee delphinium bears spikes of purple, blue, or white flowers.

ZONES: 2–7
SIZE: 5–6'h × 2–3'w
TYPE: Perennial
FORM: Upright
TEXTURE: Medium
GROWTH: Medium
LIGHT: Full sun to partial shade

MOISTURE: High
SOIL: Fertile, well-drained
FEATURES: Flowers, foliage
USES: Border
FLOWERS: ■□■

SITING: *Delphinium elatum* prefers full sun or light shade in midafternoon and fertile, well-drained soil with a pH of 5.5–7.0. This plant does not perform well in high-heat areas. Spikes of blue, lavender, purple, and white flowers appear in early and midsummer. Delphinium is a classic favorite for the cottage garden, and flowers are superb fresh cut or dried. Good companions include David Austin and 'Carefree Wonder' roses, 'David' garden phlox, baby's breath, and Claridge Druce geranium cultivars.

CARE: Plant 12–36" apart in late spring or fall. Apply slow-release granular plant food at time of planting or begin using water-soluble plant food 3 weeks after planting in spring. Delphiniums are heavy feeders, so pay attention to soil pH and fertility. Cease feeding 6–8 weeks prior to first frost date. Water deeply when the soil is dry.

Stake delphinium so the support is not visible and does not compete visually with the blooms.

Tall cultivars usually require sturdy staking or may be placed against fences or walls for support. Deadhead by cutting back spent spikes to encourage small, flowering side shoots. Cut to the ground in autumn after frost withers the foliage.

PROPAGATION: Delphinium propagation is difficult. Fresh seed (less than 6 months old) produces the best germination rates and requires no pretreatment. Store packaged seed purchased in winter in the refrigerator until ready to sow. Germination occurs in 12–18 days at 70–75°F. Divide in early spring. Dig around the root clump and lift. Use a sharp spade to slice through the root system.

PESTS AND DISEASES: Snails and slugs are common pests. Diseases include powdery mildew, bacterial leaf and fungal leaf spot, Southern blight, and root rot.

RELATED SPECIES: 'Berghimmel' reaches 6' tall and has wind-resistant stems with white blooms and a yellow bee (center); 'Jubelruf' reaches 6' tall, has wind-resistant stems, and bears semidouble bright blue flowers with a white bee; and 'Rosemary Brock' reaches 5' tall and bears semidouble mauve flowers with darker sepal tips and a brown bee.

CHRYSANTHEMUM
Dendranthema ×grandiflorum *den-DRAN-theh-muh gran-dih-FLOR-uhm*

Garden chrysanthemums are a traditional sign of autumn in the landscape. They are also known as mums.

ZONES: 4–9
SIZE: 1–3'h × 12–24"w
TYPE: Perennial
FORM: Rounded
TEXTURE: Medium
GROWTH: Medium
LIGHT: Full sun
MOISTURE: High

SOIL: Fertile, well-drained
FEATURES: Flowers, foliage
USES: Border, container
FLOWERS: ■■▨■ □■■

SITING: Garden chrysanthemum prefers full sun and fertile, well-drained soil with a pH of 5.5–7.0. Flowers appear in late summer and autumn in shades of crimson, orange, yellow, pink, cream, and purple. It is a short-lived perennial in Zones 4 and 5 and may be grown as an annual in cool areas. Companions include 'Purpureum' fennel and 'Sky Racer' purple moor grass.

CARE: Plant 12–24" apart in spring or fall. Apply slow-release granular plant food at time of planting, or begin using water-soluble plant food 3 weeks after planting in spring. Cease feeding 6–8 weeks prior to first frost date. Water deeply whenever the soil is dry. Cut back in spring and early summer if more compactness is desired. Cut to the ground in autumn after frost withers the foliage, or leave erect for winter viewing in mild locations.

PROPAGATION: Divide every 3 years in spring to maintain vigor. Dig around the root clump and lift.

PESTS AND DISEASES: Pests include aphids, earwigs, nematodes, spider mites, fourlined plant bug and whiteflies. Viruses cause stunting, yellowing, and puckering of leaves. Other diseases include powdery mildew, crown gall, rust, and botrytis.

Pinch mum tips in spring to encourage compact growth.

Cut back in fall once foliage is disfigured by frost.

Mulch with straw for added cold protection.

SWEET WILLIAM
Dianthus barbatus dy-AN-thubs bahr-BAYT-ubs

Sweet william is an old-fashioned favorite in the garden.

ZONES: 3–8
SIZE: 26"h × 12"w
TYPE: Biennial
FORM: Upright
TEXTURE: Medium
GROWTH: Medium
LIGHT: Full sun to partial shade
MOISTURE: Medium
SOIL: Fertile, well-drained
FEATURES: Flowers, foliage
USES: Border, container
FLOWERS: ■■□

SITING: Sweet William prefers full sun in its northern range and afternoon shade in the Deep South. Soil should be fertile but well-drained with a pH of 7.0–7.5. Clusters of pink, red, white, or various combinations and hues of these colors appear in late spring and early summer. Light to medium green leaves may be tinged with bronze. Plants are old-fashioned favorites and often appear in cottage gardens and nostalgic grandmother's gardens. The fragrant flowers are prized for cutting and for dried arrangements. Plants are suitable for early color in borders or containers. Good garden companions include 'Silver Carpet' lamb's-ears, lemon thyme, pansies, and violas.

CARE: Plant 12" apart in spring or fall. Apply slow-release plant food, such as Miracle-Gro Shake 'n Feed All Purpose, at time of planting or begin using water-

Deadhead sweet William to stimulate reblooming.

soluble plant food, such as Miracle-Gro Water Soluble All Purpose, 3 weeks after planting in spring. Follow label directions for amount and frequency. Cease feeding 6–8 weeks prior to first frost date. Water deeply whenever the soil is dry. Apply 3" of vegetative mulch to help retain soil moisture and add organic matter to the soil as it decomposes. In the South, plants can be grown as perennials if the flowers are removed before seeds form. Cut to the ground in autumn after frost withers foliage or leave erect for winter viewing in warmer locations and cut back in early spring to encourage new growth and upright habit.

PROPAGATION: Plants reseed in the landscape, which is the easiest and most reliable method of reproduction. Plants grown from seed take two seasons to bloom. Sprinkle seeds over the soil mix and cover lightly. Thoroughly moisten and keep moist, not soggy, until seeds germinate. Germination occurs in 7–10 days at 60–70°F. Transplant 13–20 days after sowing. After germination, reduce temperature to 55–59°F.

PESTS AND DISEASES: Insect pests include slugs, snails, aphids, and caterpillars. Diseases include crown rot, rust, and powdery mildew.

PINK
Dianthus chinensis dy-AN-thubs chih-NEN-sibs

Pink cultivars appear in a variety of patterns and attractive colors. It is also known as China pink or annual pink.

ZONES: 7–10
SIZE: 6–24"h × 6–12"w
TYPE: Annual
FORM: Mound
TEXTURE: Fine
GROWTH: Fast
LIGHT: Full sun to partial shade
MOISTURE: Medium
SOIL: Fertile, well-drained
FEATURES: Flowers, foliage
USES: Bedding, container
FLOWERS: ■■□

SITING: Pink prefers full sun in its northern range and light afternoon shade in warmer areas. Soil should be fertile and well-drained with a pH of 7.0–7.5. Fringed flowers appear all summer long in red, pink, or white, often with a purple eye. Colors may appear as patterns as well as solid. The 3"-long leaves are light to medium green. Pink is often grown as an annual, but will overwinter in Zones 7 and higher. It is an exceptional bedding plant, providing cheerful summer color. Good companions in the garden include miniature roses, sweet potato vine, and 'David' garden phlox.

CARE: Plant 6–12" apart in late spring after the last frost. Apply slow-release granular plant food at time of planting or begin using water-soluble plant food 3 weeks after planting. Water deeply when the soil is dry. Apply 3" of vegetative mulch to help retain soil moisture and add organic matter to the soil as it decomposes. Deadheading will hasten reblooming but can be tedious due to the large number of blooms on each plant. Plants will self-seed but will not become invasive. Remove plants just prior to or after the first frost.

PROPAGATION: Sprinkle seeds over the soil mix and cover lightly. Thoroughly moisten and keep moist, not soggy, until seeds germinate. Germination occurs in 7 days at 70–75°F. Transplant 18–25 days after sowing. After germination, reduce the temperature to 50–56°F.

PESTS AND DISEASES: Slugs, grasshoppers, chipmunks, squirrels, and deer are common pests. In poorly drained soils and high humidity, crown rot may be a problem.

RELATED SPECIES: Baby Doll Series cultivars have patterned red to white flowers, 'Fire Carpet' has red blooms, and 'Parfait' has weather-resistant bicolored blooms.

COTTAGE PINK

Dianthus plumarius dy-AN-thuhs ploo-MAYR-ee-uhs

Cottage pink, also known as grass pink, is an old-fashioned favorite for the blooming cottage garden.

ZONES: 4–8
SIZE: 8–20"h × 15–24"w
TYPE: Perennial
FORM: Mound
TEXTURE: Fine
GROWTH: Slow
LIGHT: Full sun
MOISTURE: Medium
SOIL: Fertile, well-drained
FEATURES: Flowers, foliage
USES: Border, container
FLOWERS: ■□

SITING: Cottage pink prefers full sun and fertile, well-drained, alkaline soil with a pH of 7.0–7.5. Clove-scented toothed flowers appear spring through summer in rose, pink, and white. Evergreen foliage is gray-green and grasslike. Plant cottage pink in the border, the cottage garden, and in containers. Companions include 'Bonica,' 'Carefree Wonder,' 'Iceberg,' and 'The Fairy' roses.

CARE: Plant 12–24" apart in spring or fall. Apply slow-release granular plant food at time of planting or begin using water-soluble plant food 3 weeks after planting in spring. Cease feeding 6–8 weeks prior to first frost date. Water deeply whenever the soil is dry. Cut back immediately after flowering to look tidy. Cut to the ground in autumn after frost withers the foliage or leave evergreen foliage erect for winter viewing in milder locations.

Lift the entire clump to divide cottage pink. Slice through it with a sharp spade.

PROPAGATION: Divide every 2–3 years in spring to maintain vigor.
PESTS AND DISEASES: Slugs, grasshoppers, chipmunks, squirrels, and deer are common pests. Leaf spots may occur in high humidity and poor air circulation. Proper spacing and air circulation reduce susceptibility to disease.
RELATED SPECIES: 'Prairie Pink' has blue-green foliage and large, fragrant double pink flowers; 'Queen of Sheba' has single cream-colored blooms speckled with pink; and 'Raspberry Tart' has semidouble red flowers with a deep red center.

Separate offshoots. Relocate and replant them in the garden.

FRINGED BLEEDING HEART

Dicentra eximia dy-SEHN-truh eks-EE-mee-uh

Fringed bleeding heart blooms sporadically all summer.

ZONES: 3–8
SIZE: 24"h × 18"w
TYPE: Perennial
FORM: Irregular
TEXTURE: Fine
GROWTH: Medium
LIGHT: Full to partial shade
MOISTURE: Medium
SOIL: Fertile, well-drained
FEATURES: Flowers, foliage
USES: Flowers, foliage
FLOWERS: ■□

SITING: Fringed bleeding heart tolerates full shade or partial shade and prefers fertile, well-drained soil with a pH of 5.5–7.0.

Nodding stems of heart-shaped pink flowers appear in late spring and intermittently through early autumn. The red-tinted gray-green stems of deeply lobed leaflets add a graceful element to the landscape. The foliage of this low-maintenance perennial remains attractive throughout the growing season. Place in large swaths in woodland gardens, at the foot of irrigated trees and shrubs, in odd-numbered groups in the shade border, or in containers for delightful early-season color and interest. Companions that complement the gray-tinged foliage include lady's mantle, Japanese painted fern, 'Elegans' Siebold hosta, and 'Mrs. Moon' Bethlehem sage.

CARE: Plant 18" apart in spring or fall. After planting, water deeply and add 3" of mulch around, but not touching, the plants. Mulch helps retain soil moisture and as it breaks down, adds organic matter to the soil. Apply slow-release granular plant food at time of planting, or begin using water-soluble plant food 3 weeks after planting in spring. Cease feeding 6–8 weeks prior to first frost date. Water deeply whenever the soil becomes dry, letting the soil dry slightly between waterings. Cut plants to the ground in autumn after frost withers the foliage.

PROPAGATION: Plants reliably self-seed in the landscape. Divide every 3 years or when vigor declines, in spring or fall. Dig around the root clump and lift. Use a sharp spade to slice through the root system. Reset portions that contain healthy roots and top shoots, then water and mulch. Discard any pieces that do not contain both healthy roots and top shoots.

PESTS AND DISEASES: Plants are relatively pest free when their cultural preferences (sun, soil, moisture) are met. Slugs and snails are occasional pests.

RELATED SPECIES: The cultivar 'Alba' has pure white blooms and deeply divided foliage, 'Adrian Bloom' has deep carmine-red flowers, and 'Bountiful' has purplish-pink flowers.

COMMON BLEEDING HEART
Dicentra spectabilis *dy-SEHN-truh spek-TAH-bih-lihs*

Common bleeding heart bears spectacular heart-shaped blooms in late spring.

ZONES: 3–9
SIZE: 4'h × 2'w
TYPE: Perennial
FORM: Irregular
TEXTURE: Fine
GROWTH: Medium
LIGHT: Full to partial shade

MOISTURE: Medium
SOIL: Fertile, well-drained
FEATURES: Flowers, foliage
USES: Woodland, border, container
FLOWERS: ■□

SITING: Common bleeding heart prefers full or partial shade and fertile, well-drained soil with a pH of 5.5–7.0. Long, arching stems of pendant pink flowers with white inner petals appear in late spring and early summer. After flowering the foliage dies back. This old-fashioned plant adds grace and delicacy to woodland gardens or shade borders. Flowers are superb additions to fresh-cut arrangements. Companions include 'Elegans' Siebold hosta, heart-leaf brunnera, and 'Mrs. Moon' Bethlehem sage.

CARE: Plant 15–24" apart in spring or fall in fertile soil high in organic matter. After planting, water deeply and add 3" of mulch around, but not touching, the plant.

Interplant hosta with bleeding heart to cover space left after bleeding heart dies back in summer.

Apply slow-release granular plant food at time of planting or begin using water-soluble plant food 3 weeks after planting in spring. Water deeply whenever the soil becomes dry.

PROPAGATION: Plants lightly self-seed in the landscape. Divide every 3 years, or when vigor declines, in spring or fall. Dig around the root clump and lift. Use a sharp spade to slice through the root system. Reset portions that contain healthy roots and top shoots, then water and mulch. Discard any pieces that do not contain both healthy roots and top shoots.

PESTS AND DISEASES: Plants are relatively pest free when their cultural preferences (sun, soil, moisture) are met. Slugs and snails are occasional pests. Wet soil during the summer may contribute to disease problems.

RELATED SPECIES: The cultivar 'Alba' has pure white blooms and the same attractive foliage. Dutchman's breeches (*D. cucullaria*) bears long, arching stems of curious white flowers with a yellow tip in early spring. Deeply divided leaves are light and airy and bluish green. After flowering, the foliage dies back.

GAS PLANT
Dictamnus albus *dik-TAM-nuhs AL-bus*

Gas plant, also known as dittany, bears white flowers in early summer.

ZONES: 3–8
SIZE: 15–36"h × 24"w
TYPE: Perennial
FORM: Upright
TEXTURE: Medium
GROWTH: Slow
LIGHT: Full sun to partial shade

MOISTURE: Medium
SOIL: Moderately fertile, well-drained
FEATURES: Flowers, foliage
USES: Border
FLOWERS: □■

SITING: Gas plant prefers full sun or partial shade from the afternoon sun and well-drained, moderately fertile soil with a pH of 5.5–7.0. Flowers and unripe fruit produce a volatile oil that can be ignited in hot weather. Roots resent transplanting and disturbance. Plant in groups in borders for best effect. Companions include 'Fire King' yarrow, beardlip penstemon, smooth white penstemon, and 'Hameln' fountain grass.

CARE: Plant 18–24" apart in spring or fall. Feed with slow-release granular plant food at time of planting or begin using water-soluble plant food 3 weeks after planting in spring. Cease feeding 6–8 weeks prior to first frost date. This low-maintenance

Wear gloves when working with gas plant to protect skin from oils that may cause irritation similar to that of poison ivy.

perennial is drought tolerant once established, but new transplants require ample and frequent moisture. Prune plants to the ground in late fall or leave erect for winter interest and cut back in early spring.

PROPAGATION: All propagation techniques are difficult for gas plant. Gather seed from plants and sow immediately in a protected outdoor site. Germination should occur the following spring. Division may damage the crown of the parent plant. A sharp spade and clean cuts yield greater success. Avoid bruising, pulling, and ripping of roots. Plunge a sharp spade straight through the center of the crown to slice through the root system. Reset portions that contain healthy roots and top shoots, then water and mulch. Discard any pieces that do not contain both healthy roots and top shoots.

PESTS AND DISEASES: Plants are relatively pest free when their cultural preferences are met.

RELATED SPECIES: The cultivar 'Purpureus' has purple flowers with darker purple veins, 'Ruber' has pinkish-purple flowers, and 'Albiflorus' has white flowers with yellow veins.

FOXGLOVE
Digitalis purpurea *dihj-ih-TAH-lihs per-PER-ee-uh*

Common foxglove is a traditional English garden plant.

ZONES: 3–8
SIZE: 3–6'h × 24"w
TYPE: Biennial
FORM: Upright
TEXTURE: Medium
GROWTH: Medium
LIGHT: Full sun to partial shade

MOISTURE: Medium
SOIL: Fertile, well-drained
FEATURES: Flowers, foliage
USES: Border, woodland
FLOWERS: ■■□

SITING: Foxglove prefers full sun or partial shade from the afternoon sun and fertile, well-drained soil with a pH of 5.5–7.0. Tall spikes of purple, pink, or white flowers appear in early summer. Plant in cottage gardens, mixed perennial borders, along fencerows, and in bright woodland gardens. Companions include 'Fire King' yarrow, 'Apothecary's' rose, 'The Rocket' ligularia, and 'Stargazer' lily.

CARE: Plant 18" apart in spring or fall in fertile soil high in organic matter. After planting, water deeply and add 3" of mulch around, but not touching, the plants. Apply slow-release granular plant food at time of planting or begin using water-soluble plant food 3 weeks after planting in spring. Water deeply whenever the soil becomes dry. Remove flower stalks after blooms have faded or leave

Collect foxglove seed to sow in a new area.

erect long enough for seeds to drop if self-seeding is desired. If plants do not self-seed in the landscape, plan to replace every year or two with container stock.

PROPAGATION: Plants frequently self-seed in the landscape. To sow indoors sprinkle seeds over the soil mix and leave them exposed to light; do not cover. Thoroughly moisten and keep moist, not soggy, until seeds germinate. Germination occurs in 5–10 days at 60–65°F. Transplant seedlings 15–20 days after sowing. After germination, reduce temperature to 55–60°F.

PESTS AND DISEASES: Diseases include Southern blight, anthracnose, and fungal leaf spot.

RELATED SPECIES: The cultivar 'Alba' has white flowers, 'Apricot' has apricot flowers, Excelsior Hybrids come in pastel shades, and Foxy Hybrids have carmine, pink, cream, and white flowers with flecks of maroon. Yellow foxglove *(D. grandiflora)* reaches 3–4' tall and 24–36" wide and has pale yellow blooms with brown veins. Strawberry foxglove *(D. ×mertonensis)* is a perennial with strawberry-pink blooms; divide every 2–3 years to maintain vigor. Strawberry foxglove plants come true from seed.

PURPLE CONEFLOWER
Echinacea purpurea *ek-in-AY-see-ah per-PER-ee-ah*

Purple coneflower is a superb low-maintenance native perennial for the summer garden.

ZONES: 3–9
SIZE: 4'h × 18"w
TYPE: Perennial
FORM: Upright
TEXTURE: Medium
GROWTH: Medium
LIGHT: Full sun
MOISTURE: Medium

SOIL: Fertile, well-drained
FEATURES: Flowers, foliage
USES: Border, container
FLOWERS: ■□

SITING: Purple coneflower prefers full sun and fertile, well-drained soil with a pH of 5.5–7.5. Rosy-purple flowers appear from midsummer into autumn. Purple coneflower is magnificent in a full-sun border planted in groups or placed in mixed container plantings. Flowers attract butterflies and are excellent for cutting. Good companions include 'Husker Red' smooth white penstemon, 'Purpureum' purple fountain grass, 'David' garden phlox, and 'Goldsturm' black-eyed Susan.

CARE: Plant 18" apart in early spring or fall. Apply slow-release granular plant food at time of planting or begin using water-soluble plant food 3 weeks after planting in spring. Cease feeding 6–8 weeks prior to first frost date. Water deeply when the soil dries. Remove faded flower stalks to

Butterflies are attracted to the blooms of purple coneflower.

stimulate reblooming. Prune back in fall if frost withers the foliage; in warmer areas leave erect for late-season viewing and prune back in early spring.

PROPAGATION: Divide in fall or early spring. Dig around the root clump and lift. Use a sharp spade to slice through the root system. Reset portions that contain healthy roots and top shoots.

PESTS AND DISEASES: Plants are relatively pest free. Moderate soil fertility helps create strong, robust foliage that is not as easily penetrated by pests. Powdery mildew, aster yellows, and bacterial leafspot may occur.

RELATED SPECIES: The cultivar 'Finale White' has 4" single white flowers with a greenish-brown disk, 'Magnus' has 7" deep purple flowers with a deep orange disk, 'Robert Bloom' has rich crimson-tinted mauve flowers with a deep orange-brown disk, 'The King' has large deep carmine flowers with an orange-brown disk, and 'White Swan' has honey-scented pure white flowers with an orange-brown disk. Pale purple coneflower *(E. pallida)* has light purple blooms and tolerates poor soil.

GLOBE THISTLE
Echinops ritro EK-ihn-ops REE-troh

Globe thistle bears attractive steel blue, spherical flowers.

ZONES: 3–9
SIZE: 24"h × 18"w
TYPE: Perennial
FORM: Upright
TEXTURE: Coarse
GROWTH: Fast
LIGHT: Full sun
MOISTURE: Medium to low

SOIL: Moderately fertile, well-drained
FEATURES: Flowers, foliage
USES: Border, container
FLOWERS: ■

SITING: Globe thistle prefers full sun and moderately fertile soil but tolerates well-drained sandy soils with low fertility. It prefers a pH of 6.5–7.5. It is drought tolerant and extremely low maintenance. Plant in groups in borders or in mixed container plantings. Flowers attract butterflies and are excellent for cutting and drying. Good companions include purple coneflower, 'Snowbank' white boltonia, Russian sage, gaura, and 'Kobold' blazing star.

CARE: Plant 18" apart in spring or fall. Apply slow-release granular plant food at time of planting. Cease feeding 6–8 weeks prior to first frost date. Water deeply when the soil is dry. Even though the plant is low maintenance and drought tolerant, it performs better if watered during dry spells. Plants self-seed in the landscape.

If this is not desired, deadhead blooms immediately after flowering. Prune back in fall if frost withers foliage; in warmer areas, leave erect for late-season viewing, and prune back in early spring.

PROPAGATION: Divide in spring or fall.

PESTS AND DISEASES: Plants are relatively pest free when their cultural preferences are met.

RELATED SPECIES: The cultivar 'Blue Glow' has light blue flowers, 'Taplow Blue' is a strong performer with deep blue flowers, and 'Veitch's Blue' has bright blue blooms.

1 To divide globe thistle, cut back stems to 6" high.

2 Plunge a sharp spade through the root system.

3 Replant pieces that contain healthy roots and shoots.

CUSHION SPURGE
Euphorbia polychroma (epithymoides) yew-FOR-bee-uh pahl-ee-KROH-muh (ee-pith-ih-MOY-deez)

Cushion spurge, also known as euphorbia, bears yellow flowers in midspring.

ZONES: 4–9
SIZE: 15"h × 24"w
TYPE: Perennial
FORM: Rounded
TEXTURE: Medium
GROWTH: Fast
LIGHT: Full sun to partial shade
MOISTURE: Medium

SOIL: Moderately fertile, well-drained
FEATURES: Flowers, foliage
USES: Border, container
FLOWERS: ■
FALL COLOR: ■ ■

SITING: Cushion spurge prefers moderately fertile, well-drained soil with a pH of 5.5–7.0. In cooler regions plants do best in full sun; in warmer areas plants prefer afternoon shade. Chartreuse bracts surround yellow flowers in midspring. Dark green leaves turn red, maroon, or orange in autumn. Plant at the front of a border or use in container plantings. Good companions include 'Moonbeam' threadleaf coreopsis, 'Rotfuchs' spike speedwell, and 'Rosea' showy evening primrose.

Cut back cushion spurge immediately after bloom to stimulate rebloom and compact foliar growth.

CARE: Plant 18–24" apart in spring or fall. Apply slow-release granular plant food at time of planting. Cease feeding 6–8 weeks prior to first frost date. Water deeply when the soil is dry. Even though the plant is low maintenance and drought tolerant, it performs better if watered during dry spells. Plants prolifically self-seed in the landscape. If this is not desired, deadhead blooms immediately after flowering. Prune back in fall if frost withers foliage; in warmer areas, leave erect for late-season viewing, and prune back in early spring.

PROPAGATION: Divide in spring or fall. Dig around the root clump and lift. Use a sharp spade to slice through the root system. Reset portions that contain healthy roots and top shoots, then water and mulch. Discard the older woody central portion.

PESTS AND DISEASES: Plants are relatively pest free when their cultural preferences (sun, soil, moisture) are met.

RELATED SPECIES: The cultivar 'Emerald Jade' is smaller than the species and has attractive autumn hues, 'Midas' has bright yellow bracts and flowers, and 'Purpurea' has purple leaves and yellow flowers.

QUEEN-OF-THE-PRAIRIE

Filipendula rubra *fihl-ih-PEN-doo-lah ROO-bruh*

Queen-of-the-prairie, also known as meadowsweet, bears pink plumes of flowers in summer.

ZONES: 3–9
SIZE: 6–8'h × 4'w
TYPE: Perennial
FORM: Rounded
TEXTURE: Medium
GROWTH: Fast
LIGHT: Full sun
MOISTURE: Medium to high

SOIL: Moderately fertile
FEATURES: Flowers, foliage
USES: Border, wetland
FLOWERS: ■

SITING: Queen-of-the-prairie prefers full sun and moderately fertile soil with a pH of 5.5–7.0. Plants tolerate boggy conditions as well. Plumes of pink to peach flowers appear in early and midsummer. Toothed lobed leaves reach up to 8" across and are dramatic in the landscape. Plant in odd-number groups in a large perennial border, along the river's edge, or in boggy ground. Good companions include 'Variegatus' sweet flag in wetlands and 'Gracillimus' maiden grass and spiderwort in other sites.

CARE: Plant 3–4' apart in spring or fall. Apply slow-release granular plant food at time of planting. Follow label directions for amount and frequency. Cease feeding 6–8 weeks prior to first frost date. If planting in a wetland or on the bank of a natural body of water, avoid plant foods and chemical pesticides to prevent chemicals from leaching into the water. Water deeply when the soil is dry. Apply 3" of vegetative mulch in summer and winter to help retain soil moisture. Prune back in fall if frost withers the foliage; in warmer areas, leave erect for late-season viewing and prune back in early spring.

PROPAGATION: Divide in fall. Dig around the root clump and lift. Use a sharp spade to slice through the root system. Reset portions that contain healthy roots and top shoots, then water and mulch. Discard any pieces that do not contain both healthy roots and top shoots.

PESTS AND DISEASES: Diseases include powdery mildew, leaf spot, and rust.

RELATED SPECIES: The cultivar 'Venusta' has deep rose flowers that lighten as they age. Queen-of-the-meadow (*F. ulmaria*) bears creamy white flowers in summer, reaches 24–36" high and 24" wide, and prefers afternoon shade. *F. ulmaria* 'Aurea' has brilliant yellow leaves in spring that lighten as the season progresses.

FUCHSIA

Fuchsia hybrids *FYEW-shuh*

Fuchsia hybrids are popular plants for hanging baskets.

ZONES: 8–10
SIZE: 6–36"h × 12–24"w
TYPE: Perennial
FORM: Irregular
TEXTURE: Medium
GROWTH: Medium
LIGHT: Full sun to partial shade

MOISTURE: High
SOIL: Moist, fertile, well-drained
FEATURES: Flowers, foliage
USES: Container, border
FLOWERS: ■ □ ■ ■

SITING: Fuchsia hybrids prefer full sun or partial afternoon shade and moist, well-drained soil with a pH of 5.5–7.0. The flowers are usually pendant and tubular, often bicolored, and appear in early summer into autumn. They come in a variety of forms that include single, semidouble, and double. Triphylla Group fuchsias have long tubes, single flowers, and leaves that are sometimes purple underneath. They are more tolerant of heat than other fuchsias. *F. procumbens* flowers are erect; foliage is mid- to light-green, sometimes purplish below. Fuchsias are typically grown as annuals and are attractive in hanging baskets, in containers, or in borders. Good companions for containers include 'Sapphire' and 'Lilac Fountains' lobelia and sweet woodruff.

Remove fallen blossoms to promote sanitation.

CARE: Plant 12–18" apart in late spring after the last frost. Apply slow-release granular plant food at time of planting, or begin using water-soluble plant food 3 weeks after planting in spring. Follow label directions for amount and frequency. Apply 3" of vegetative mulch to help retain soil moisture and add organic matter to the soil as it decomposes. Shear back plant if more compactness is desired. Deadheading will stimulate reblooming but may be tedious considering the multitude of blooms. Spent blooms typically fall and should be removed to promote sanitation and reduce pest infestations. Remove plants after the first frost in cooler climates.

PROPAGATION: Sow seed at 60–75°F in spring. Thoroughly moisten and keep moist, not soggy, until seeds germinate. Transplant outdoors after the last frost.

PESTS AND DISEASES: Insect pests include thrips, whiteflies, and aphids. Diseases include Southern blight, rust, crown gall, and crown and root rot.

BLANKET FLOWER

Gaillardia ×grandiflora *guh-LARD-ee-uh grand-ih-FLOR-uh*

Blanket flower attracts butterflies. It blooms profusely in dry, sunny sites.

ZONES: 3–8
SIZE: 36"h × 18"w
TYPE: Perennial
FORM: Upright
TEXTURE: Medium
GROWTH: Medium
LIGHT: Full sun
MOISTURE: Medium

SOIL: Fertile, well-drained
FEATURES: Flowers, foliage
USES: Border, container
FLOWERS: ■ ■

SITING: Blanket flower prefers full sun and fertile, well-drained soil but tolerates soil with low fertility. The preferred pH is 5.5–7.0. Daisylike flowers reach 3–5" across and are bright yellow with a red base and a mahogany central disk. Flowers appear from early summer into early autumn, attract butterflies, and are good in fresh-cut arrangements. This short-lived perennial adds cheerful color to a border or container. Companions include 'Snowbank' white boltonia, rosemary, threadleaf coreopsis, and creeping zinnia.

CARE: Plant 18" apart in spring or fall. Apply slow-release granular plant food at time of planting or begin using water-soluble plant food 3 weeks after planting in spring. Cease feeding 6–8 weeks prior to first frost date. Water deeply when the soil is dry. Apply 3" of vegetative mulch in summer to help retain soil moisture. Deadhead blooms to stimulate reblooming. Cut back hard in late summer to early fall to stimulate fall bloom and new foliage growth. Do not feed at this time; new growth is susceptible to frost damage. Plants overwinter better if not cut back after frost. Trim damaged foliage in early spring.

PROPAGATION: Divide in spring or fall. Dig around the root clump and lift. Seed-grown plants will flower intermittently during the first season, with exuberance during the second. Sprinkle seeds over the soil mix and leave exposed to light; do not cover. Thoroughly moisten and keep moist, not soggy, until seeds germinate. Germination occurs in 5–15 days at 70–75°F. Transplant 30–42 days after sowing.

PESTS AND DISEASES: Insect pests include aphids, slugs, and snails. Diseases include powdery mildew, downy mildew, rust, and bacterial leaf spot.

RELATED SPECIES: The cultivar 'Baby Cole' has 3" bright red ray florets with yellow tips and a burgundy disk, 'Red Plume' has brick red flowers, 'Tokajer' has dark orange flowers, and 'Kobold' has deep red flowers with yellow tips and a red disk.

1 Deadhead spent flowers to stimulate season-long bloom.

2 After deadheading, blanket flower will continue to develop new flower buds.

COMMON SNOWDROP

Galanthus nivalis *gal-AN-thus nih-VALL-iss*

Common snowdrop appears in late winter, often in snow.

ZONES: 3–9
SIZE: 4"h × 4"w
TYPE: Perennial
FORM: Upright
TEXTURE: Fine
GROWTH: Medium
LIGHT: Partial shade
MOISTURE: High

SOIL: Moist, fertile, well-drained
FEATURES: Flowers, foliage
USES: Naturalizing, border, woodland
FLOWERS: ☐

SITING: Snowdrops prefer partial shade and fertile, humus-rich, moist, well-drained soil with a pH of 5.5–7.0. Blooms are pendulous, ½" long, and creamy white with a spot of green at the tip of each petal. Flowers are sweet scented and appear in late winter, often emerging through snow. Leaves are narrow and erect. Plant great swaths, hundreds of bulbs, for the best effect; a few will not catch the eye. Snowdrops add appeal to alpine gardens, rock gardens, dwarf conifer gardens, and woodland gardens. Good companions include Christmas rose, Lenten rose, and winter aconite.

CARE: Plant bulbs 4" apart and 3" deep in autumn in well-drained soil. Apply slow-release granular plant food at time of planting. Follow label directions for amount and frequency. Snowdrops prefer even moisture and will not tolerate water-soaked soils in summer or winter. Apply 3" of vegetative mulch in summer and winter to help retain soil moisture and add organic matter to the soil as it decomposes.

PROPAGATION: Lift clumps and separate bulbs after flowering, but before the foliage dies down. Replant the bulbs at the proper spacing, water, and mulch.

PESTS AND DISEASES: Plants are vulnerable to narcissus bulb fly and botrytis.

RELATED SPECIES: The cultivar 'Flore Pleno' has double flowers and produces many offsets, 'Lady Elphinstone' has double flowers and gray-green foliage, 'Magnet' has large flowers and is a bit taller and more vigorous than the species, and 'Scharlockii' has slender flowers spotted with green on the outer petals.

SWEET WOODRUFF
Galium odoratum GAL-ee-uhm o-der-AH-tuhm

Sweet woodruff, also known as bedstraw, is an attractive ground cover for light shade.

ZONES: 4–8
SIZE: 18"h × 18"w
TYPE: Perennial
FORM: Spreading
TEXTURE: Fine
GROWTH: Fast
LIGHT: Partial shade
MOISTURE: Medium

SOIL: Fertile, well-drained
FEATURES: Flowers, foliage
USES: Ground cover, container, border
FLOWERS: □

SITING: Sweet woodruff prefers partial shade but tolerates full shade. Fertile, well-drained soil with a pH of 5.5–7.0 is ideal. Star-shaped flowers appear from late spring to midsummer. Whorls of slightly prickly deep green leaves on square stems create a handsome loose and open ground cover even when the plant is bloomless. Dried foliage smells like new-mown hay. Sweet woodruff is best at the feet of broadleaf evergreens, in shade borders, or dripping from containers. Good companions include hosta, rhododendron, and coral bell hybrids.

Sweet woodruff runners pull up easily.

CARE: Plant 12–36" apart in spring or fall. The closer the plants, the faster the ground-cover effect. Apply slow-release granular plant food at time of planting. Water deeply when the soil is dry. Even though the plants are low maintenance, they perform best if they receive ample moisture during dry spells. Excessive sun exposure and dry soil causes the foliage to yellow and prematurely die back. Plants spread by creeping rhizomes in the landscape but are easily pulled up if they are unwanted. Prune back in fall if frost wilts the foliage; in milder areas, leave erect for late-season viewing, and prune back in early spring.

PROPAGATION: Divide in spring or fall. Dig around the root clump and lift. Use a sharp spade to slice through the root system. Reset portions that contain healthy roots and top shoots, then water and mulch. Discard any pieces that do not contain both healthy roots and top shoots.

PESTS AND DISEASES: Plants are relatively pest free. Occasional disease problems include powdery mildew, rust, and fungal leaf spot.

WHITE GAURA
Gaura lindheimeri GAW-ruh lind-HEYE-mer-eye

White gaura produces white flowers all summer long. Pink forms of gaura are also commonly available.

ZONES: 5–9
SIZE: 5'h × 3'w
TYPE: Perennial
FORM: Upright
TEXTURE: Fine
GROWTH: Medium
LIGHT: Full sun
MOISTURE: Medium

SOIL: Fertile, well-drained
FEATURES: Flowers, foliage
USES: Border, container
FLOWERS: □ ▓

SITING: White gaura prefers full sun and fertile, well-drained soil but tolerates drought, light afternoon shade, and humidity. The preferred pH is 6.5–7.5. Light, airy racemes of pink buds open to white flowers from late spring to early autumn. Slender stems and leaves add to the airy quality of the plant. Gaura's unique see-through effect and extensive bloom time make it a welcome addition to perennial borders. Place in odd-numbered groups in borders or containers. Good companions include 'Iceberg' rose, Siberian iris, globe thistle, and 'Goldsturm' black-eyed Susan.

CARE: Plant 24–36" apart in spring or fall. Apply slow-release granular plant food at

Shear back foliage in early summer to create a more compact habit.

time of planting. Water deeply when the soil is dry. Even though the plants are low maintenance and drought tolerant, they perform better if watered during dry spells. Apply 3" of vegetative mulch in summer to help retain soil moisture. Flowers are considered self-cleaning and do not need to be deadheaded unless the occasional brown hue is not acceptable. Leave plants standing in fall until they wilt from frost, then prune back. Plants are short-lived, especially in cooler climates, and may need replacing every 2–3 years.

PROPAGATION: Sprinkle seeds over the soil mix and leave exposed to light; do not cover. Thoroughly moisten and keep moist, not soggy, until seeds germinate. Germination occurs in 5–12 days at 70–72°F. Transplant 20–28 days after sowing. After transplanting, reduce temperature to 50°F.

PESTS AND DISEASES: Insect pests include aphids and beetles. Disease pests include rust, leaf spot, and powdery mildew.

RELATED SPECIES: The cultivar 'Corrie's Gold' has gold-and-cream variegated leaves, and 'Crimson Butterflies' reaches 15" tall and has vibrant pink blooms and burgundy-stained foliage.

ENDRESS'S GERANIUM
Geranium endressii *jer-AY-nee-uhm ehn-DREE-see-eye*

Endress's geranium blooms on and off all summer with light pink flowers.

ZONES: 5–8
SIZE: 18"h × 24"w
TYPE: Perennial
FORM: Spreading
TEXTURE: Medium
GROWTH: Fast
LIGHT: Full sun to partial shade

MOISTURE: Medium
SOIL: Moderately fertile, well-drained
FEATURES: Flowers, foliage
USES: Border, container
FLOWERS: ■

SITING: Endress's geranium prefers full sun or light shade in the afternoon and well-drained, moderately fertile soil with a pH of 5.5–7.0. Erect, trumpet-shaped light pink flowers appear in early summer to early autumn and darken as they age. Endress's geranium prefers cooler climates and stops flowering in southern midsummer heat. Plants are welcome additions to the front of a border or spilling from a mixed container planting. Good companions include 'Kobold' blazing star, lavender, and 'Bressingham White' Carpathian harebell.

CARE: Plant 18" apart in spring or fall. Apply slow-release granular plant food at time of planting or begin using water-soluble plant food 3 weeks after planting in spring. Cease feeding 6–8 weeks prior to first frost date. Water deeply whenever the soil is dry. Deadhead blooms to stimulate reblooming, The tradeoff to deadheading is the loss of the cranesbill-like fruit, which will not form unless seeds are allowed to develop. Leaves are evergreen and may be left for winter viewing unless disfigured by frost.

PROPAGATION: Divide in spring or fall every 2–3 years to maintain vigor. Dig around the root clump and lift.

PESTS AND DISEASES: Plants are relatively pest free when their cultural preferences are met. Occasional diseases include downy mildew, powdery mildew, and bacterial blight.

RELATED SPECIES: The cultivar 'Wargrave Pink' is a vigorous grower with many salmon-pink blooms in summer. 'Claridge Druce' (*G. ×oxonianum*) is a hybrid between *G. endressii* and *G. versicolor*. It has pink flowers with darker veins. 'Russell Prichard' (*G. ×riversleaianum*) is a cross of *G. endressii* and *G. traversii*.

BLOODY CRANESBILL
Geranium sanguineum *jer-AY-nee-uhm san-GWIHN-ee-uhm*

Bloody cranesbill blooms even in high heat. It is also known as hardy geranium.

ZONES: 4–8
SIZE: 8"h × 12"w
TYPE: Perennial
FORM: Rounded
TEXTURE: Fine
GROWTH: Medium
LIGHT: Full sun to partial shade
MOISTURE: Medium

SOIL: Moderately fertile, well-drained
FEATURES: Flowers, foliage, fruits
USES: Border, container
FLOWERS: ■
FALL COLOR: ■

SITING: Bloody cranesbill prefers full sun or light shade in the afternoon and well-drained, moderately fertile soil with a pH of 5.5–7.0. Magenta-pink flowers with darker veins and a white eye appear from early summer to early autumn. Bloody cranesbill is the best-suited perennial cranesbill for southern landscapes due to its heat tolerance. Good companions include 'Bressingham White' Carpathian harebell, 'Monroe White' lilyturf, and 'Silver Carpet' lamb's-ears.

CARE: Plant 12" apart in spring or fall. Apply slow-release granular plant food at time of planting. Water deeply when the soil is dry. Even though the plants are low maintenance and drought tolerant, they perform better if watered during dry spells. Deadhead blooms to stimulate reblooming. Leaves are evergreen in mild climates. In cool climates leaves turn crimson in autumn and may be left for winter viewing unless disfigured by frost.

PROPAGATION: Divide in spring or fall every 2–3 years to maintain vigor.

PESTS AND DISEASES: Plants are relatively pest free when their cultural preferences are met. Occasional diseases include downy mildew, powdery mildew, and bacterial blight.

RELATED SPECIES: The cultivar 'Album' has white flowers, 'Elsbeth' has pink flowers with darker veins and leaves that become vibrant red in autumn, 'Cedric Morris' has rose-magenta blooms, 'John Elsley' is prostrate with rose-pink flowers and deep green leaves, and 'Shepherd's Warning' is compact with pink blooms.

1 Cut back plants to stimulate more compact foliage.

2 Several weeks later, healthy new growth emerges.

1 Divide plants by lifting the entire plant.

2 Separate plants by pulling apart the root system.

3 Reset pieces that contain healthy roots and shoots.

GLOBE AMARANTH
Gomphrena globosa gom-FREE-nuh glub-BOS-uh

Globe amaranth, also known as gomphrena, bears a multitude of globe-shaped flowers in summer.

ZONES: NA
SIZE: 12–24"h × 12"w
TYPE: Annual
FORM: Upright
TEXTURE: Medium
GROWTH: Fast
LIGHT: Full sun

MOISTURE: Medium
SOIL: Moderately fertile, well-drained
FEATURES: Flowers, foliage
USES: Border, container
FLOWERS: ■ ■ □ ■

SITING: Globe amaranth prefers full sun and moderately fertile, well-drained soil with a pH of 5.5–7.0. Erect spikes of cloverlike flowers with vibrant pink, purple, or ivory bracts appear from summer through autumn. Opposite leaves are bright green. Plants are relatively low maintenance, even drought tolerant, and seem weather resistant. Flowers are superb fresh cut or dried. Plant in containers or in odd-numbered groups in borders. Good garden companions include 'The Fairy' and 'Iceberg' roses, germander, and baby's breath.

CARE: Plant 12" apart in late spring after the last frost. Apply slow-release granular plant food at time of planting or begin using water-soluble plant food 3 weeks after planting in spring. Apply 3" of vegetative mulch to help retain soil moisture and add organic matter to the soil as it decomposes. Cut back plant if more compactness is desired. Deadhead to

Harvest flowers in their prime and hang them upside down in small bundles in a dry location away from direct sunlight.

stimulate reblooming. Remove plants either just before the first frost or right afterward in cooler climates.

PROPAGATION: Sprinkle seed over the soil mix and leave exposed to light or cover; either is acceptable. Thoroughly moisten and keep moist, not soggy, until seeds germinate. Germination occurs in 10–14 days at 72°F. Transplant 20–25 days after sowing. After transplanting, reduce temperature to 68°F.

PESTS AND DISEASES: Plants are relatively pest free when their cultural preferences (sun, soil, moisture) are met.

RELATED SPECIES: The cultivar 'Aurea Superba' has orange-yellow flowers with red-tinged bracts, 'Buddy' is more compact with vibrant purple flower bracts, 'Nana' has dark red flower bracts, and 'Strawberry Fields' has orange-red bracts. *G. haageana* 'Lavender Lady' has lavender flower bracts.

ANNUAL BABY'S BREATH
Gypsophila elegans jip-SOF-uh-luh EL-eh-genz

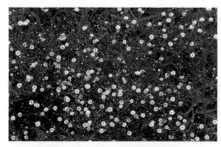

Annual baby's breath provides a light, airy quality to landscape plantings.

ZONES: NA
SIZE: 24"h × 12"w
TYPE: Annual
FORM: Rounded
TEXTURE: Fine
GROWTH: Medium
LIGHT: Full sun

MOISTURE: Medium
SOIL: Light, well-drained
FEATURES: Flowers
USES: Border, container
FLOWERS: □ ■

SITING: Annual baby's breath prefers full sun and light, moderately fertile, well-drained alkaline soil (pH 6.5–7.5). Tiny, starlike white or pink blooms appear on slender stalks in summer. Long-lasting flowers are ideal fresh cut or dried. Lance-shaped leaves are silvery green. Use in a mixed container plantings or in airy groups in perennial borders or rose gardens. Good companions include roses, purple coneflower, and globe amaranth.

CARE: Plant 12" apart in late spring after the last frost. Apply slow-release granular plant food at time of planting or begin using water-soluble plant food 3 weeks after planting in spring. Follow label directions for amount and frequency. Apply 3" of vegetative mulch to help retain soil moisture and add organic matter to the soil as it decomposes. Deadhead to stimulate reblooming. Remove plants just

before the first frost or right afterward when foliage is disfigured.

PROPAGATION: Sprinkle seeds over the soil mix and leave exposed to light or lightly cover; either is acceptable. Thoroughly moisten and keep moist, not soggy, until seeds germinate. Germination occurs in 10–15 days at 70–80°F. Transplant 21–28 days after sowing. After transplanting, reduce temperatures to 68°F.

PESTS AND DISEASES: Insect pests include slugs and snails. Diseases include crown gall, and crown and stem rot.

RELATED SPECIES: The cultivar 'Carminea' has carmine-rose flowers, 'Compacta Plena' has double light pink to white flowers, 'Covent Garden' has large white flowers, 'Red Cloud' has dark carmine-pink flowers, and 'Rosea' bears soft rose-pink flowers.

BABY'S BREATH
Gypsophila paniculata *jip-SOF-uh-luh pan-ik-yew-LAHT-ah*

Baby's breath lightly and artistically fills the space between other plants.

ZONES: 3–8
SIZE: 4'h × 4'w
TYPE: Perennial
FORM: Rounded
TEXTURE: Fine
GROWTH: Medium
LIGHT: Full sun
MOISTURE: Medium
SOIL: Moderately fertile, well-drained
FEATURES: Flowers
USES: Border, container
FLOWERS: □ ■

SITING: Baby's breath prefers full sun and light, moderately fertile, well-drained, alkaline soil (pH 6.5–7.5). Clouds of tiny white flowers appear in mid- to late summer, adding a delicate, airy quality to the landscape. Silvery-green leaves are 2–3" long and linear. Plant in drifts in borders or as part of mixed container plantings. Good companions include roses, lilies, daylilies, and 'Kobold' blazing star.

CARE: Plant 36" apart in spring or fall. Apply slow-release granular plant food at time of planting or begin using water-soluble plant food 3 weeks after planting in spring. Cease feeding 6–8 weeks prior to first frost date. Water deeply whenever the soil is dry. Deadhead blooms to stimulate reblooming and, if cut early, to dry for later use. Prune back in fall if frost withers the foliage; in milder areas, leave erect for late-season viewing and prune back in early spring.

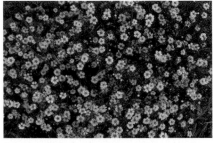

Creeping baby's breath hugs the ground. This is the pink-flowered form.

PROPAGATION: Baby's breath is difficult to transplant and difficult to divide. The most common form of propagation is tissue culture, not practical for the home gardener. Cultivars do not come true from seed, and seed-grown plants are generally inferior to vegetatively propagated plants. To sow seed, sprinkle seeds over the soil mix and leave exposed to light. Germination occurs in 5–10 days at 70–80°F. Transplant 15–20 days after sowing.

PESTS AND DISEASES: Insect pests include slugs and snails. Diseases include crown gall and crown and stem rot.

RELATED SPECIES: The cultivar 'Bristol Fairy' has double clear white flowers, 'Compacta Plena' is dwarf with double white flowers, 'Double Snowflake' has an abundance of double pure white flowers, 'Flamingo' has double soft pink flowers, and 'Viette's Dwarf' is 12–16" tall with double pale pink flowers. Creeping baby's breath (*G. repens*) is an attractive ground-hugging, semievergreen perennial hardy in Zones 4–7. Plants have star-shape white or pink blooms and bluish-green leaves.

SNEEZEWEED
Helenium autumnale *hel-EEN-ee-uhm aw-tuhm-NAH-lee*

Sneezeweed, also known as Helen's flower, has attractive daisylike flowers.

ZONES: 3–8
SIZE: 5'h × 18"w
TYPE: Perennial
FORM: Upright
TEXTURE: Medium
GROWTH: Fast
LIGHT: Full sun
MOISTURE: High, medium
SOIL: Fertile, moist, well-drained
FEATURES: Flowers, foliage
USES: Border, container, wetlands
FLOWERS: ■ ■

SITING: Common sneezeweed prefers full sun and fertile, well-drained soil with a pH of 5.5–7.0. Plants tolerate wet soils and may be planted in boggy areas. Daisylike yellow or orange flowers appear from late summer into midautumn. Plant in groups in a border, in a mixed container planting, or in a wetlands area. Companions for well-drained soil include 'Autumn Joy' sedum, Russian sage, and bluebeard. Wetlands companions include 'Variegatus' sweet flag and goatsbeard.

CARE: Plant 18" apart in spring or fall. Apply slow-release granular plant food at time of planting or begin using water-soluble plant food 3 weeks after planting in spring. Water deeply whenever the soil is dry. If planting in a wetland, avoid plant foods or chemical pesticides. Deadhead blooms to stimulate reblooming. Leave plants standing in fall until they wither from frost, then cut back.

PROPAGATION: Divide in spring or fall every 3 years to maintain vigor. Seed germination occurs in 8–12 days at 72°F. Transplant 28–35 days after sowing.

PESTS AND DISEASES: Powdery mildew and rust may occur.

RELATED SPECIES: 'Grandicephalum' has large yellow flowers, 'Peregrinum' has mahogany flowers with a yellow border, 'Rubrum' flowers are dark red, and 'Superbum' flowers are wavy and yellow.

Divide sneezeweed in spring or fall. Start by digging the entire clump.

Slice through the clump with a sharp spade and replant pieces that contain healthy roots and shoots.

ANNUAL SUNFLOWER
Helianthus annuus *heel-ee-AN-thus AN-yew-uhs*

Annual sunflower's seeds attract a variety of wildlife to the garden.

ZONES: NA
SIZE: 3–15'h × 2'w
TYPE: Annual
FORM: Upright
TEXTURE: Coarse
GROWTH: Fast
LIGHT: Full sun
MOISTURE: Medium

SOIL: Moderately fertile, moist, well-drained
FEATURES: Flowers, foliage, seed head
USES: Border, naturalizing, container
FLOWERS: ■ ■

SITING: Annual sunflower prefers full sun and moderately fertile, well-drained, alkaline soil (pH 6.5–7.5). Large, daisylike yellow flowers with a dark brown or mahogany central disk appear in summer. Hairy, toothed leaves are dark green and noticeable. Flowers attract butterflies and are excellent fresh cut; seeds attract birds. Staking is usually needed. Plant in groups at the back of an informal border, along a fence, or against a shed or barn.

CARE: Plant 24" apart in late spring after the last frost. Apply slow-release granular plant food at time of planting or begin using water-soluble plant food 3 weeks after planting. Water deeply whenever the soil is dry. Apply 3" of vegetative mulch in summer to help retain soil moisture. Leave seed heads for birds to feast on or cut back after blooms fade to promote tidiness. Remove plants just before the first frost or right afterward in cooler climates. Cover bare soil with 3" of vegetative mulch during the winter to protect topsoil.
PROPAGATION: Sprinkle seed over the soil mix and cover lightly. Thoroughly moisten and keep moist, not soggy, until seeds germinate. Germination occurs in 5–10 days at 68–72°F.
PESTS AND DISEASES: Diseases include downy mildew, powdery mildew, rust, and fungal leaf spot. Pests include caterpillars, beetles, weevils, and cutworms.
RELATED SPECIES: The cultivar 'Autumn Beauty' has 6" yellow-, bronze-, and red-tinted flowers, 'Music Box' has 4" flowers in shades of yellow and red with a black disk, 'Russian Giant' reaches 11' tall and has large yellow flowers, and 'Teddy Bear' reaches 3' tall, has double golden-yellow flowers, and with its short stature is ideal for growing in containers.

'Teddy Bear' sunflower produces double flowers on dwarf plants.

Stake tall sunflowers early when the root system is small. Use expandable stakes so the stake can grow as the plant grows.

MANY-FLOWERED SUNFLOWER
Helianthus ×multiflorus *heel-ee-AN-thus mull-tih-FLOR-uhs*

Many-flowered sunflower produces numerous smaller flowers in summer.

ZONES: 3–9
SIZE: 6'h × 3'w
TYPE: Perennial
FORM: Upright
TEXTURE: Coarse
GROWTH: Fast
LIGHT: Full sun
MOISTURE: Medium

SOIL: Moderately fertile, moist, well-drained
FEATURES: Flowers, foliage
USES: Border, container
FLOWERS: ■

SITING: Many-flowered sunflower prefers full sun and moderately fertile, moist, well-drained, alkaline soil (pH 6.5–7.5). Yellow flowers with a brownish-yellow disk appear from late summer to midautumn. Lance-shaped leaves are dark green and slightly hairy. Plants perform well in borders or in large mixed container plantings. Good companions include 'Purpureum' fennel, Kansas gayfeather, and 'Summer Pastels' yarrow.
CARE: Plant 24–36" apart in spring or fall. Apply slow-release granular plant food at time of planting or begin using water-soluble plant food 3 weeks after planting in spring. Follow label directions for amount and frequency. Cease feeding 6–8 weeks prior to first frost date. Water deeply whenever the soil is dry. Apply 3" of vegetative mulch in summer to help retain soil moisture and add organic matter to the soil as it decomposes. Cut back when frost withers the foliage; in milder areas, leave erect for late-season viewing and cut back in early spring.
PROPAGATION: Divide in spring or fall every 3 years to maintain vigor. Dig around the root clump and lift. Use a sharp spade to slice through the root system. Reset portions that contain healthy roots and top shoots, then water and mulch. Discard any pieces that do not contain both healthy roots and top shoots.
PESTS AND DISEASES: Diseases include downy mildew, powdery mildew, rust, and fungal leaf spot. Pests include caterpillars, beetles, weevils, and cutworms.
RELATED SPECIES: 'Capenoch Star' has light yellow flowers, 'Flore Pleno' has double golden flowers, 'Loddon Gold' has double vivid golden flowers, and 'Triomphe de Gand' has golden-yellow flowers.

STRAWFLOWER
Helichrysum bracteatum (Xerochrysum) *hehl-ih-KRIS-uhm brak-tee-AH-tuhm (zee-roh-KRIS-um)*

Strawflowers feel papery to the touch.

ZONES: NA
SIZE: 3–5'h × 12"w
TYPE: Annual
FORM: Upright
TEXTURE: Medium
GROWTH: Medium
LIGHT: Full sun
MOISTURE: Medium

SOIL: Moderately fertile, moist, well-drained
FEATURES: Flowers, foliage
USES: Border, container
FLOWERS: ■ ■ ■ □

SITING: Strawflower prefers full sun and moderately fertile, moist, well-drained soil with a pH of 5.5–7.0. Bright papery bracts in yellow, red, pink, and white appear from late spring into autumn. Strawflowers are simple and easy to dry if harvested early in their bloom cycle. Lance-shaped leaves are gray-green. Plant in odd-numbered, multicolored groups in the border or in containers. Good companions include 'Blackie' sweet potato vine, lemon thyme, and fennel.

CARE: Plant 12" apart in late spring after the last frost. Apply slow-release granular plant food at time of planting or begin using water-soluble plant food 3 weeks

Harvest strawflowers before they open for an elegant dried blossom.

after planting. Water deeply when the soil feels dry 2" below the surface. Plants are drought tolerant but look best when watered during dry spells. Apply 3" of vegetative mulch to help retain soil moisture. Remove plants just before the first frost or right afterward in cooler climates. Cover bare soil with 3" of vegetative mulch during the winter to protect the topsoil.

PROPAGATION: Sprinkle seeds over the soil mix and cover lightly. Thoroughly moisten and keep moist, not soggy, until seeds germinate. Germination occurs in 7–10 days at 70–75°F. Transplant 20–26 days after sowing. After transplanting, reduce temperature to 60–65°F.

PESTS AND DISEASES: Plants are relatively pest free when their cultural preferences are met.

RELATED SPECIES: The cultivar 'Dwarf Hot Bikini' has assorted bright-colored blooms, 'Frosted Sulphur' bears double pale yellow flowers, King Size Series bears double flowers in mixed colors, Monstrosum Series also produces double flowers in a range of colors, and 'Sky Net' bears creamy white flowers with a hint of pink.

SUNFLOWER HELIOPSIS
Heliopsis helianthoides *heel-ee-AHP-sihs heel-ee-an-THOY-deez*

Sunflower heliopsis is also known as false sunflower, heliopsis, or oxeye.

ZONES: 3–9
SIZE: 3–6'h × 24"w
TYPE: Perennial
FORM: Upright
TEXTURE: Medium
GROWTH: Medium
LIGHT: Full sun
MOISTURE: Medium

SOIL: Moderately fertile, moist, well-drained
FEATURES: Flowers, foliage
USES: Container, border
FLOWERS: ■

SITING: Sunflower heliopsis prefers full sun and moderately fertile, moist, well-drained soil with a pH of 5.5–7.0. Daisylike yellow flowers with a yellow central disk appear from midsummer to early autumn. Lance-shaped, toothed medium green leaves reach 6" long. Cultivars of this short-lived perennial have better form and habit than the species, though they may still require staking. Flowers are good for cutting. Plant in odd-numbered groups in borders or use in the center of a mixed container planting. Good companions include purple coneflower, 'Sissinghurst' verbena, and 'Vivid' obedient plant.

CARE: Plant 36" apart in spring or fall. Apply slow-release granular plant food at time of planting or begin using water-soluble plant food 3 weeks after planting in spring. Follow label directions for amount and frequency. Cease feeding 6–8 weeks prior to first frost date. Water deeply whenever the soil is dry. Apply 3" of vegetative mulch in summer to help retain soil moisture and add organic matter to the soil as it decomposes. Stake tall plants if stems flop. Deadhead blooms to stimulate reblooming. Prune back in fall if frost withers the foliage; in milder areas, leave erect for late-season viewing and prune back in early spring.

PROPAGATION: Propagate by seed, division, or cuttings. Sprinkle seeds over the soil mix and leave uncovered, exposed to light. Thoroughly moisten and keep moist, not soggy, until seeds germinate. Germination occurs in 3–10 days at 70°F. Transplant 11–20 days after sowing. Divide in spring or fall every 2–3 years to maintain vigor. Dig around the root clump and lift. Use a sharp spade to slice through the root system. Reset portions that contain healthy roots and top shoots, then water and mulch. Discard any pieces that do not contain both healthy roots and top shoots.

PESTS AND DISEASES: Aphids are a known pest; diseases include powdery mildew, aster yellows, and rust.

RELATED SPECIES: The cultivar 'Ballerina' reaches 3' tall and has single golden flowers, 'Jupiter' has single orange-yellow flowers, 'Karat' has single yellow flowers, 'Incomparablis' has double yellow-orange flowers, 'Lohfelden' has semidouble orange-golden flowers, 'Sonneschild' has double bright golden flowers, and 'Zinniflora' has double deep golden yellow flowers.

HELIOTROPE

Heliotropium arborescens *heel-ee-oh-TROP-ee-uhm ar-bor-ES-ehns*

Heliotrope has vanilla-scented flowers and leaves with a hint of purple. It is also known as cherry pie plant.

ZONES: NA
SIZE: 4'h × 12–18"w
TYPE: Annual
FORM: Upright
TEXTURE: Medium
GROWTH: Medium
LIGHT: Full sun
MOISTURE: Medium

SOIL: Fertile, moist, well-drained
FEATURES: Flowers, foliage
USES: Border, container
FLOWERS: ■■□

SITING: Heliotrope prefers full sun and fertile, moist, well-drained soil with a pH of 5.5–7.0. Plants are short-lived perennials usually grown as annuals. Clusters of deep violet-blue or lavender-blue flowers, 3–4" across, appear in summer. The fragrant flowers are reminiscent of vanilla and coveted by perfumers. Deep green leaves, often with a touch of purple, have prominent veins. Plant in odd-numbered groups in borders or use freely in containers. Good companions include 'Iceberg' rose and tall cosmos as well as 'Summerwine' and 'Summer Pastels' yarrow.

CARE: Plant 12" apart in late spring after the last frost. Apply slow-release granular plant food at time of planting or begin using water-soluble plant food 3 weeks after planting. When the soil feels dry 2" below the surface, water deeply. Apply 3" of vegetative mulch to help retain soil moisture and add organic matter to the soil as it decomposes. Remove plants just before the first frost or right afterward in cooler climates. Cover bare soil with 3" of vegetative mulch during the winter to preserve the topsoil.

PROPAGATION: Sprinkle seeds over the soil mix and cover lightly. Thoroughly moisten and keep moist, not soggy, until seeds germinate. Germination occurs in 4–8 days at 70–72°F. Transplant in 14–21 days. After transplanting, reduce temperature to 62–65°F.

PESTS AND DISEASES: Plants are vulnerable to whiteflies, aphids, leaf spot, and rust.

RELATED SPECIES: The cultivar 'Alba' bears fragrant white flowers, 'Chatsworth' has fragrant purple flowers, 'Florence Nightingale' had pale mauve-tinted flowers, 'Iowa' has deep purple flowers and blue-tinted leaves, 'Lord Roberts' has light violet-blue flowers, 'Marine' reaches 18" tall and has very deep violet-blue flower clusters up to 6" across, and 'White Lady' reaches 12" tall and bears white flowers with pink-stained buds.

LENTEN ROSE

Helleborus orientalis *HELL-eh-bor-uhs or-ee-ehn-TAL-ihs*

Lenten rose bears unique flowers in midwinter. It is also known as hellebore.

ZONES: 4–9
SIZE: 18"h × 18"w
TYPE: Perennial
FORM: Upright
TEXTURE: Medium
GROWTH: Medium
LIGHT: Full to partial shade

MOISTURE: Medium
SOIL: Fertile, moist, well-drained
FEATURES: Flowers, foliage
USES: Border, woodland
FLOWERS: □■■

SITING: Lenten rose is the easiest of the hellebores to grow. It prefers full to partial shade with shelter from the afternoon sun. The soil should be fertile, moist, well-drained, and alkaline (pH 6.5–7.5). Thick stems support nodding, saucer-shaped white flowers that are sometimes stained green and pale pink. Flowers appear from midwinter into midspring. Basal leathery leaves are deep green and evergreen.

Their bold texture is a pleasant addition to the landscape. Place this low-maintenance perennial in odd-numbered groups at the front of shade perennial borders, or scatter in groups throughout the irrigated woodland garden. Good companions include Japanese painted fern, 'Magnet' snowdrop, 'Mrs. Moon' lungwort, and European wild ginger.

CARE: Plant 18" apart in spring or fall. Apply slow-release granular plant food at

Trim away dead or brown leaves in late winter or early spring.

time of planting or begin using water-soluble plant food 3 weeks after planting in spring. Cease feeding 6–8 weeks prior to first frost date. Water deeply whenever the soil is dry. Apply 3" of vegetative mulch in summer and winter to help retain soil moisture. There is no need to prune back in fall because the foliage is evergreen.

PROPAGATION: Plants self-sow in the landscape. Handle and move newly emerged seedlings carefully.

PESTS AND DISEASES: Plants are relatively pest free when their cultural preferences are met. Leaf spot and black rot may appear occasionally.

RELATED SPECIES: *H. orientalis* ssp. *abchasicus* has pale green flowers stained reddish purple outside, ssp. *guttatus* has creamy white flowers spotted with maroon inside, and Millet Hybrids have larger white, pink, or red flowers. Bearsfoot hellebore (*H. foetidus*) has nodding, bell-shape green flowers, sometimes with a purple rim, that appear from midwinter to midspring. Lobed, deep green leaves smell putrid when crushed but are handsome additions to the shaded landscape. Christmas rose (*H. niger*) has saucer-shape white flowers, sometimes stained with pale pink and green, that appear from early winter to early spring.

DAYLILY
Hemerocallis hybrids   *hehm-er-oh-KAL-iss*

Daylilies are low-maintenance perennials tolerant of most sites.

ZONES: 3–10
SIZE: 6–48"h × 12–36"w
TYPE: Perennial
FORM: Irregular
TEXTURE: Medium
GROWTH: Medium
LIGHT: Full sun to part shade

MOISTURE: Medium
SOIL: Fertile, moist, well-drained
FEATURES: Flowers, foliage
USES: Border, container
FLOWERS: ■ ■ ■ □ ■ ■

SITING: Daylilies prefer full sun and fertile, moist, well-drained soil but tolerate drought and low fertility. The preferred pH is 5.5–7.0. Daylily flowers are trumpet shaped, and most last only one day. Some daylilies are repeat bloomers and will produce flowers on and off all season. Daylilies are classic low-maintenance perennials for a border. Dwarf selections are best for containers. Daylilies reign supreme when naturalized in large drifts.

CARE: Plant 12–36" apart in spring or fall. Apply slow-release granular plant food at time of planting or begin using water-soluble plant food 3 weeks after planting in spring. Cease feeding 4–6 weeks prior to first frost date. Water deeply whenever the soil is dry. Apply 3" of vegetative mulch in

Deadhead daylilies to keep the plants attractive while the additional blooms open.

summer to help retain soil moisture. Prune back if frost withers foliage; in milder areas leave erect for late-season viewing and prune back in early spring.

PROPAGATION: Divide in spring or fall every 3 years to control growth. Dig around the root clump and lift. Established clumps may be thick and dense and difficult to cut through. A sharp ax may be required. Otherwise, back-to-back garden forks can be used to pry apart the root system. Reset potions that contain healthy roots and top shoots.

PESTS AND DISEASES: Plants are relatively pest free when their cultural preferences are met. Snails and slugs are occasional problems; daylily rust is a new disease.

RELATED SPECIES: There are more than 30,000 named daylily cultivars. The cultivar 'Hyperion' reaches up to 48" tall and has fragrant rich yellow flowers midseason, 'Catherine Woodbury' reaches 2' tall and has antique-toned lavender-pink flowers, 'Eenie Weenie' reaches 10" tall and has yellow flowers with fluted edges, and 'Stella de Oro' reaches 12" tall and has reblooming bright golden yellow flowers.

CORAL BELLS
Heuchera sanguinea   *HOO-ker-uh san-GWIHN-ee-uh*

Coral bells are low-maintenance perennials for sun or shade.

ZONES: 3–8
SIZE: 12–24"h × 12"w
TYPE: Perennial
FORM: Rounded
TEXTURE: Fine
GROWTH: Medium
LIGHT: Full sun to partial shade

MOISTURE: Medium
SOIL: Fertile, moist, well-drained
FEATURES: Flowers, foliage
USES: Border, container
FLOWERS: ■ □ ■

SITING: Coral bells prefer full sun in the North and partial shade in the South. Plants prefer fertile, moist but well-drained soil with a pH of 5.5–7.0. Tubular red, white, or pink flowers appear on slender stalks in summer. Plant at the front of a shade border or add to mixed container plantings. Companions for shade include astilbes, hostas, and Japanese painted fern.

CARE: Plant 18" apart in spring or fall. After planting, water deeply and add 3" of mulch around, but not touching, the plants. Apply slow-release granular plant food at time of planting or begin using water-soluble plant food 3 weeks after planting in spring. Water deeply whenever the soil is dry. Prune in fall if frost withers foliage; in milder areas, leave erect for late-season viewing, and prune back in early spring.

PROPAGATION: The species may be propagated by seed, but all desirable cultivars need to be vegetatively propagated. Divide in spring or fall every 3 years to maintain vigor.

PESTS AND DISEASES: Powdery mildew, rust, and leaf spot are occasional pests.

RELATED SPECIES: The cultivar 'Apple Blossom' bears pale pink flowers, 'Brandon Pink' has coral-pink flowers, 'Cherry Splash' has green and gold leaf marbling, 'Firesprite' has red flowers, 'Northern Fire' has silver marbled leaves and bright red flowers, and 'Pearl Drops' bears arching stems of white flowers stained pink. Purple-leaf coral bells (*H. macrantha* × *H. americana*) is grown primarily for its colorful foliage. 'Palace Purple' has dark purple leaves. 'Chocolate Ruffles' is deep maroon, and 'Pewter Veil' is silvery.

1
Trim away dead leaves from heuchera in late fall or spring.

2
***Heuchera americana* has marbled young foliage with copper tints.**

HOSTA
Hosta hybrids *HAH-stub*

Hostas offer mounds of delightful shapes and textures for the shade.

ZONES: 3–8
SIZE: 2–48"h × 2–48"w
TYPE: Perennial
FORM: Rounded
TEXTURE: Medium
GROWTH: Medium
LIGHT: Part to full shade

MOISTURE: Medium
SOIL: Fertile, moist, well-drained
FEATURES: Foliage, flowers
USES: Border, ground cover, container
FLOWERS: ☐ ■ ■

SITING: Hosta prefers partial or full shade and fertile, moist but well-drained soil with a pH of 5.5–7.0. Mounds of heart-shape, oval, or lance-shape leaves in green, blue, yellow, and silver hues are the star attraction. Stalks of bell- or spider-shape blue, lavender, or white flowers appear in summer. Interesting and low maintenance, hostas are elite members of the classic perennial shade border. Plant in odd-numbered groups in borders, in woodland gardens, in containers, or at the base of irrigated woody plants.

CARE: Plant 18–36" apart in spring or fall. Apply slow-release granular plant food at time of planting or begin using water-soluble plant food 3 weeks after planting in spring. Follow label directions for amount and frequency. Cease feeding 6–8 weeks prior to first frost date. When the soil feels dry 2" below the surface, water deeply. Apply 3" of vegetative mulch in summer and winter to help retain soil moisture and add organic matter to the soil as it decomposes. Some hosta aficionados snip off developing flowers, feeling that they detract from the foliage. Cut the plant back in fall once frost withers the foliage.

PROPAGATION: Many hostas do not require division to remain vigorous and are long-lived. They may be divided in spring or fall. Dig around the root clump and lift. Use a sharp spade to slice through the root system. Reset portions that contain healthy roots and top shoots, then water and mulch. Discard any pieces that do not contain both healthy roots and top shoots.

PESTS AND DISEASES: Plants are relatively pest free when their cultural preferences are met. Slugs and snails are notorious pests.
RELATED SPECIES: Fortune's hosta *(H. fortunei)* reaches 24" high and wide and has mounds of heart-shape green to gray-green leaves. Lance leaf hosta *(H. lancifolia)* reaches 24" high and 18" wide and has pointed leaves that add drama to the edge of a border. Fragrant hosta *(H. plantaginea)* reaches 30" high and 24" wide and has large, heart-shape yellowish-green leaves and sweetly fragrant white flowers in late summer. Thousands of other hosta varieties are available to suit most any shade gardener's preferences.

Divide hosta by lifting the entire plant from its growing bed.

Plunge a sharp spade through the crown and root system.

Select pieces with healthy roots and shoots to reset in the garden.

SIEBOLD HOSTA
Hosta sieboldiana *HAH-stuh sih-bold-ee-AN-uh*

Siebold hosta is a large excellent low-maintenance perennial for shade with heart-shaped blue-green or blue-gray leaves.

ZONES: 3–8
SIZE: 36"h × 4'w
TYPE: Perennial
FORM: Rounded
TEXTURE: Medium
GROWTH: Medium
LIGHT: Part to full shade

MOISTURE: Medium
SOIL: Fertile, moist, well-drained
FEATURES: Foliage
USES: Border, woodland, container
FLOWERS: ■

SITING: Siebold hosta prefers partial to full shade and fertile, moist but well-drained soil with a pH of 5.5–7.0. Leaves reach 10–20" long and are heart-shape or rounded and an appealing blue-green to blue-gray. In early summer, bell-shape blooms appear first as pale lavender, then fade to white. Good companions include heart-leaf brunnera, 'Deutschland' astilbe, bugbane, 'Mrs. Moon' Bethlehem sage, and European wild ginger.
CARE: Plant 36" apart in spring or fall. Apply slow-release granular food at time

Plant Siebold hosta 36" apart in triangular formation for best effect.

of planting or begin using water-soluble plant food 3 weeks after planting in spring. Cease fertilizing 6–8 weeks prior to first frost date. Water deeply whenever the soil is dry. Apply 3" of vegetative mulch in summer and winter to help retain soil moisture. Some hosta aficionados snip off developing flowers, feeling they detract from the foliage. Cut back in fall once frost withers the foliage.
PROPAGATION: Siebold hosta does not need dividing to maintain vigor. Should more plants be desired, division is easy. Dig around the root clump and lift. Use a sharp spade to slice through the root system. Reset portions that contain healthy roots and top shoots, then water and mulch. Discard any pieces that do not contain both healthy roots and top shoots.
PESTS AND DISEASES: Plants are relatively pest free when their cultural preferences are met. Slugs and snails are common pests. Control with traps or baits.
RELATED SPECIES: 'Aurea' has golden yellow leaves; var. *elegans* has puckered, heart-shape bluish leaves. 'Frances Williams' has puckered, heart-shape bluish-green leaves with an irregular golden edge.

WAVY HOSTA
Hosta undulata *HAH-stuh uhn-dyew-LAH-tuh*

Wavy hosta has twisted or wavy leaves with white splashes.

ZONES: 3–8
SIZE: 12–18"h × 18"w
TYPE: Perennial
FORM: Rounded
TEXTURE: Medium
GROWTH: Medium
LIGHT: Full to part shade

MOISTURE: Medium
SOIL: Fertile, moist, well-drained
FEATURES: Foliage, flowers
USES: Border, container
FLOWERS: ■

SITING: Wavy hosta prefers partial to full shade and fertile, moist but well-drained soil with a pH of 5.5–7.0. Twisted or wavy leaves are 6" long and bright green with splashes of bright white in the center or margins. Light lilac flowers appear in midsummer. Plants withstand sun better than most hostas. Place in a border or use in shady container plantings. Good companions include goatsbeard, bugbane, sweet woodruff, and Cascade Series lobelia.
CARE: Plant 36" apart in spring or fall. Apply slow-release granular plant food at time of planting or begin using water-soluble plant food 3 weeks after planting in spring. Cease feeding 6–8 weeks prior to first frost date. Water deeply whenever the soil is dry. Apply 3" of vegetative mulch in summer and winter to help retain soil moisture. Prune back in fall once frost withers the foliage.
PROPAGATION: Wavy hosta does not need dividing to maintain vigor. Should more plants be desired, division is easy.
PESTS AND DISEASES: Plants are relatively pest free when their cultural preferences are met. Slugs and snails are common pests. Control with traps or bait.
RELATED SPECIES: *H. u.* var. *albo-marginata* has leaves with cream margins, and blue hosta (*H. ventricosa*) has bluegreen leaves.

1 Hosta foliage naturally turns yellow in fall.

2 Cut back hosta after frost disfigures foliage.

3 Pruned plants are ready for winter mulch.

CHAMELEON PLANT

Houttuynia cordata *hoo-TOO-nee-uh kor-DAH-tuh*

Chameleon plant, also known as houttuynia, has colorful foliage and spreads rapidly.

ZONES: (5) 6–11
SIZE: 6–12"h × 18"w
TYPE: Perennial
FORM: Spreading
TEXTURE: Medium
GROWTH: Fast
LIGHT: Full sun to part shade

MOISTURE: Wet
SOIL: Moderately fertile, moist
FEATURES: Foliage, flowers
USES: Ground cover, wetland, container
FLOWERS: □

SITING: Chameleon plant prefers full sun to partial shade and moist soil with a pH of 5.5–7.0. Plants have colorful foliage with splashes of blue-green, gray-green, and red. Greenish yellow flowers emerge in summer and turn white with age. Plants are invasive and should be used only where they can be managed and removed when necessary. Containers are ideal for constraining plants.

CARE: Plant 18–24" apart in spring or fall. Plants quickly spread to fill in gaps and make a solid ground cover. Chameleon plant requires constant moisture for best growth. On dry sites, the foliage will turn brown and tattered unless plants are given supplemental watering. If planting in a wetland, avoid plant foods and chemical pesticides to prevent chemicals from leaching into water bodies. Water deeply when the soil is dry. In wetlands, apply 3" of vegetative mulch in winter to help protect roots. In containers, expect to see the roots emerge from the drainage holes.

PROPAGATION: Divide in spring. Dig around the root clump and lift. Use a sharp spade to slice through the root system. Reset portions that contain healthy roots and top shoots, then water and mulch. Discard any pieces that do not contain both healthy roots and top shoots.

PESTS AND DISEASES: Slugs and snails are common pests.

RELATED SPECIES: The cultivar 'Chameleon' is less invasive than the species and has leaves splashed with green, pale yellow, and red.

HYACINTH

Hyacinthus orientalis *hi-uh-SIHN-thus or-ee-ehn-TAL-is*

Hyacinth bulbs produce lovely fragrant bell-shaped flowers in spring.

ZONES: 4–8
SIZE: 8–12"h × 6"w
TYPE: Perennial
FORM: Upright
TEXTURE: Medium
GROWTH: Slow
LIGHT: Full sun

MOISTURE: Medium
SOIL: Moderately fertile, well-drained
FEATURES: Flowers
USES: Border, container, massing
FLOWERS: ■ ■ ■ □

SITING: Hyacinth prefers full sun and moderately fertile, well-drained soil with a pH of 5.5–7.0. Bell-shape, intensely fragrant blue, violet, pink, or white flowers appear in spring. Strap-shape, glossy leaves are deep green. Plant in drifts in borders, mass in beds around irrigated deciduous trees, or use in container plantings. The fragrance is unmistakable and usually greatly admired.

CARE: Plant bulbs outdoors 4" deep and 4–6" apart in fall. Apply slow-release granular plant food at time of planting. Follow label directions for amount and frequency. Water deeply whenever the soil is dry. Apply 3" of organic mulch in summer and winter to help retain soil moisture and add organic matter to the soil as it decomposes.

PROPAGATION: Unearth the bulbs in summer, when dormant, and separate offsets that form around each bulb. Replant healthy, firm bulbs 4–6" apart in moderately fertile, well-drained soil, then water and mulch.

PESTS AND DISEASES: Problems include aphids, botrytis, and bulb rot. Site in well-drained soil and keep dry in summer.

1 To enjoy hyacinth blooms indoors, fill a bulb-forcing jar with water.

2 Place the bulb so that just the base is immersed in the water.

3 Maintain the water level to keep the bulb base immersed and watch the roots, shoots, and flowers grow.

AARON'S BEARD

Hypericum calycinum *hi-PEER-ih-kuhm kal-ih-KYN-uhm*

Aaron's beard spreads rapidly. It is also known as St. Johnswort.

ZONES: 4–9
SIZE: 24"h × 36"w
TYPE: Woody perennial
FORM: Spreading
TEXTURE: Medium
GROWTH: Fast
LIGHT: Full to part shade
MOISTURE: Medium
SOIL: Moderately fertile, moist, well-drained
FEATURES: Flowers, foliage
USES: Ground cover
FLOWERS: ■

SITING: Aaron's beard prefers partial to full shade and moderately fertile, moist, well-drained soil with a pH of 5.5–7.0. Bright yellow flowers with pronounced stamens appear from midsummer to midautumn. Evergreen leaves are dark green on top and lighter below. Plants are invasive and should be placed on banks, along fence lines, and other areas where they can ramble.

CARE: Plant 36" apart in spring or fall. Apply slow-release granular plant food at time of planting. Water deeply when the soil is dry. Apply 3" of vegetative mulch in summer and winter to help retain soil moisture and add organic matter to the soil as it decomposes. Cut plants back to the ground in spring to remove winter-tattered shoots and leaves. In the South plants often succumb to heat and drop their leaves in summer.

PROPAGATION: Divide in spring. Dig around the root clump and lift. Use a sharp spade to slice through the root system. Reset portions that contain healthy roots and top shoots, then water and mulch. Discard any pieces that do not contain both healthy roots and top shoots.

PESTS AND DISEASES: Problems include scale, rust, and leaf spot.

RELATED SPECIES: Some species such as tutsan (*H. androsaemum*) have become commonly used in cut flower arrangements for their ornamental seed capsules that change from greenish-yellow to red and eventually black. Golden cup St. Johnswort (*H. patulum*) is an evergreen shrub that bears clusters of 2" yellow flowers in summer. 'Hidcote' and 'Sungold' are popular cultivars. *H. ×moserianum* is a hybrid of Aaron's beard and golden St. Johnswort. It has 3" yellow blooms.

EVERGREEN CANDYTUFT

Iberis sempervirens *ih-BEER-ihs sehm-purr-VY-renz*

Evergreen candytuft produces mounds of white flowers in spring.

ZONES: 3–9
SIZE: 12"h × 18"w
TYPE: Perennial
FORM: Rounded
TEXTURE: Medium
GROWTH: Medium
LIGHT: Full sun
MOISTURE: Medium
SOIL: Moderately fertile, well-drained
FEATURES: Flowers, foliage
USES: Border, container
FLOWERS: □

SITING: Evergreen candytuft prefers full sun and moderately fertile, well-drained alkaline soil (pH of 6.5–7.5). Tiny white flowers appear in late spring and early summer and cover the top of the plant. Deep green leaves, evergreen and 1" long, create appeal long after the flowers have faded. The mound-shaped habit is also pleasing. Candytuft is a low-maintenance top-performing perennial when its cultural preferences are met. Plant in odd-number groups at the front of a border or add to a container planting and allow it to spill over the sides. Good companions include sea pink, 'Strawberry Vanilla Latte' lily, 'Strawberry Shortcake' lily, 'Royal Wedding' Oriental poppy, 'Beauty of Livermere' Oriental poppy, germander, and 'Iceberg' rose.

CARE: Plant 18" apart in spring or fall. Apply slow-release granular plant food at time of planting. Cease feeding 6–8 weeks prior to first frost date. When the soil feels dry 2" below the surface, water deeply. Apply 3" of vegetative mulch in summer and winter to help retain soil moisture and add organic matter to the soil as it decomposes. Shear back one-third of the plant after blooming to maintain the compact, rounded habit. Plants are evergreen and do not need to be cut back in fall unless foliage is disfigured by frost.

PROPAGATION: Seed produces variable flower color and size. Cultivars are propagated by cuttings taken after flowering. Sprinkle seeds over the soil mix and leave exposed to light; do not cover. Thoroughly moisten and keep moist, not soggy, until seeds germinate. Germination occurs in 14–22 days at 60–65°F. Transplant 14–21 days after sowing. Reduce the temperature to 50°F after transplanting the seedlings.

PESTS AND DISEASES: Plants are relatively pest free when their cultural preferences are met.

RELATED SPECIES: The cultivars 'Autumn Beauty' and 'Autumn Snow' bear white flowers in spring and fall, 'Climax' has spoon-shape leaves, 'Compacta' and 'Schneeflocke' are compact and dense, and 'Weisser Zwerg' is also compact with short, linear leaves.

Shear evergreen candytuft back after bloom is complete to stimulate compact, dense foliar growth.

NEW GUINEA IMPATIENS

Impatiens hawkeri *ihm-PAY-shenz HAW-ker-eye*

New Guinea impatiens has solid or variegated foliage and an assortment of flower colors to choose from.

ZONES: NA
SIZE: 18–36"h × 18"w
TYPE: Annual
FORM: Rounded
TEXTURE: Medium
GROWTH: Slow
LIGHT: Partial shade to full sun

MOISTURE: Medium
SOIL: Fertile, moist, well-drained
FEATURES: Flowers, foliage
USES: Border, container
FLOWERS: ■ ■ ■ ■ □

SITING: New Guinea impatiens prefers partial shade, but can be grown in full sun with adequate moisture. Provide fertile, moist, well-drained soil with a pH of 5.5–7.0. Vibrant shades of orange, salmon, rose, pink, scarlet, lavender, or white flowers appear in summer and are complemented by bronze-and-yellow variegated or solid bronze foliage. Plants are grown as annuals in most areas. New Guinea impatiens is well suited as a bedding plant, in containers, and planted in odd-number groups in the border. Good companions include hellebore, 'Palace Purple' heuchera, and 'Husker Red' beard tongue.

CARE: Plant 12–18" apart in late spring. Apply slow-release granular plant food at time of planting or begin using water-soluble plant food 3 weeks after planting in spring. Water deeply when the soil is dry. Apply 2–3" of organic mulch in summer to help retain soil moisture and add organic matter to the soil as it decomposes. Remove plants just before the first frost or right afterward.

PROPAGATION: Take cuttings in summer. Cut pieces that contain two healthy leaves and at least three nodes. Insert exposed nodes into moist soil mix, keeping leaves above the soil level. Supply bottom heat and keep the soil mix and cuttings moist, not soggy, until root and top shoot growth is evident, then transplant.

PESTS AND DISEASES: Diseases include impatiens necrotic spot virus, fungal leaf spot, and verticillium wilt.

RELATED SPECIES: Cultivars with single flowers include 'Big Top' with white flowers, 'Showboat' with pinkish-purple flowers, and 'Star Dancer' with lavender flowers and striped leaves. Cultivars with double flowers include 'Apple Blossom', with pink flowers and 'Damask Rose' with deep red flowers.

IMPATIENS

Impatiens walleriana *ihm-PAY-shenz wall-air-ee-AN-uh*

Impatiens is often used as a bedding plant for shady spaces. It is also known as busy Lizzie or touch-me-not.

ZONES: NA
SIZE: 6–24"h × 12–24"w
TYPE: Annual
FORM: Irregular
TEXTURE: Fine
GROWTH: Medium
LIGHT: Part to full shade

MOISTURE: Medium
SOIL: Fertile, moist, well-drained
FEATURES: Flowers, foliage
USES: Bedding, container
FLOWERS: □ ■ ■ ■ ■

SITING: Impatiens prefers partial shade and fertile, well-drained soil with a pH of 5.5–7.0. Orange, pink, red, purple, and white flowers appear in summer. Foliage is light to bright green and sometimes has red-stained leaves and stems. Plants are usually grown as annuals. They are well suited as bedding plants for shade and in containers. Good container companions include heart-leaf bergenia, 'Husker Red' beard-tongue, and 'Carpet of Snow' sweet alyssum.

CARE: Plant 12–24" apart in late spring. Apply slow-release granular plant food at time of planting or begin using water-soluble plant food 3 weeks after planting in spring. Water deeply when the soil is dry. Apply 3" of vegetative mulch in summer to help retain soil moisture and add organic matter to the soil as it decomposes. Remove plants either just before the first frost or right afterward.

PROPAGATION: Sprinkle seeds over the soil mix and cover lightly. Thoroughly moisten and keep moist, not soggy, until seeds germinate. Germination occurs in 10–20 days at 75–78°F. Transplant 14–21 days after sowing. Reduce the temperature to 60°F after transplanting.

PESTS AND DISEASES: Diseases include impatiens necrotic spot virus, fungal leaf spot, and verticillium wilt.

RELATED SPECIES: The cultivar 'Starbright' has a white star in the center of pink, red, violet, and orange flowers; Swirl Series has hues of pink and orange flowers rimmed with deep pink; and Super Elfin Series reaches only 10" tall and comes in pastels and traditional tones.

A container of impatiens is a great way to brighten up a shady garden.

If roots are pot-bound, slice vertically through them and fan root ends out.

SWEET POTATO
Ipomoea batatas *ib-pub-MAY-ah bab-TAH-tubs*

Ornamental sweet potato adds striking color to a container garden. 'Tricolor' has green and white leaves tinged in pink.

ZONES: 9–11
SIZE: 1'h × 5–15'w
TYPE: Perennial
FORM: Upright
TEXTURE: Coarse
GROWTH: Fast
LIGHT: Full sun
MOISTURE: Medium

SOIL: Moderately fertile, well-drained
FEATURES: Leaves, stems
USES: Container, arbor
FLOWERS: ■

SITING: Sweet potato vine prefers full sun, shelter from drying winds, and moderately fertile, well-drained soil with a pH of 5.5–7.0. Leaves are lobed, heart-shaped, or entire. Choice cultivars for the ornamental landscape include chartreuse and purplish-black leaf and stem colors. Trumpet-shaped lavender flowers appear in summer. Sweet potato vine adds texture and color to container plantings. Container companions for the chartreuse-color vine include purple fountain grass, 'Crimson Butterflies' gaura, and 'Patty's Plum' Oriental poppy. Container companions for the purple-black vine include 'Karl Foerster' feather reed grass, gulf muhly, and 'Evelyn' beard tongue.

CARE: Plant 12–24" apart in late spring. Apply slow-release plant food, such as Miracle-Gro Shake 'n Feed All Purpose, at the time of planting or begin using water-soluble plant food, such as Miracle-Gro Water Soluble All Purpose, 3 weeks after planting in spring. Follow label directions for amount and frequency. Water deeply when the soil is dry. Apply 3" of vegetative mulch in summer to help retain soil moisture and add organic matter to the soil as it decomposes. Remove plants just before the first frost or right afterward. Cover bare soil with 3" of vegetative mulch during the winter to preserve the topsoil.

PROPAGATION: Take cuttings in summer. Cut pieces that contain two healthy leaves and at least three nodes. Insert exposed nodes into moist soil mix, keeping leaves above the soil level. Cover trays with plastic to increase humidity. Supply bottom heat and keep the soil mix and cuttings moist, not soggy, until root and top shoot growth is evident, then transplant.

PESTS AND DISEASES: Diseases include rust, fungal leaf spot, stem rot, and wilt.

RELATED SPECIES: The cultivar 'Blackie' has lobed purplish-black leaves. 'Black Heart' and 'Margarita' are other popular cultivars.

MORNING GLORY
Ipomoea tricolor *ib-pub-MAY-ah TRY-kub-ler*

Morning glory blossoms are sky blue and the vines climb quickly.

ZONES: NA
SIZE: 6–12'h × 5'w
TYPE: Annual
FORM: Upright
TEXTURE: Medium
GROWTH: Fast
LIGHT: Full sun
MOISTURE: Medium

SOIL: Moderately fertile, well-drained
FEATURES: Flowers, foliage
USES: Container, arbor
FLOWERS: ■ ■ ■

SITING: Morning glory vine prefers full sun and fertile, well-drained soil with a pH of 5.5–7.0. Funnel-shape, azure-blue flowers appear in summer. Heart-shape leaves and fast-twining stems are bright medium green. Grow the vine on an arbor or a trellis or allow it to spill from a container. Good container companions include 'Bravado' purple coneflower, 'Whirling Butterflies' gaura, 'Casa Blanca' lily, and 'Carpet of Snow' alyssum.

CARE: Plant 12–24" apart in late spring where plants will receive at least 6 hours of unobstructed sunlight. Apply slow-release granular plant food at time of planting. Follow label directions for amount and frequency. (Excessive nitrogen plant foods may result in vigorous vines but limited flowering.) Water deeply when the soil is dry. Apply 3" of vegetative mulch in summer to help retain soil moisture and add organic matter to the soil as it decomposes. Remove plants just before the first frost or right afterward. Cover bare soil with 3" of vegetative mulch during winter to preserve the topsoil.

PROPAGATION: Seed morning glory directly in place in the garden.

PESTS AND DISEASES: Diseases include rust, fungal leaf spot, stem rot, and wilt.

RELATED SPECIES: The cultivar 'Crimson Rambler' has red flowers with white throat, 'Heavenly Blue Improved' has sky blue flowers with a pale center, 'Flying Saucers' has marbled blue and white flowers, and 'Wedding Bells' has rosy-blue flowers.

1 **Soak seeds overnight before sowing to speed germination.**

2 **Plant seeds directly in the landscape as they resent transplanting. Chain link fencing or a trellis provide good support.**

BEARDED IRIS
Iris bearded hybrids *EYE-rihs*

Bearded iris is a traditional favorite for the perennial border. It blooms in a rainbow of colors and bicolors.

ZONES: 3–9
SIZE: 6–36"h × 12–24"w
TYPE: Perennial
FORM: Upright
TEXTURE: Medium
GROWTH: Medium
LIGHT: Full sun to partial shade

MOISTURE: Medium
SOIL: Fertile, well-drained
FEATURES: Flowers, foliage
USES: Border
FLOWERS: ☐ ■ ■ ■ ■ ■ ■

SITING: Bearded iris prefers full sun, or light afternoon shade in warmer climates, and fertile, well-drained soil with a pH of 5.5–7.0. Flower colors include shades of blue, purple, red, white, yellow, orange, and pink. Flowers have flashy standard (upright) petals, fall (drooping) petals, and beards. Beards are colored or white hairs in the center of the fall petals. Flowers appear in early spring to early summer. Shallow-rooted thick rhizomes produce fans of sword-shaped leaves. Bearded iris are classified into groups according to their size and bloom time. Groups—in ascending order of height and bloom time—include miniature dwarf bearded, standard dwarf bearded, intermediate bearded, miniature tall bearded, border bearded, and tall bearded. Plant in odd-numbered groups in a border or create an all-iris bed for the best effect. Fresh-cut flowers are spectacular and usually quite fragrant. Good companions include false indigo, delphinium, and 'Butterfly Blue' or 'Pink Mist' pincushion flower.

CARE: Plant 12–24" apart, depending on the cultivar, in fall or early spring. Plant rhizomes horizontally 1" deep, with tops exposed. Apply slow-release, low-nitrogen granular plant food at time of planting and each spring. Too much nitrogen will produce lush leaves but reduce flowering.

Louisiana iris performs well in high heat.

Add bonemeal to the soil at planting time. Water deeply when the soil is dry. Add 3" of vegetative mulch outside of the root zone; avoid placing it over the rhizomes.

PROPAGATION: Iris should be divided due to overcrowding or reduced vigor, usually every 3–4 years. Divide in mid- to late summer. Dig around the rhizomes and lift. Use a sharp spade or pruners to cut through the root system. Cut back foliage to 6". Reset portions that contain healthy roots and top shoots, then water and mulch. Discard pieces that are hollow, woody, soft, and do not contain both healthy roots and top shoots. Plants often have reduced flowering the first season after division but flower freely the second season.

PESTS AND DISEASES: Pests include iris borer, iris weevil, thrips, slugs, and snails. Diseases include rhizome rot, crown rot, and leaf spot.

RELATED SPECIES: Dwarf bearded iris (*I. pumila*) reaches 4–6" high, has gray-green leaves, and bears purple, blue, or yellow flowers in spring. Japanese iris (*I. ensata*) reaches 36" high and bears flowers with reduced standards in shades of purple and reddish purple in early summer; leaves have a pronounced midrib. Louisiana iris (*I. fulva*) reaches 18–36" high and bears nonbearded bright red to rust and occasionally yellow flowers in early summer. Louisiana iris prefers moist soil and hot summers. It may spread fast but is suited for Southern heat.

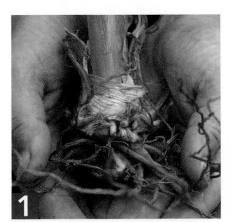

1 Divide and plant bare-root rhizomes of iris in late summer.

2 Fan the roots and cover with 1" of soil, but leave the tops of rhizomes exposed.

3 Apply a thin layer of organic mulch and water thoroughly.

SIBERIAN IRIS

Iris sibirica *EYE-ribs si-BEER-ib-kub*

Siberian iris is a low-maintenance perennial with elegant blooms and grasslike foliage.

ZONES: 3–9
SIZE: 18–48"h × 24"w
TYPE: Perennial
FORM: Upright
TEXTURE: Medium
GROWTH: Fast
LIGHT: Full sun to part shade

MOISTURE: Moist
SOIL: Moderately fertile, well-drained
FEATURES: Flowers, foliage
USES: Border, container
FLOWERS: ■■□

SITING: Siberian iris prefers full sun and moderately fertile, well-drained soil with a pH of 5.5–7.0. Elegant beardless flowers, often with blue-hue petals, are held well above the foliage in early summer. Fall petals are dark-veined and marked with white or gold. Leaves are narrow and grasslike. This low-maintenance perennial is trouble-free, long-lived, and attractive throughout the growing season. Plant in odd-number groups in the middle or back of a perennial border or in containers. Good companions include false indigo and 'Biokovo' cranesbill.

CARE: Plant 18–24" apart in fall or early spring. Apply slow-release granular plant food at time of planting. When the soil feels dry 2" below the surface, water deeply. Apply 3" of vegetative mulch in summer and winter to reduce weed seed germination, retain soil moisture, and keep soil temperatures stable. Trim plants to the ground in late fall after frost disfigures the foliage.

PROPAGATION: In moderately fertile soil, plants may be divided every 3 years to maintain vigor. In rich soils division is needed sooner to maintain vigor and control growth. Dig around the root clump and lift. Use a sharp spade to slice through the root system. The larger the portion, the larger the resulting plant during the first year. Smaller pieces may take 2–3 years to reach mature size and bloom. Reset portions that contain healthy roots and top shoots. Discard any pieces that do not contain both healthy roots and top shoots. Water deeply and apply 3" of vegetative mulch around the plants.

PESTS AND DISEASES: Plants are relatively pest free when cultural requirements (sun, soil, moisture, planting depth) are met.

RELATED SPECIES: *I. sibirica* 'Alba' bears white flowers, 'Ann Dasch' has dark blue flowers with yellow on the falls, 'Butter and Sugar' bears white-and-yellow flowers, 'Caesar's Brother' has deep purple flowers, 'Ego' bears brilliant blue flowers, 'Ewen' has burgundy blooms, 'Papillon' bears light blue flowers, and 'Wisley White' has white flowers with a yellow splash on the falls. Sweet iris (*I. pallida*) reaches 2–4' high and bears soft blue flowers with a yellow beard in early summer. Leaves are gray-green and sometimes evergreen. The rhizomes are powdered or dried in pea-size chunks to use as a fixative (holds scents for a long time) for potpourri. Yellow flag iris (*I. pseudacorus*) prefers moist, even wet, soils. Flowers are yellow with a deeper yellow splash on each fall. Leaves are gray-green. Reticulated iris (*I. reticulata*) has a bulb instead of rhizomes, reaches 4–6" high, and produces fragrant purple-and-gold blooms in late winter or early spring. Dutch iris (*I. xiphium* hybrids) bear blue or violet or occasionally white, yellow, or mauve flowers in spring and early summer. They are hardy to Zone 5.

Siberian iris foliage is attractive throughout the growing season.

Sweet iris, with variegated foliage, is an old-fashioned but under-used iris.

Yellow flag iris performs well in moist soils or standing water.

COMMON TORCH LILY

Kniphofia uvaria *nye-FO-fee-uh oo-VAR-ee-uh*

Common torch lily blooms add drama to the landscape. It is also known as red hot oker.

ZONES: 5–9
SIZE: 4'h × 4'w
TYPE: Perennial
FORM: Irregular
TEXTURE: Coarse
GROWTH: Medium
LIGHT: Full sun to part shade

MOISTURE: Medium
SOIL: Fertile, moist, well-drained
FEATURES: Flowers, foliage
USES: Border, container
FLOWERS: ■ ■ ■

SITING: Torch lily prefers full sun and fertile, moist, well-drained soil with a pH of 5.5–7.0. In warm climates provide shelter from afternoon sun. Spectacular flowers display red buds opening to orange and fading to yellow in summer. Flowers attract bees and butterflies and are excellent fresh cut. Good companions include 'Moonbeam' threadleaf coreopsis, 'Gracillimus' maiden grass, and 'Sonnenwende' evening primrose.

CARE: Plant 24–36" apart in late spring. Apply slow-release granular plant food at time of planting. When the soil feels dry 2" below the surface, water deeply. Deadhead spent blooms to encourage

Remove faded flower stalks of common torch lily to keep the plants attractive.

reblooming. Leave plants erect for winter interest, then cut back in early spring.

PROPAGATION: Divide in spring or early summer. Plants may take two seasons to recover their normal bloom cycle after division. Sprinkle seeds over the soil mix and leave exposed to light; do not cover. Thoroughly moisten and keep moist, not soggy, until seeds germinate. Germination occurs in 20–27 days at 65–75°F. Transplant 30–45 days after sowing. Reduce the temperature to 60°F after transplanting. Seed-grown plants will take three seasons to fully flower.

PESTS AND DISEASES: Plants are relatively pest free when cultural requirements (sun, soil, moisture, planting depth) are met. Wet soil often results in crown rot.

RELATED SPECIES: The cultivar 'Bressingham Comet' is dwarf-bearing and has orange flowers with red tips, 'Bressingham Torch' bears bright orange flowers intermittently throughout the summer and early autumn, 'Rosea Superba' reaches 36" high and bears rose red flowers that turn white, and 'White Fairy' reaches 3' high and bears white flowers in early summer.

SPOTTED DEADNETTLE

Lamium maculatum *LAM-ee-uhm mahk-yew-LAT-uhm*

Spotted deadnettle cultivars have green-and-white splashed leaves that brighten shady spaces.

ZONES: 4–8
SIZE: 8"h × 3'w
TYPE: Perennial
FORM: Spreading
TEXTURE: Medium
GROWTH: Fast
LIGHT: Full to part shade

MOISTURE: Medium
SOIL: Moderately fertile, moist, well-drained
FEATURES: Flowers, foliage
USES: Ground cover, container
FLOWERS: ■ □

SITING: Spotted deadnettle cultivars prefer full or partial shade and moderately fertile, evenly moist, well-drained soil with a pH of 5.5–7.0. Cultivars, rather than the invasive species, are best for landscape use. Whorls of vibrant pink flowers appear in late spring and early summer. Place spotted deadnettle at the feet of woody plants in an irrigated bed, as a ground cover for a partially shaded slope, or in a shady container planting. Good companions include 'Elegans' siebold hosta, heart-leaf brunnera, 'Mrs. Moon' Bethlehem sage, and 'Sissinghurst White' lungwort.

In hot climates shear back lamium to promote compact growth.

CARE: Plant 12–36" apart in spring or fall. The closer the spacing, the faster the ground will be covered. Apply slow-release granular plant food at time of planting or begin using water-soluble plant food 3 weeks after planting in spring. When the soil feels dry 2" below the surface, water deeply. In the South, shear plants after first bloom to promote compact growth.

PROPAGATION: Divide cultivars in spring. Dig around the root clump and lift. Use a sharp spade to slice through the root system. Reset portions that contain healthy roots and top shoots.

PESTS AND DISEASES: Slugs and snails are pests. Diseases include powdery mildew, downy mildew, and leaf spot. Well-drained soil is essential. Standing water, as well as prolonged dry soil, may cause death of spotted deadnettle.

RELATED SPECIES: The cultivar 'Beacon Silver' has pale pink flowers and silver leaves edged in green, heat-tolerant 'White Nancy' has white flowers and silver leaves edged in green, 'Aureum' has pink flowers and gold leaves stained white, and 'Beedham's White' has white flowers and chartreuse leaves.

LANTANA
Lantana camara *lahn-TAHN-uh KAHM-er-uh*

Lantana offers vibrant nonstop summer color for hot, dry places.

ZONES: 8–10
SIZE: 3–6'h × 3–6'w
TYPE: Woody shrub
FORM: Spreading
TEXTURE: Medium
GROWTH: Fast
LIGHT: Full sun
MOISTURE: Medium to dry

SOIL: Moderately fertile, well-drained
FEATURES: Flowers, foliage
USES: Ground cover, container, border
FLOWERS: ■ ■ ■ ■ ☐

SITING: Lantana prefers full sun and moderately fertile, well-drained soil with a pH of 5.5–7.5. Plants are woody shrubs commonly grown as annuals; they are drought tolerant once established. Plants and flowers are toxic, so keep them away from children. Flowers appear from late spring to late autumn in colors including shades of cream, yellow, red, orange, and pink. Fragrant foliage is wrinkled, toothed, and deep green. Stems may be slightly prickly. Flowers attract butterflies, and fruits attract birds. Use as a ground cover for a sunny bank or garden bed, place in a border for bright color, or use in container plantings. Good companions include maiden grass, fountain grass, wax myrtle, and Northern bayberry.

Butterflies are attracted to the colorful blooms of lantana.

CARE: Plant 3–6' apart in late spring. Apply slow-release granular plant food at time of planting. Follow label directions for amount and frequency. Plants receiving too much nitrogen may have lush leaves but fewer flowers. When the soil becomes dry 2–3" below the surface, water deeply. Water transplants well until they are established. Apply 3" of vegetative mulch in summer and winter to help retain soil moisture and add organic matter to the soil as it decomposes. Prune woody growth back to the ground in late winter or early spring.

PROPAGATION: Plants often self-sow in the landscape. To sow indoors, sprinkle seeds over the soil mix and cover lightly. Keep moist, not soggy, until seeds germinate. Provide temperatures of 60–65°F until germination occurs.

PESTS AND DISEASES: Insect pests include whiteflies and spider mites. Diseases include leaf spot and rust.

RELATED SPECIES: Dwarf 'Arlequin' has deep pink and yellow flowers, 'Brazier' bears bright red flowers, and 'Cream Carpet' has creamy white flowers. 'Miss Huff' and 'Mozelle' are hardy to Zone 7.

SWEET PEA
Lathyrus odoratus *LATH-ih-ruhs o-dor-AT-uhs*

Sweet peas have old-fashioned nostalgic appeal with heady fragrance.

ZONES: NA
SIZE: 10'h × 5'w
TYPE: Annual
FORM: Climber
TEXTURE: Medium
GROWTH: Fast
LIGHT: Full sun to part shade

MOISTURE: Medium
SOIL: Fertile, well-drained
FEATURES: Flowers, foliage
USES: Trellis, container, ground cover
FLOWERS: ■ ■ ■ ☐

SITING: Sweet pea prefers full sun or light dappled shade and fertile, well-drained soil with a pH of 5.5–7.0. Fragrant flowers appear from summer into early autumn. Place in a woody plant border to grow through shrubs, on an arbor or trellis for bright color, or in a container to wind through other plants. Good container companions include 'Southern Belle' hibiscus, 'Blue Bird' rose of Sharon, and 'Butterfly Blue' pincushion flower.

CARE: Plant 12–24" apart in early spring in fertile soil high in organic matter. Apply slow-release granular plant food at time of planting or begin using water-soluble plant food 3 weeks after planting in spring. Follow label directions for amount and frequency. Water deeply when the soil is

Sweet peas climb on brushwood, a trellis, an arbor or shrubby plants. Start them off by training tendrils onto the support.

dry. Apply 3" of vegetative mulch in summer to help retain soil moisture and add organic matter to the soil as it decomposes. Plants grown on an arbor or a trellis may need additional support. Deadhead spent blooms to encourage reblooming. Remove plants either just before the first frost or right afterward when foliage is disfigured. Cover bare soil with 3" of vegetative mulch during winter to preserve the topsoil.

PROPAGATION: To increase germination, nick the seed coat with a nail file or rub with sandpaper. Then soak seeds in water for 12 hours. Sprinkle seed over the soil mix and cover. Thoroughly moisten and keep moist, not soggy. Provide temperatures of 55–60°F until seeds germinate.

PESTS AND DISEASES: Diseases include powdery mildew, Pythium root rot, and rust. Pests include slugs and snails.

RELATED SPECIES: Spencer cultivars reach 6–8' high and produce a wide palette of solid, bicolor, picotee, and mixed colors. The Bijou Group reaches 20" high and bears flowers in shades of pink, white, red, and blue.

LAVENDER

Lavandula angustifolia lah-VAN-dyu-lah ahn-gust-ih-FOL-ee-uh

Lavender's popularity dates back to the Middle Ages.

ZONES: 5–8
SIZE: 3'h × 3'w
TYPE: Perennial
FORM: Rounded
TEXTURE: Fine
GROWTH: Slow
LIGHT: Full sun
MOISTURE: Medium

SOIL: Moderately fertile, well-drained
FEATURES: Flowers, foliage
USES: Border, container
FLOWERS: ■■□

SITING: Lavender prefers full sun and well-drained soil with a pH of 5.5–7.5. Silvery leaves contain volatile oils, which account for the classic lavender scent. The spikes of fragrant lavender flowers that appear in summer attract bees and butterflies and are excellent fresh cut or dried. Good garden companions include Culver's root, spike speedwell, lemon thyme, and gayfeather.

CARE: Plant 18–24" apart in spring. Apply slow-release granular plant food at time of planting. The soil must drain freely for lavender to thrive. Deadhead spent blooms to encourage reblooming. Shear back after first flowering to promote compact habit. Cut back in late spring once new growth is visible. To dry lavender, clip flower stalks

Snip lavender stalks while they are in the bud stage and hang upside down to dry in a shady, dry location.

before they fully open and secure in 1"- or smaller-diameter bundles. Hang bundles upside down in a dry, shaded area. When they are dry, place in an airtight container until ready to use.

PROPAGATION: Plants may be layered in summer. Pin a branch to the ground so that nodes contact the soil. When roots have formed, snip the branch from the parent plant, leaving some green top growth to accompany the new root system. To increase germination rate, chill seed at 35–40°F for 4–6 weeks. Germination occurs in 14–21 days at 65–75°F. Transplant 20–35 days after sowing then reduce the temperature to 60°F.

PESTS AND DISEASES: Fusarium root rot may be a problem. Plants grown in wet soil conditions usually succumb to disease.

RELATED SPECIES: 'Hidcote' reaches 24" high, has deep purple flowers, and is more compact and tidy than the species; 'Munstead' reaches 18" high and has blue-purple flowers; and 'Nana Alba' reaches 12" high and has white flowers. 'Rosea,' 'Jean Davis,' and 'Lodden's Pink' have pink flowers. The cultivar 'Lavender Lady' may be grown from seed.

SHASTA DAISY

Leucanthemum ×superbum lu-KAHN-thuh-muhm su-PEHR-buhm

Shasta daisy produces excellent fresh cut flowers or a long-lasting garden display.

ZONES: 4–8
SIZE: 36"h × 24"w
TYPE: Perennial
FORM: Upright
TEXTURE: Medium
GROWTH: Medium
LIGHT: Full sun to part shade

MOISTURE: Medium
SOIL: Moderately fertile, well-drained
FEATURES: Flowers, foliage
USES: Border, container
FLOWERS: □

SITING: Shasta daisy prefers full sun or light afternoon shade and moderately fertile, well-drained soil with a pH of 5.5–7.0. Plants may be short lived in the South. White flowers with a yellow central disk appear from early summer through early autumn. Flowers are excellent for cutting. Plants are well suited for the perennial borders or containers. Good companions include 'Bonica' and 'Carefree Wonder' roses, Kansas gayfeather, and 'Silver Carpet' lamb's-ears.

CARE: Plant 18–24" apart in spring or fall. Apply slow-release granular plant food at time of planting. Water deeply when the soil is dry. Apply 3" of vegetative mulch in summer and winter to reduce weed seed germination, retain soil moisture, and keep soil temperatures stable. Deadhead spent blooms to encourage reblooming. Prune back in fall once frost withers the foliage.

PROPAGATION: Divide in spring or fall.

PESTS AND DISEASES: Diseases include crown gall, powdery mildew, leaf spots, and rust. Aphids and slugs may be troublesome.

RELATED SPECIES: 'Alaska' has single white flowers, 'Phyllis Smith' bears single white blooms with twisted petals, 'Snow Lady' has single white flowers, 'Cobham Gold' has double white flowers, and 'Wirral Pride' bears double flowers.

Remove side shoots from Shasta daisy during division.

Replant pieces that contain healthy roots and top shoots.

SPIKE GAYFEATHER
Liatris spicata   LEE-ah-trihs spih-KAH-tuh

Spike gayfeather, also known as blazing star, is a low-maintenance perennial with spectacular pinkish purple flowers.

ZONES: 3–9
SIZE: 3'h × 18"w
TYPE: Perennial
FORM: Upright
TEXTURE: Coarse
GROWTH: Medium
LIGHT: Full sun
MOISTURE: Medium

SOIL: Moderately fertile, moist, well-drained
FEATURES: Flowers, foliage
USES: Border, container, cut flower
FLOWERS: ▪▫

SITING: Spike gayfeather prefers full sun and moderately fertile, moist, well-drained soil with a pH of 6.5–7.5. Once established, plants are reliably low maintenance and troublefree. Pinkish-purple flower spikes appear from mid- to late summer into early autumn. Flowers attract bees and butterflies and are excellent fresh cut or dried. Plant in perennial borders or use in mixed container plantings. Good companions include 'David' garden phlox, 'Iceberg' rose, 'Gracillimus' or 'Morning Light'

Spike gayfeather cultivars other than 'Kobold' may need staking to keep them upright during bloom.

maiden grass, Russian sage, 'Snowbank' white boltonia, and purple coneflower.

CARE: Plant 18–24" apart in spring or fall. Apply slow-release granular plant food at time of planting. Cease feeding 6–8 weeks prior to first frost date. Water deeply when the soil is dry. The cultivar 'Kobold' does not need staking; the species and other cultivars may. Deadhead spent blooms to keep plants tidy. Prune back in fall once frost withers the foliage, or leave erect in warmer zones for winter viewing.

PROPAGATION: Divide in spring or fall.

PESTS AND DISEASES: Slugs and snails are pests. Diseases include leaf spot, rust and aster yellows.

RELATED SPECIES: 'Kobold' is shorter than the species at only 24" high. 'Alba,' 'Floristan,' and 'Snow Queen' bear white flowers, and 'Blue Bird' has bluish flowers. Kansas gayfeather (*L. pychnostachya*) reaches 5' high; it is well adapted in the Midwest, provided soil is moderately fertile and sun is ample. If the soil is too rich, excessive nitrogen is applied, or there is too little sunlight, plants may become floppy. Staking is not normally necessary when cultural requirements are met.

BIGLEAF LIGULARIA
Ligularia dentata   lihg-yew-LAR-ee-uh dehn-TAH-tuh

Bigleaf ligularia is a big plant for moist soil.

ZONES: 3–8
SIZE: 3–5'h × 3'w
TYPE: Perennial
FORM: Irregular
TEXTURE: Coarse
GROWTH: Medium
LIGHT: Part shade to full sun

MOISTURE: Medium to high
SOIL: Moderately fertile, moist
FEATURES: Flowers, foliage
USES: Border, wetland
FLOWERS: ▪

SITING: Bigleaf ligularia prefers full sun, with light afternoon shade in warmer climates, and deep, fertile, moist soil with a pH of 5.5–7.0. Daisylike yellow-orange flowers with a brown center appear from summer into early autumn. Place this plant in an informal area where the soil is reliably moist. Good companions include 'Variegatus' sweet flag and yellow flag iris.

CARE: Plant 24–36" apart in spring or fall. Apply slow-release granular plant food at time of planting. Water deeply when the soil begins to dry. Apply 3" of vegetative mulch in summer and winter to help retain soil moisture. Deadhead spent blooms to encourage reblooming.

1

Ligularia often wilts in the afternoon, even when soil moisture is adequate.

2

If soil is dry, water deeply.

PROPAGATION: If plants are not deadheaded, they self-seed in the landscape. To reproduce desirable cultivars, divide in spring or fall.

PESTS AND DISEASES: Plants are relatively pest free when cultural requirements (sun, soil, planting depth, moisture) are met. Slugs and snails may be pests.

RELATED SPECIES: The cultivar 'Desdemona' has orange flowers and leaves that are stained burgundy underneath, 'Gregynog Gold' bears pyramidal spikes of orange flowers and has saw-edged leaves, 'Othello' bears deep orange flowers and dark purple leaves. *L. stenocephala* 'The Rocket' is the best suited ligularia for a part-shade border and for ornamental use. 'The Rocket' bears spikes of yellow flowers in early and late summer. Foliage is bold, triangular-shaped, and toothed. It is not uncommon to see leaves wilting in midafternoon in Zone 5, even in moist soil in partial shade. They spring back up by early evening.

TURK'S-CAP LILY
Lilium superbum *LIHL-ee-uhm su-PEHR-buhm*

Turk's cap lily bears pendulous flowers that attract butterflies.

ZONES: 3–8
SIZE: 4–10' h ×
4–6"w
TYPE: Perennial
FORM: Upright
TEXTURE: Medium
GROWTH: Medium
LIGHT: Full sun to
partial shade

MOISTURE: Medium
SOIL: Fertile, moist,
well-drained
FEATURES: Flowers
USES: Container,
woodland, border
FLOWERS: ■ ■ ■ ■
　　　　　□

SITING: Turk's-cap lily prefers full sun or light afternoon shade and fertile, moist, well-drained soil with a pH of 5.5–7.0. Pendulous recurved orange flowers appear in mid- to late summer. Flowers have burgundy spots and are green-splashed near the base. Mid- to bright green leaves appear in whorls on purple-stained green stems. An abundance of flowers with recurved petals nodding well above the foliage ensures the popularity of these lilies. The flowers attract butterflies. Place in large swaths at the edge of a bright woodland, in odd-number groupings in a border, or in containers. Good container companions include the chartreuse-leaved sweet potato vine and the black-leaved 'Blackie' sweet potato vine, 'Moonbeam' threadleaf coreopsis, and 'Corries Gold' gaura.

CARE: Plant 6–12" apart and two to three times deeper than their diameter in spring or fall in fertile soil high in organic matter. To increase organic matter, add 1–2" of composted food and leaf waste, composted animal manure, mushroom compost, peat moss, or bagged humus to the planting bed and till in to a depth of 12–15". Add bonemeal and slow-release granular plant food at time of planting. Apply 3" of vegetative mulch in summer and winter to reduce weed seed germination, retain soil moisture, and keep soil temperatures stable. Water deeply when the soil begins to dry. Remove flowers when they fade to reduce seed set. Take as little stem as possible with cut flowers. Allow the foliage to die back naturally after blooms fade.

PROPAGATION: In spring dig down to the bulb and gently pull off the largest of the small bulbs that are attached to the main bulb. Re-cover the main bulb and plant bulblets in prepared soil 12" away from other plants. Water deeply and apply 3" of vegetative mulch.

PESTS AND DISEASES: Diseases include botrytis and viruses. Slugs and snails may feed on foliage; deer, rabbits, and groundhogs may eat top growth.

RELATED SPECIES: Asiatic and Oriental hybrids bear scented flowers in summer. 'Casa Blanca' bears large, fragrant white flowers in mid- to late summer, and 'Star Gazer' has star-shaped pinkish-red flowers with dark red spots in early summer. Both add beauty to container plantings as well as the border. Aurelian hybrid lilies (*L.* ×*aurelianense*) are crosses between *L. henryi* and *L. sargentiae*. Some popular cultivars include 'Black Beauty', a deep crimson flower with recurved petals and 'Pink Perfection', with trumpet-shaped pink flowers. Martagon lily (*L. martagon*) is also known as Turk's cap lily for its nodding reddish-purple blooms borne on plants 4–6' tall.

Plucking the anthers from a white lily keeps the pollen from staining the bloom.

Cut back lily foliage in fall if it has not died back naturally.

For winter protection from cold, insulate lilies with evergreen boughs.

BLUE LILYTURF

Liriope muscari ler-EYE-oh-pee muhsk-AR-ee

Blue lilyturf is a reliable evergreen ground cover for sun or shade.

ZONES: 6–10
SIZE: 12"h × 18"w
TYPE: Perennial
FORM: Rounded
TEXTURE: Medium
GROWTH: Medium
LIGHT: Full sun to full shade

MOISTURE: Medium to low
SOIL: Moderately fertile, well-drained
FEATURES: Flowers, foliage, berries
USES: Ground cover, container
FLOWERS: ■ ■ □

SITING: Blue lilyturf tolerates full sun, part shade, or full shade (afternoon shade is preferred in the South) and prefers moderately fertile, well-drained soil with a pH of 5.5–7.0. Protect from strong winds and wet soils in all climates. Spikes of tiny purple blooms appear from late summer through autumn. Dense clumps of narrow, arching dark green evergreen leaves are tolerant of most sun and soil situations. Deep blue berries follow blooms and last until frost. Plants are drought tolerant once established. Plants are commonly used as ground covers in tree and shrub beds, as a turf substitute, and in containers. Full-sun companions include 'Fairy Princess' and 'Krinkled White' peonies, Russian sage, bluebeard, and 'Vivid' obedient plant. Part-shade companions include 'Amethystina' toad lily and 'Frances Williams' and 'Gold Standard' hostas.
CARE: Plant 12–18" apart in late spring. Apply slow-release granular plant food at time of planting. Cease feeding 4–6 weeks prior to first frost date. Give transplants ample water until they are established. Otherwise, water only when the soil becomes dry 2–3" below the surface. Apply 3" of vegetative mulch in summer and winter to help retain soil moisture. Deadhead spent blooms. Shear back in early spring to promote new growth. An easy way to accomplish this task is to set a lawnmower at its highest setting and mow off the tattered overwintering foliage.
PROPAGATION: Divide in spring or fall. Dig around the tubers and lift. Use a sharp spade to slice through the root system. Reset portions that contain healthy roots and top shoots, then water and mulch. Discard any pieces that do not contain both healthy roots and top shoots.
PESTS AND DISEASES: Plants are relatively pest free when cultural requirements (sun, soil, planting depth, moisture) are met. Wet soil may render plants susceptible to diseases such as anthracnose and root rot.
RELATED SPECIES: The cultivar 'Grandiflora' is taller than the species, with narrow, arching leaves and lavender flowers; 'Variegata' leaves are gold-striped; 'John Burch' leaves have a yellow-green center stripe; 'Silvery Midget' leaves are variegated white; 'Monroe White' has an abundance of white flowers; and 'Curly Twist' has curiously twisted leaves.

CREEPING LILYTURF

Liriope spicata lehr-EYE-oh-pee spihk-AH-tuh

Creeping lilyturf is a superb ground cover for sun or shade. It is also known as creeping liriope. Pictured is 'Silver Dragon'.

ZONES: 5–10
SIZE: 10"h × 18"w
TYPE: Perennial
FORM: Rounded
TEXTURE: Medium
GROWTH: Medium
LIGHT: Full sun, part shade, full shade

MOISTURE: Medium
SOIL: Moderately fertile, well-drained
FEATURES: Flowers, foliage, berries
USES: Ground cover, border, container
FLOWERS: ■ □

SITING: Creeping lilyturf prefers moderately fertile, well-drained soil with a pH of 5.5–7.0. It tolerates full sun, part shade, or full shade. Plants are drought tolerant once established. Spikes of tiny lavender to white flowers appear in late summer. Dark semievergreen leaves are narrow and grasslike. Deep blue berries follow blooms and persist until frost. Use as a ground cover for tree and shrub beds, as a turf replacement, in a border, and in containers. Good shade companions include 'Sunspot' heucherella, 'Silver Falls' Japanese painted fern, and 'Variegatum' Solomon's seal.
CARE: Plant 15–18" apart in spring or fall. Apply slow-release granular plant food at time of planting or begin using water-soluble plant food 3 weeks after planting in spring. Water deeply when the soil is dry. Deadhead spent blooms. Shear back in early spring to promote new growth.
PROPAGATION: Divide in spring or fall.
PESTS AND DISEASES: Plants are relatively pest free when cultural requirements are met. Anthracnose and root rot are diseases associated with wet soils. Slugs and snails may be pests.
RELATED SPECIES: The cultivar 'Alba' has white flowers, and 'Silver Dragon' has striped silver leaves, pale purple flowers, and white-green fruit.

1 Lift clumps in spring or fall for division.

2 Divide roots with a sharp spade.

3 Reset pieces that contain healthy roots and shoots.

CARDINAL FLOWER
Lobelia cardinalis *lob-BEEL-yuh kard-ihn-AHL-ihs*

Cardinal flower's red blooms attract hummingbirds.

ZONES: 3–9
SIZE: 36"h × 12"w
TYPE: Perennial
FORM: Upright
TEXTURE: Medium
GROWTH: Medium
LIGHT: Full sun to part shade

MOISTURE: Medium to high
SOIL: Fertile, moist, well-drained
FEATURES: Flowers, foliage
USES: Border, woodland, container
FLOWERS: ■■□

SITING: Cardinal flower prefers full sun in northern zones and afternoon shade in the South and deep, fertile, moist yet well-drained soil with a pH of 5.5–7.0. Red flowers appear from summer to early autumn. Bright green leaves are sometimes stained bronze. Flowers attract bees, butterflies, and hummingbirds. Good companions include red ginger lily, 'Marmorata' and 'Crow Feather' Allegheny foamflowers, 'Persian Carpet' heuchera, and 'Superba' featherleaf rodgersia.

CARE: Plant 12" apart in late spring. Apply slow-release granular plant food at time of planting. If planting in a wetland, avoid plant foods and chemical pesticides. When the soil feels almost dry 2" below the surface, water deeply. Deadhead spent

Water plants deeply when the soil feels dry 2" below the surface.

blooms to encourage reblooming. Plants are short-lived perennials and may need to be replaced or divided every 2 years. Prune back in fall once frost withers the foliage.

PROPAGATION: Plants self-seed in the landscape. To sow indoors, sprinkle seeds over the soil mix and leave exposed to light; do not cover. Thoroughly moisten and keep moist, not soggy, until seeds germinate. Germination occurs in 8–12 days at 70°F. Transplant 25–30 days after sowing. After transplanting, reduce temperature to 60–65°F.

PESTS AND DISEASES: Rust and slugs are possible.

RELATED SPECIES: The cultivar 'Alba' bears white flowers, 'Rosea' has pink flowers, and 'Ruby Slippers' has dark red flowers.

LOBELIA
Lobelia erinus *lob-BEEL-yuh eh-RIN-uhs*

Lobelia is a fine-textured plant for bright shade.

ZONES: NA
SIZE: 4–10"h × 6–12"w
TYPE: Annual
FORM: Spreading
TEXTURE: Fine
GROWTH: Medium
LIGHT: Part shade

MOISTURE: Medium
SOIL: Fertile, well-drained
FEATURES: Flowers, foliage
USES: Border, container
FLOWERS: ■■□■

SITING: Lobelia prefers afternoon shade and fertile, moist, yet well-drained soil with a pH of 5.5–7.0. Two-lipped blue, purple, white, or pink flowers appear from summer through early autumn. Mid- to dark green leaves are sometimes stained bronze. Place in odd-number groups in the part-shade border, at the edge of a container, or where plants cascade over the rim of a rock wall. Good companions include 'Pictum' Japanese painted fern, heart-leaf brunnera, 'Elegans' Siebold hosta, 'Mrs. Moon' lungwort, and lady's mantle.

CARE: Plant 6–12" apart in late spring. Apply slow-release granular plant food at time of planting or begin using water-soluble plant food 3 weeks after planting in spring. Follow label directions for amount and frequency. When the soil begins to feel dry, water deeply. Maintain moist but not soggy soil. If using an irrigation system, maintain deep, infrequent waterings and avoid delivering a light sprinkle every day. Apply 2–3" of organic mulch around, but not touching, the plants in summer to help retain soil moisture and add organic matter to the soil as it decomposes. Deadhead spent blooms to encourage reblooming. Remove plants just before the first frost or right afterward when foliage is disfigured.

PROPAGATION: Sprinkle seeds over the soil mix and leave exposed to light; do not cover. Thoroughly moisten and keep moist, not soggy, until seeds germinate. Germination occurs in 15–20 days at 70–80°F. Transplant 20–25 days after sowing. After transplanting, reduce the temperature to 60–65°F.

PESTS AND DISEASES: Rust and slugs are possible problems that may develop.

RELATED SPECIES: The cultivar 'Alba' has white flowers, 'Blue Moon' has deep blue flowers, 'Cobalt Blue' has cobalt blue blooms, 'Crystal Palace' has vibrant bright blue flowers, 'Pink Flamingo' is upright with pink flowers, and 'Sapphire' has vibrant sapphire-blue flowers.

SWEET ALYSSUM

Lobularia maritima *lobb-yew-LAHR-ee-uh mar-ih-TIM-uh*

Sweet alyssum is a fine-textured fragrant plant for full sun locations.

ZONES: NA
SIZE: 4–12"h × 10–12"w
TYPE: Annual
FORM: Spreading
TEXTURE: Fine
GROWTH: Fast
LIGHT: Full sun to part shade

MOISTURE: Medium
SOIL: Moderately fertile, well-drained
FEATURES: Flowers, foliage
USES: Border, ground cover, container
FLOWERS: □ ■ ■

SITING: Sweet alyssum prefers full sun and moderately fertile, well-drained soil with a pH of 5.5–7.5. Tiny, cross-shape, fragrant, bright white, sometimes purple or pink flowers appear in summer. Leaves are slightly hairy and gray-green. Plant this dainty, cascading annual at the edge of a border or spilling from a mixed container planting. Good companions include pink coreopsis, 'Stargazer' lily, and 'Purpureum' fennel.

CARE: Plant 6–12" apart in late spring. Apply slow-release granular plant food at time of planting or begin using water-soluble plant food 3 weeks after planting in spring. Water deeply when the soil is dry. Apply vegetative mulch around, but not touching, the plants in summer to help

Plant sweet alyssum as an edging plant for the flower border or in a container.

retain soil moisture. Shear back after first bloom to encourage reblooming. Remove plants just before the first frost or right afterward when foliage is disfigured.

PROPAGATION: Sprinkle seeds over the soil mix and leave exposed to light; do not cover. Thoroughly moisten and keep moist, not soggy, until seeds germinate. Germination occurs in 8–10 days at 78–80°F. After germination, reduce temperature to 50–55°F. Transplant into the garden when temperatures warm and all frost danger has passed.

PESTS AND DISEASES: Slugs, flea beetles, downy mildew, clubroot, and white blister are occasional pests.

RELATED SPECIES: Alice Series cultivars are compact and bear white, pink, or purple flowers; Basket Series cultivars are strong spreaders and bear rosy red, violet-blue, peach, and white flowers; 'Carpet of Snow' is low growing with white flowers; 'Navy Blue' is low and compact with deep purple flowers; 'New Purple' is low growing with purple flowers turning lighter at the margins; 'Oriental Nights' bears early-flowering rich purple blooms; and 'Wonderland Rose' bears rosy pink flowers.

LUPINE

Lupinus hybrids *lup-EYE-nuhs*

Lupines are classic English perennial border plants. They require cool weather for best garden performance.

ZONES: 4–8
SIZE: 20–36"h × 12–30"w
TYPE: Perennial
FORM: Upright
TEXTURE: Medium
GROWTH: Fast
LIGHT: Full sun to part shade

MOISTURE: Medium
SOIL: Fertile, well-drained
FEATURES: Flowers, foliage
USES: Border, container
FLOWERS: ■ ■ ■ ■ ■ ■ □

SITING: Lupine prefers full sun or partial afternoon shade and fertile, well-drained soil with a pH of 5.5–6.8. Plants are short-lived perennials often grown as annuals. Cool summer temperatures are ideal. Lupine resists heat, humidity, and transplanting. Spikes of pealike blooms appear in summer. Place in groups in borders or use in container plantings. Good companions include alyssum, pink coreopsis, sweet woodruff, and 'Caesar's Brother' Siberian iris.

CARE: Plant 12–30" apart, depending on the cultivar, in late spring. Apply slow-release granular plant food at time of planting or begin using water-soluble plant food 3 weeks after planting. Cease feeding 6–8 weeks prior to first frost date if growing as a perennial. Water deeply when the soil is dry. Apply 3" of vegetative mulch in summer. Deadhead spent blooms to encourage reblooming unless self-sown seedlings are

Apply mulch to lupine to keep roots cool.

desired, then leave flowers until they drop their seeds. Trim back in fall once frost withers the foliage.

PROPAGATION: Plants lightly self-seed in the landscape. Divide in spring. Soak seed in water for 24 hours before sowing. Sprinkle seed over the soil mix and cover lightly. Germination occurs in 6–12 days at 65–75°F. Transplant 18–30 days after sowing. After transplanting, reduce temperature to 50–55°F.

PESTS AND DISEASES: Diseases include Southern blight, powdery mildew, downy mildew, rust, and stem rot.

RELATED SPECIES: Russell hybrids reach 36" high and bear spikes of flowers in red, blue, pink, white, and yellow. Gallery hybrids reach 20" high and bear spikes of blue, yellow, rose, red, and white flowers. 'Catherine of York' bears orange and yellow flowers in early and midsummer, 'Chandelier' reaches 36" high and bears spikes of yellow flowers, and 'The Chatelaine' reaches 36" high and bears pink and white flowers. Texas bluebonnet (*L. texensis*) is a stunning annual that bears bluish-purple flowers in summer.

GOOSENECK LOOSESTRIFE

Lysimachia clethroides *lihs-ih-MAHK-ee-uh klehth-ROY-deez*

Gooseneck loosestrife flowers attract butterflies and bees.

ZONES: 3–9
SIZE: 36"h × 24"w
TYPE: Perennial
FORM: Upright
TEXTURE: Medium
GROWTH: Fast
LIGHT: Full sun to partial shade

MOISTURE: Medium to high
SOIL: Fertile, moist, well-drained
FEATURES: Flowers, foliage
USES: Border, container
FLOWERS: □

SITING: Gooseneck loosestrife prefers full sun or light afternoon shade in warmer climates, and fertile, well-drained, moist soil with a pH of 5.5–7.0. The rhizomes spread rapidly in moist soil. Arching white flowers resemble the profile of a goose head. Flowers attract bees and butterflies and are excellent fresh cut. Place plants in groups in perennial borders, naturalize along a stream bank, or use in container plantings. Good companions include 'Kobold' blazing star, purple coneflower, 'Goldsturm' black-eyed Susan, and 'Filagran' Russian sage.

CARE: Plant 24–36" apart in spring or fall. Apply slow-release granular plant food at time of planting. Cease feeding 4–6 weeks prior to first frost date. Maintain moist soil. When the soil begins to feel dry, water deeply. Apply 3" of vegetative mulch in summer and winter to reduce weed seed germination, retain soil moisture, and keep soil temperatures stable. Deadhead spent blooms to encourage reblooming. Prune plants back to ground level in fall once frost withers the foliage.

PROPAGATION: This plant vigorously reproduces in the landscape by spreading rhizomes. It can easily become invasive. Division will reduce plant size and restore vitality to tired plants. Divide in spring. Dig around the root clump and lift. Use a sharp spade to slice through the root system. Reset portions that contain healthy roots and top shoots, then water and mulch.

PESTS AND DISEASES: Rust and leaf spot may occasionally occur.

1 Lift the plant in the spring to divide it.

2 Tease the roots apart by hand, or slice through them with a sharp spade.

3 Reset portions that contain healthy roots and shoots.

PLUME POPPY

Macleaya cordata *mahk-LAY-uh kor-DAH-tuh*

Plume poppy fills large spaces in sun or bright shade.

ZONES: 4–9
SIZE: 8'h × 3'w
TYPE: Perennial
FORM: Upright
TEXTURE: Coarse
GROWTH: Fast
LIGHT: Full sun to partial shade
MOISTURE: Medium to high

SOIL: Moderately fertile, moist, well-drained
FEATURES: Foliage, flowers
USES: Border, naturalizing, container
FLOWERS: □ ■

SITING: Plume poppy prefers full sun and moderately fertile, well-drained soil, although it tolerates moist soil and part shade. The preferred pH is 5.5–7.0. Plants spread rapidly. Large, lobed leaves are 8" across, blue-gray above, and silver beneath. Plumes of creamy white flowers appear from mid- to late summer. Plants are focal points; parade them in odd-number groups in the center of borders or in groups along a bank or anywhere they can spread freely. Large containers will restrain their spread. Good container companions include flowering kale, 'Tricolor' sweet potato vine, and gooseneck loosestrife.

CARE: Plant 36" apart in fall or spring. Apply slow-release granular plant food at time of planting. Cease feeding 6–8 weeks prior to first frost date. Water deeply when the soil is dry. Apply 3" of vegetative mulch around, but not touching, the plants in summer to help retain soil moisture. Deadhead spent blooms, or cut for use in fresh arrangements, to encourage reblooming. Prune back in fall once frost withers the foliage, or leave erect in warmer zones for winter viewing and trim back in spring.

PROPAGATION: Plume poppy reseeds readily in the landscape, sometimes becoming invasive. Transplant self-sown seedlings or divide existing clumps in spring. Dig around the root clump and lift. Use a sharp spade to slice through the root system. Reset portions that contain healthy roots and top shoots.

PESTS AND DISEASES: Plants are relatively pest free when cultural requirements (sun, soil, planting depth, moisture) are met. Slugs are occasional pests.

RELATED SPECIES: The cultivar 'Alba' bears white flowers, and 'Flamingo' has mauve-pink flowers.

HOLLYHOCK MALLOW
Malva alcea 'Fastigiata' *MAHL-vuh al-SEE-uh*

Hollyhock mallow is a low-maintenance perennial with spectacular blooms.

ZONES: 3–8
SIZE: 36"h × 24"w
TYPE: Perennial
FORM: Upright
TEXTURE: Medium
GROWTH: Medium
LIGHT: Full sun
MOISTURE: Medium

SOIL: Moderately fertile, well-drained
FEATURES: Flowers, foliage
USES: Border, container
FLOWERS: ■

SITING: Hollyhock mallow prefers full sun and moderately fertile, well-drained soil with a pH of 5.5–7.0. Five-petal, rosy pink flowers are produced from summer into autumn. Attractive seedpods follow the flowers. Place in the middle of the border or island bed. Good companions include 'Snowbank' white boltonia, 'Iceberg' and 'The Fairy' roses, 'Moonbeam' threadleaf coreopsis, and 'Butterfly Blue' and 'Miss Willmott' pincusion flowers.

CARE: Plant 18–24" apart in spring or autumn. Apply slow-release granular plant

Cut back the spent blossoms of hollyhock mallow after it has finished blooming to promote new growth.

food at time of planting or begin using water-soluble plant food 3 weeks after planting in spring. Cease feeding 6–8 weeks prior to first frost date. Water deeply when the soil is dry. Apply 3" of vegetative mulch around, but not touching, the plants in summer to help retain soil moisture. 'Fastigiata' doesn't need staking. Deadhead spent blooms to encourage reblooming or leave some to allow for self-seeding in the landscape. Prune back in fall once frost withers the foliage.

PROPAGATION: To exactly reproduce the cultivar, propagate vegetatively, not by seed. Divide in spring or fall. Otherwise, sprinkle seeds over the soil mix and ightly cover. Thoroughly moisten and keep moist, not soggy, until seeds germinate. Germination occurs in 3–6 days at 70–75°F. Transplant 15–20 days after sowing. After transplanting, reduce temperature to 60–65°F.

PESTS AND DISEASES: Plants are relatively pest free when cultural requirements (sun, soil, planting depth, moisture) are met. Japanese beetle may be a pest in the North; in the South plants seem more susceptible to spider mites and thrips.

OSTRICH FERN
Matteuccia struthiopteris (pennsylvanica) *mah-TU-see-uh struth-ee-OHP-ter-ihs (pen-sil-VAN-ih-kuh)*

Ostrich fern is a large plant for shady sites in cooler climates.

ZONES: 3–8
SIZE: 5'h × 3'w
TYPE: Perennial
FORM: Irregular
TEXTURE: Medium
GROWTH: Medium
LIGHT: Partial shade
MOISTURE: Medium to high

SOIL: Fertile, moist, well-drained
FEATURES: Flowers, foliage
USES: Border, woodland, container

SITING: Ostrich fern prefers afternoon shade and fertile, well-drained, moist soil with a pH of 5.5–7.0. It spreads by rhizomes and may be invasive in cooler climates. Plants dislike the excessive heat and humidity of southern climates. Place groups in the middle of a shaded island bed, at the back of a border, or in a woodland garden. Good companions include 'Ursula's Red' Japanese painted fern, 'Superba' Chinese astilbe, and common bugbane.

CARE: Plant 36" apart in fall or spring in fertile soil high in organic matter. Apply slow-release granular plant food at time of planting. Apply 3" of vegetative mulch around, but not touching, the plants in summer and winter. Mulch reduces weed seed germination, holds moisture in the soil, and as it decomposes, adds organic matter to the soil. When the soil begins to feel dry 2" below the surface, water deeply. Vegetative fronds are withered by the first frost; fertile fronds last the winter. Trim plants back in spring if the fronds look ragged.

PROPAGATION: Plants will produce offspring in the landscape through spreading rhizomes. Divide in early spring. Dig around the rhizomes and lift. Use a sharp spade to slice through the root system. Reset portions that contain healthy roots and top shoots, then water and mulch. Discard any pieces that do not contain both healthy roots and top shoots.

PESTS AND DISEASES: Plants are relatively pest free when cultural requirements (sun, soil, planting depth, moisture) are met.

Dig plantlets that sprout from spreading rhizomes in early spring.

VIRGINIA BLUEBELL
Mertensia virginica *mehr-TEHN-see-uh ver-JIHN-ih-kuh*

Virginia bluebell flower buds are pink and open to bluish purple.

ZONES: 3–7
SIZE: 18"h × 8–10"w
TYPE: Perennial
FORM: Upright
TEXTURE: Medium
GROWTH: Slow
LIGHT: Part shade
MOISTURE: Medium to high

SOIL: Fertile, well-drained
FEATURES: Flowers, foliage
USES: Border, woodland, container
FLOWERS: ■■□

SITING: Virginia bluebell prefers afternoon shade and fertile, well-drained, moist soil with a pH of 5.5–7.0. Pink buds and flowers emerge in mid- to late spring and quickly turn vibrant sky blue or purple-blue. Leaves will yellow in summer and disappear by midsummer. Good companions to cover the empty space left in summer include the perennials 'Elegans' Siebold hosta and 'Superba' featherleaf

Plant shade-tolerant annuals such as impatiens among Virginia bluebells to provide color through summer.

rodgersia, and the annuals New Guinea impatiens, impatiens, and lobelia.
CARE: Plant 8–12" apart in spring in fertile soil high in organic matter. To increase organic matter, add 1–2" of compost to the planting bed and till in to a depth of 12–15". Apply slow-release granular plant food at time of planting. Apply 3" of vegetative mulch around, but not touching, the plants in summer and winter. Mulch reduces weed seed germination, holds moisture in the soil, and, as it decomposes adds organic matter to the soil. Because the plant is dormant during summer, little water is needed at that time.
PROPAGATION: Divide very early in spring before the plant blooms. Dig around the root clump and lift. Use a sharp spade to slice through the root system. Reset portions that contain healthy roots and top shoots, then water and mulch. Discard any pieces that do not contain both healthy roots and top shoots.
PESTS AND DISEASES: Slugs and snails are common pests. Diseases include rust and powdery mildew.

BEEBALM
Monarda didyma *muh-NAHR-duh DIHD-ih-muh*

Beebalm flowers attract hummingbirds and butterflies. Beebalm is also known as Oswego tea.

ZONES: 3–9
SIZE: 36"h × 24"w
TYPE: Perennial
FORM: Upright
TEXTURE: Medium
GROWTH: Medium
LIGHT: Full sun to partial shade
MOISTURE: Medium to high

SOIL: Moderately fertile, moist, well-drained
FEATURES: Flowers, foliage
USES: Border, naturalizing, container
FLOWERS: ■ ■ ■□

SITING: Beebalm tolerates full sun or light afternoon shade and needs good air circulation. It prefers moderately fertile, well-drained soil with a pH of 5.5–7.0. Whorls of scarlet red or pink flowers appear in mid- to late summer. The fragrant foliage is hairy underneath. Flowers attract hummingbirds, bees, and butterflies. Place in borders, add to container plantings, or naturalize. Good companions include daylily, sweet flag iris, and gaura.
CARE: Plant 18–24" apart in spring or autumn. Apply slow-release granular plant food at time of planting. Maintain moist soil. No staking is needed. Deadhead spent blooms to encourage reblooming. Trim back in fall once frost withers the foliage.
PROPAGATION: Divide in spring, once new growth is seen, or in autumn.

PESTS AND DISEASES: Reduce susceptibility to powdery mildew by selecting mildew-resistant cultivars, selecting sites with good air circulation, keeping soil moist, not soggy or bone dry, and avoiding overcrowding.
RELATED SPECIES: Cultivars with resistance to powdery mildew include 'Aquarius', with pink flowers and bronze-stained foliage; 'Bowman', with purple flowers; 'Gardenview Scarlet', with large bright red flowers; 'Marshall's Delight', with pink flowers; and 'Violet Queen', with violet-purple flowers.

1 **To divide beebalm, cut back the foliage to 3–4" above ground level.**

2 **Lift the entire plant and plunge a sharp spade through the roots.**

3 **Reset pieces with healthy roots and shoots.**

GRAPE HYACINTH
Muscari botryoides *muhs-KAH-ree boht-ree-OY-deez*

Grape hyacinths add pink, purple, or white flower clusters to the landscape in spring.

ZONES: 3–8
SIZE: 6–8"h × 6"w
TYPE: Perennial
FORM: Irregular
TEXTURE: Medium
GROWTH: Medium
LIGHT: Full sun
MOISTURE: Medium to high

SOIL: Moderately fertile, moist, well-drained
FEATURES: Flowers, foliage
USES: Border, naturalizing, container
FLOWERS: ■□■

SITING: Grape hyacinth prefers full sun and moderately fertile, moist, yet well-drained soil with a pH of 5.5–7.0. Dense clusters of white, pink, or bright sky-blue flowers appear in spring. Leaves are grasslike and medium green. Drifts of grape hyacinth in borders or rock gardens, at the feet of woody shrubs, in containers, or naturalized add delightful color and texture to the spring landscape. Good companions include rosemary, evergreen candytuft, and sea pink.

Remove spent flower heads before seedpods form to reduce self-seeding in the landscape.

CARE: Plant 6" apart and 4" deep in autumn in large groups. Add bonemeal to the soil at planting time. Apply slow-release granular plant food in spring after the last frost and growth is visible or use water-soluble plant food. Follow label directions for amount and frequency. Maintain moist, not soggy, soil. If using an irrigation system, maintain deep, infrequent waterings; avoid delivering a light sprinkle every day. Apply 3" of vegetative mulch in summer and winter to help retain soil moisture and add organic matter to the soil as it decomposes. When applying mulch, do not let it touch plant stems.

PROPAGATION: Plants will self-sow in the landscape. Remove offsets that grow from the parent bulb and reset them in summer.

PESTS AND DISEASES: Virus diseases may occur but are not common.

WOODLAND FORGET-ME-NOT
Myosotis sylvatica *meye-uh-SOHT-iss sill-VAHT-ib-kuh*

Woodland forget-me-not produces sky blue blooms in partial shade.

ZONES: 3–9
SIZE: 6–12"h × 6"w
TYPE: Perennial
FORM: Upright
TEXTURE: Medium
GROWTH: Medium
LIGHT: Partial shade
MOISTURE: Medium

SOIL: Moderately fertile, moist, well-drained
FEATURES: Flowers, foliage
USES: Border, woodland, container
FLOWERS: ■■□

SITING: Woodland forget-me-not prefers afternoon shade and moderately fertile, well-drained, moist soil with a pH of 5.5–7.0. Plants do not thrive in high heat and humidity. Bright blue flowers with a yellow eye appear from spring to early summer. Leaves are 2–3" long, hairy, pointed, and gray-green. Plants are commonly grown as biennials and may not last more than two seasons. Place in odd-number groups in the border, in swaths in the woodland, in containers, or scattered about the feet of irrigated woody plants. Good companions include 'Mrs. Moon' and 'Sissinghurst' lungwort, Lenten rose, and bear's foot hellebore.

CARE: Plant 10–12" apart in spring or fall. Apply slow-release granular plant food at time of planting, or begin using water-soluble plant food after the last frost and growth is visible. Follow label directions for amount and frequency. Maintain moist, not soggy, soil. When the soil feels dry 2" below the surface, water deeply. If using an irrigation system, maintain deep, infrequent waterings and avoid delivering a light sprinkle every day. Apply 3" of vegetative mulch in summer and winter to help retain soil moisture. When applying mulch, do not let it touch plant stems.

PROPAGATION: Plants self-sow in the landscape. To start indoors, sprinkle seeds over the soil mix and leave exposed to light; do not cover. Thoroughly moisten and keep moist, not soggy, until seeds germinate. Germination occurs in 7–14 days at 68–72°F. Transplant 15–25 days after sowing. Reduce the temperature to 55°F after transplanting. Seed-grown plants may flower lightly the first season and fully the second.

PESTS AND DISEASES: Botrytis and powdery mildew are common diseases. Slugs and snails are pests.

RELATED SPECIES: The Ball Series consists of compact 6" plants in blue, pink or white. 'Blue Bird' has bright blue flowers on plants 12" tall. Alpine forget-me-not (*M. alpestris*) is a short-lived perennial bearing blue flowers on plants 8" tall. It is hardy in Zones 4–8. Water forget-me-not (*M. scorpioides*) grows on wet sites. It is hardy in Zones 5–9.

DAFFODIL
Narcissus hybrids *nahr-SIHS-uhs*

Daffodil flowers are excellent fresh cut or dried or simply enjoyed in the landscape for their bright, cheery blooms.

ZONES: 3–8
SIZE: 5–24"h × 6–12"w
TYPE: Perennial
FORM: Upright
TEXTURE: Medium
GROWTH: Medium
LIGHT: Full sun to partial shade

MOISTURE: Medium
SOIL: Moderately fertile, well-drained
FEATURES: Flowers, foliage
USES: Border, naturalizing, container
FLOWERS: ■□

SITING: Daffodils prefer full sun or light afternoon shade and moderately fertile, well-drained soil with a pH of 5.5–7.0. Daffodils are classified into groups based on their flower form: trumpet, large cupped, small cupped, double, triandrus, cyclamineus, jonquilla, tazetta, poeticus, wild or other species, and split corona. Flowers are usually yellow or white. Daffodils may be used in groups in borders, naturalized among deciduous trees, in turf, and in container plantings. They may also be forced for indoor enjoyment during the winter.

CARE: Plant 6–12" apart in autumn, depending on the cultivar and location. Plant bulbs two to three times deeper than their diameter. Add bonemeal to the soil at planting time. Apply low-nitrogen, high-potassium plant food after flowering. Allow foliage to die back naturally so bulb can store enough energy to produce flowers the following season. Avoid braiding foliage or folding and wrapping it with rubber bands. Add 1" of vegetative mulch to daffodil planting beds. Keep soil moist during the growing season, but allow it to dry somewhat in summer to coincide with the bulbs' dormancy.

PROPAGATION: After flowering, when leaves fade, or in early autumn before new roots form, lift clumps and separate bulbs. Replant, water, and mulch.

PESTS AND DISEASES: Pests include viruses, fungal diseases, bulb scale mite, and large narcissus bulb fly.

1 Dig wide holes to hold clusters of bulbs.

2 Place the bulbs' basal plate down in hole.

JONQUIL
Narcissus jonquilla *nahr-SIHS-uhs jahn-KWIL-uh*

Jonquils bear yellow or white fragrant flowers in early spring.

ZONES: 4–8
SIZE: 6–20"h × 6–12"w
TYPE: Perennial
FORM: Upright
TEXTURE: Medium
GROWTH: Medium
LIGHT: Full sun to partial shade

MOISTURE: Medium
SOIL: Moderately fertile, well-drained
FEATURES: Flowers, foliage
USES: Border, naturalizing, container
FLOWERS: ■□

SITING: Jonquils are one classification of narcissus. Plants prefer full sun or light afternoon shade and moderately fertile, well-drained soil with a pH of 5.5–7.2. The species *jonquilla*, or jonquil, produces one to six fragrant yellow or white flowers per stem in early to midspring. Leaves are basal and somewhat cylindrical or rushlike. Flowers are excellent fresh cut and dried. Jonquils may be used in groups in borders or naturalized among deciduous trees, along lake banks, in pastures, in turf, or in container plantings. They may also be forced for indoor enjoyment.

CARE: Plant 6–12" apart in autumn, depending on the cultivar and location. Plant bulbs two to three times deeper than their diameter. Add bonemeal to the soil at planting time. Apply low-nitrogen, high-potassium plant food after flowering. Follow label directions for amount. Allow foliage to die back naturally so bulbs can store enough energy to produce flowers the following season. Avoid braiding foliage or folding and wrapping it with rubber bands. Add 1" of vegetative mulch to planting beds. Keep soil moist during the growing season, but allow it to dry somewhat in summer to coincide with the bulbs' dormancy.

PROPAGATION: After flowering, when leaves fade, or in early autumn before new roots form, lift clumps and separate bulbs. Replant, water, and mulch.

PESTS AND DISEASES: Problems include viruses, fungal diseases, bulb scale mite, and large narcissus bulb fly.

RELATED SPECIES: The cultivar 'Bell Song' reaches 12" high and bears one or two nodding white flowers with a pale pink cup; 'Dainty Miss' reaches 18" high and has white flowers with a green-eye cup; 'Intrigue' reaches 12" high and bears yellow flowers with a long, white frilly cup; 'Lintie' reaches 8" and has yellow flowers with an orange cup; 'Pink Angel' reaches 12" high and bears white flowers with a pink-edge, green-eye, white cup; and 'Quail' reaches 15" high and has yellow flowers.

FLOWERING TOBACCO

Nicotiana alata *nihk-oh-she-AHN-uh ah-LAY-tuh*

Flowering tobacco is a popular container or flower border plant.

ZONES: NA
SIZE: 1.5–5'h × 1–2'w
TYPE: Annual
FORM: Upright
TEXTURE: Medium
GROWTH: Medium
LIGHT: Full sun to partial shade

MOISTURE: Medium
SOIL: Fertile, moist, well-drained
FEATURES: Flowers, foliage
USES: Border, bedding, container
FLOWERS: ■ ■ ■ □

SITING: Flowering tobacco prefers full sun and fertile, well-drained, moist soil with a pH of 5.5–7.0. Plants are short-lived perennials grown as annuals. Tubular red, pink, white, and green flowers are white inside and appear in summer. Flowers are fragrant and open fully during the night. Leaves are larger at the base of the plant. Place in odd-numbered groups in borders, mass as bedding plants, or use in mixed container plantings. Good companions include 'John Elsley' bloody cranesbill and 'Purpureum' fennel.

CARE: Plant 12" apart in late spring. Apply slow-release granular plant food at time of planting or begin using water-soluble plant food 3 weeks after planting. Follow label directions for amount and frequency. Water deeply when the soil is dry. Apply vegetative mulch around, but not touching, the plants in summer to help retain soil moisture and add organic matter to the soil as it decomposes. Deadhead spent blooms to encourage reblooming. Remove plants just before the first frost or right afterward when foliage is disfigured. Cover bare soil with 3" of organic mulch during winter to preserve the topsoil.

PROPAGATION: Sprinkle seeds over the soil mix and leave exposed to light; do not cover. Thoroughly moisten and keep moist, not soggy, until seeds germinate. Germination occurs in 10–15 days at 70–75°F. Transplanting may begin 20–25 days after sowing. After transplanting, reduce temperature to 60–65°F.

PESTS AND DISEASES: Diseases include mosaic virus, root rot, and downy mildew. Insect pests include aphids and spider mites. Control by spraying plants with a forceful water spray, or use an insecticide according to label directions.

RELATED SPECIES: Nicki Series cultivars reach 18" high and bear fragrant red, pink, white, and lime-green flowers. Sensation hybrids bear red, pink, and white flowers, and *N.* 'Lime Green' reaches 24" high and bears lime-green flowers. *N.* ×*sanderae*, reaches 24" high, and bears panicles of red (sometimes pink), white, or purple flowers. *N. sylvestris* grows to 5' tall and bears fragrant white trumpet-shaped flowers.

CUPFLOWER

Nierembergia hippomanica *neer-ehm-BERG-ee-uh hihp-oh-MAHN-ih-kuh*

Cupflower has appealing white flowers with yellow throats. This is 'Mt. Blanc'.

ZONES: 7–10
SIZE: 10"h × 10"w
TYPE: Perennial
FORM: Rounded
TEXTURE: Fine
GROWTH: Medium
LIGHT: Full sun
MOISTURE: Medium

SOIL: Moderately fertile, moist, well-drained
FEATURES: Flowers, foliage
USES: Border, container
FLOWERS: ■ □

SITING: Cupflower prefers full sun and moderately fertile, well-drained, moist soil with a pH of 5.5–7.0. Provide shelter from strong winds. Cup-shaped pale blue or white flowers with a distinctive yellow throat appear in summer. Leaves are small, narrow, and pointed. Place plants in odd-number groups at the front of the border, mass as bedding, or add to mixed container plantings. Good companions include gaura, 'Fastigiata' hollyhock mallow, and gulf muhly.

CARE: Plant 10" apart in late spring. Apply slow-release granular plant food at time of planting or begin using water-soluble plant food 3 weeks after planting. When the soil feels almost dry 2" below the surface, water deeply. Maintain moist, not soggy, soil. Apply 3" of vegetative mulch around, but not touching, the plants in summer to help retain soil moisture and add organic matter to the soil as it decomposes. Plants are self-cleaning, so flowers do not need to be deadheaded, but shear back lightly after flowering to encourage compact growth. Remove plants just before the first frost or right afterward when foliage is disfigured.

PROPAGATION: Sprinkle seeds over the soil mix and cover lightly. Thoroughly moisten and keep moist, not soggy, until seeds germinate. Germination occurs in 10–15 days at 70–75°F. Transplant 25–35 days after sowing. After transplanting, reduce the temperature to 60–65°F.

PESTS AND DISEASES: Diseases include tobacco mosaic virus.

RELATED SPECIES: *N. hippomanica* var. *violacea* bears violet-blue flowers, and 'Purple Robe' has purple-blue flowers.

'Purple Robe' cupflower makes a colorful addition to a sunny container garden.

LOVE-IN-A-MIST
Nigella damascena *neye-JEHL-uh dam-uh-SEE-nuh*

Love-in-a-mist is fine-textured and should be planted in groups for best effect.

ZONES: NA
SIZE: 24"h × 10"w
TYPE: Annual
FORM: Upright
TEXTURE: Fine
GROWTH: Fast
LIGHT: Full sun
MOISTURE: Medium

SOIL: Moderately fertile, well-drained
FEATURES: Flowers, foliage, seedpods
USES: Border, container
FLOWERS: ■ ■ □ □ ■

SITING: Love-in-a-mist prefers full sun and moderately fertile, well-drained soil with a pH of 5.5–7.5. Purplish-blue flowers lighten with age to pale blue and appear in summer. Flowers are followed by purple-and-green-striped seedpods, which are valued for use in dried arrangements. Plant in large groups; solitary plants are too slender and wispy to have a presence in the landscape. Good container companions include 'Bressingham Ruby' heart-leaf bergenia, 'Purpureum' fennel, rosemary, and lemon thyme.

Dried seedpods of love-in-a-mist are prized for flower arrangements.

CARE: Plant 6–12" apart in late spring. Apply slow-release granular plant food at time of planting. Water deeply when the soil is dry. Leave flowers to fade on plants to allow the seedpods to form. Remove plants just before the first frost or right afterward when foliage is disfigured.
PROPAGATION: Love-in-a-mist does not transplant well. Sow directly into the landscape bed after the last frost. Germination will occur in 7–14 days at 68–72°F. Germination rates may be low, so plant extra seed and thin later.
PESTS AND DISEASES: Plants are relatively pest free when cultural requirements are met.
RELATED SPECIES: Dwarf cultivars (less than 10" high) include 'Blue Midget', 'Cambridge Blue' with double blue flowers, and 'Dwarf Moody Blue' with semidouble flowers. Miss Jekyll Series reaches 18" high and bears blue, white, and pink flowers; 'Mulberry Rose' reaches 18" and has double pale pink flowers that darken with age; 'Oxford Blue' bears double large blue flowers; Persian Jewel Series bears pink, white, red, and purple flowers; and 'Red Jewel' has deep rose flowers.

OZARK SUNDROP
Oenothera macrocarpa (missouriensis) *ohn-oh-THEHR-uh mak-roh-KAR-puh (mih-zur-ee-EN-sis)*

Ozark sundrop blooms all summer long in Midwestern states. It is also known as Missouri primrose.

ZONES: 4–8
SIZE: 8"h × 24"w
TYPE: Perennial
FORM: Spreading
TEXTURE: Medium
GROWTH: Medium
LIGHT: Full sun
MOISTURE: Medium

SOIL: Moderately fertile, well-drained
FEATURES: Flowers, foliage
USES: Border, container, wall
FLOWERS: ■ ■ □

SITING: Ozark sundrop prefers full sun and moderately fertile, well-drained soil with a pH of 6.5–7.5. Plants require well-drained soil in winter as well as summer. Solitary, paper-thin, bright-yellow flowers appear from late spring to late summer. Plants do not perform well in warm-climate heat. Place them in groups at the front of borders, add to mixed container plantings,

Showy evening primrose's white or pink blooms are fragrant. It spreads quickly through the landscape.

or allow to cascade down a wall. Good companions include 'Jackanapes' crocosmia, geum, and 'Dazzler' blanket flower.
CARE: Plant 18–24" apart in spring. Apply slow-release granular plant food at time of planting. Water deeply when the soil is dry. Apply vegetative mulch around, but not touching, the plants in summer to help retain soil moisture. Deadhead spent blooms to encourage reblooming. Trim back in fall once frost withers the foliage.
PROPAGATION: Plants may self-sow in the landscape; divide in spring. To start indoors, sprinkle seed over the soil mix and leave exposed to light; do not cover. Thoroughly moisten and keep moist, not soggy, until seeds germinate. Germination occurs in 8–16 days at 70–80°F. Transplant 20–27 days after sowing. Reduce the temperature to 55°F after transplanting.
PESTS AND DISEASES: Root rot may occur in wet soils. Powdery mildew, rust, and Septoria leaf spot are other diseases.
RELATED SPECIES: Showy evening primrose (*O. speciosa*) reaches 12" high and wide and bears fragrant white flowers that occasionally turn pink. It tolerates humidity but may be invasive in fertile, moist soil.

CINNAMON FERN
Osmunda cinnamomea *ahz-MUHND-uh sihn-uh-MOHM-ee-uh*

Cinnamon fern spores resemble cinnamon sticks nestled among its fronds.

ZONES: 3–8
SIZE: 36"h × 36"w
TYPE: Perennial
FORM: Irregular
TEXTURE: Coarse
GROWTH: Medium
LIGHT: Partial to full shade
MOISTURE: Medium to high

SOIL: Fertile, moist, well-drained
FEATURES: Foliage, fiddlehead fronds, roots
USES: Border, woodland, container
FALL COLOR: ■ ■

SITING: Cinnamon fern prefers full shade or heavy mid- to late-day partial shade and fertile, well-drained, moist soil with a pH of 5.5–7.0. Fertile bright green fronds appear in spring, turn cinnamon brown with spores, then decline by midsummer. Fronds turn golden yellow in fall, then brown. Plant in groups in borders, as ground cover in the woodland, or as a focal point in container plantings. Good companions include goatsbeard, bugbane, and Siebold hosta cultivars.

CARE: Plant 36" apart in spring or fall in fertile soil high in organic matter. To increase organic matter, add 1–2" of compost to the planting bed and till in to a depth of 12–15". Apply slow-release granular plant food at time of planting.

A drip irrigation system efficiently delivers water to moisture-loving ferns.

When the soil feels dry 2" below the surface, water deeply. Apply 3" of vegetative mulch around, but not touching, the plants or rhizomes in summer and winter to help retain soil moisture and add organic matter to the soil as it decomposes. Prune back in fall once frost withers the foliage.

PROPAGATION: Divide in spring or fall. Dig around the rhizomes and lift. Use a sharp spade to slice through the root system. Reset portions that contain healthy roots and top shoots, then water and mulch. Discard any pieces that do not contain both healthy roots and top shoots.

PESTS AND DISEASES: Plants are relatively pest free when cultural requirements (sun, soil, planting depth, moisture) are met. Rust is an occasional problem.

ROYAL FERN
Osmunda regalis *ahz-MUHND-uh reh-GAHL-ihs*

Royal ferns are huge specimens for the shady landscape.

ZONES: 3–9
SIZE: 6'h × 6'w
TYPE: Perennial
FORM: Irregular
TEXTURE: Medium
GROWTH: Medium
LIGHT: Partial to full shade

MOISTURE: Medium to high
SOIL: Fertile, moist, well-drained
FEATURES: Foliage, roots
USES: Border, woodland, container
FALL COLOR: ■ ■

SITING: Royal fern prefers full to partial shade, shelter from the midday sun, and fertile, well-drained, moist soil with a pH of 5.5–7.2. Plants tolerate wet soil as well. Bright green fronds reach 3' long in spring, lengthening to 6' long in summer. Fibrous roots are visible above ground and create interest. They are used as osmunda fiber in orchid potting mix. Plant in odd-numbered groups in large borders, as tall ground cover in woodlands or at water's edge, or as a focal point in a large container planting. Good companions include goatsbeard, 'Superba' Chinese astilbe, bugbane, and 'Francis Williams' hosta.

CARE: Plant 3–6' apart in spring or fall. Apply slow-release granular plant food at time of planting. If planting in a wetland, or near water, avoid plant foods and chemical pesticides to prevent chemicals from leaching into bodies of water. Till in organic matter to create deep, humusy, fertile soil. Apply 3" of vegetative mulch around, but not touching, the plants in summer and winter to help retain soil moisture and add organic matter to the soil as it decomposes. Maintain moist soil. If using an irrigation system, maintain deep, infrequent waterings and avoid delivering a light sprinkle every day. Prune back in fall once frost withers the foliage.

PROPAGATION: Divide in spring or fall. Dig around the rhizomes and lift. Use a sharp spade to slice through the root system. Reset portions that contain healthy roots and top shoots, then water and mulch. Discard any pieces that do not contain both healthy roots and top shoots.

PESTS AND DISEASES: Plants are relatively pest free. Rust is an occasional problem.

RELATED SPECIES: The cultivars 'Crispa' and 'Cristata' have crested tips, 'Purpurescens' has purple-stained fronds in spring, and 'Undulata' fronds have wavy edges. Interrupted fern (*O. claytoniana*) tolerates drier sites and is hardy in Zones 4–8.

JAPANESE SPURGE
Pachysandra terminalis *pahk-ih-SAHN-druh ter-mihn-AHL-ihs*

Japanese spurge is an outstanding evergreen ground cover for shade. 'Silver Edge' is a variegated form.

ZONES: 4–8
SIZE: 8"h × 8"w
TYPE: Perennial
FORM: Spreading
TEXTURE: Medium
GROWTH: Medium
LIGHT: Partial to full shade
MOISTURE: Medium
SOIL: Moderately fertile, well-drained
FEATURES: Foliage, flowers
USES: Ground cover
FLOWERS: □
FALL COLOR: ■

SITING: Japanese spurge prefers full or partial shade and fertile to moderately fertile, well-drained soil with a pH of 5.5–7.0. Plants have evergreen whorls of toothed, glossy dark green leaves. Spikes of tiny white flowers appear in late spring. Plants spread quickly and will coexist with tree roots. Place in prepared beds at the feet of trees, in woody or herbaceous shade borders, or in woodland gardens. Good companions in a ground cover bed include 'Pumila' Chinese astilbe, bleeding heart, and 'Elegans' Siebold hosta.

CARE: Plant 12–24" apart in late spring or fall; the closer plants are, the faster the ground will be covered. Apply slow-release granular plant food at time of planting or begin using water-soluble plant food 3 weeks after planting, especially if plants will be competing with tree or shrub roots. Water deeply when the soil is dry. Apply 3" of vegetative mulch in summer and winter to reduce weed seed germination, retain soil moisture, and keep soil temperatures stable.

PROPAGATION: Divide in spring. Dig around the rhizomes and lift. Use a sharp spade to slice through the root system. Reset portions that contain healthy roots and top shoots, then water and mulch. Discard any pieces that do not contain both healthy roots and top shoots.

PESTS AND DISEASES: Leaf spot may be a disease problem.

RELATED SPECIES: The cultivar 'Green Carpet' is compact, 'Silver Edge' has light green leaves rimmed in silver-white, and 'Variegata' has white-variegated leaves and grows slowly.

PEONY
Paeonia officinalis *pay-OH-nee-uh uh-fish-ih-NAHL-ihs*

Peonies are long-lived plants with classic flowers for landscape viewing.

ZONES: 3–8
SIZE: 24–36"h × 24–36"w
TYPE: Perennial
FORM: Upright
TEXTURE: Medium
GROWTH: Medium
LIGHT: Full sun, partial shade
MOISTURE: Medium
SOIL: Fertile, moist, well-drained
FEATURES: Flowers, foliage
USES: Border
FLOWERS: ■■□

SITING: Peony prefers full sun or light afternoon shade and fertile, well-drained, moist soil with a pH of 6.5–7.2. Plants are very long lived. In the mixed border, lace groups through the middle of beds. Good companions include sea pink, gas plant, sweet woodruff, and evergreen candytuft.

CARE: Plant 24–36" apart and 2" deep in early autumn. Buds or "eyes" should be 1–2" below the soil surface and should face up. Add bonemeal and slow-release granular plant food to the soil at planting time. Select a food low in nitrogen. Apply 3" of vegetative mulch in summer. Plunge peony rings into the soil around the plant in early spring so the foliage can easily grow up through the structure; the rings will be hidden once the plant reaches full height. Maintain moist soil. Cut stems and leaves to the ground after frost disfigures the foliage. Remove peony rings and store until springtime. If disease was present, disinfect rings and pruning tools, and dispose of all trimmed foliage. Plants need at least 6 hours of unobstructed sunlight per day for the best flowering. Peonies rarely need division to maintain vigor.

PROPAGATION: To start new plants, dig around the tuber and lift. Use a sharp spade to slice through the root system. Reset portions that contain at least three healthy buds or "eyes," then water and mulch. Plants may take two seasons to resume normal bloom habits after division.

PESTS AND DISEASES: Diseases include botrytis, verticillium wilt, ringspot virus, and stem rot. Pests include nematodes and Japanese beetles. Wet soil almost always causes disease problems.

RELATED SPECIES: Upright tree peony (*P. suffruticosa*) reaches up to 7' high and 3–4' wide with white, red, pink, or purple flowers. Leaves have 3–5 lobes and are light green above and blue-green below.

1 Lift peony roots in late summer to divide them.

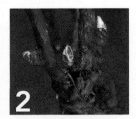

2 Make certain each division contains three or more eyes or buds.

3 Reset healthy sections shallowly, only 1–2" deep in the soil.

Remove the plant's peony ring support at the end of the season.

Cut back the foliage to ground level after frost.

ICELAND POPPY
Papaver nudicaule *pah-PAW-vehr nood-ih-KAWL-ay*

Iceland poppy has papery flowers in delicate shades of white, salmon, orange, and yellow.

ZONES: 2–8
SIZE: 18"h × 12"w
TYPE: Perennial
FORM: Upright
TEXTURE: Medium
GROWTH: Medium
LIGHT: Full sun
MOISTURE: Medium
SOIL: Fertile, well-drained
FEATURES: Flowers, foliage
USES: Border, naturalizing, container
FLOWERS: ■□■

SITING: Iceland poppy prefers full sun and deep, fertile, well-drained soil with a pH of 5.5–7.0. Plants are grown as short-lived perennials in cooler regions and as annuals in warmer regions. Solitary, fragrant, papery flowers in yellow, white, orange, or salmon-pink, up to 3" across, appear in spring and early summer. Leaves are blue-green and hairy. Flowers are excellent fresh cut. Good companions include 'Jackanapes' crocosmia, geum, and 'Dazzler' blanket flower.

CARE: Plant 12" apart in late spring. Apply slow-release granular plant food at time of planting. Apply 3" of vegetative mulch around, but not touching, the plant in summer and winter. Water deeply when the soil is dry.

PROPAGATION: Divide in spring. Dig around the root clump and lift. Use a sharp spade to slice through the root system. Reset portions that contain healthy roots and top shoots, then water and mulch. To start indoors, sprinkle seeds over the soil mix and leave exposed to light; do not cover. Thoroughly moisten and keep moist, not soggy, until seeds germinate. Germination occurs in 7–14 days at 65–75°F. Transplant 17–25 days after sowing. After transplanting, reduce temperature to 55°F.

PESTS AND DISEASES: Diseases include botrytis, powdery mildew, and root rot.

RELATED SPECIES: The cultivar 'Champagne Bubbles' bears flowers in pastel shades, 'Garden Gnome' has bright-colored flowers and is dwarf, 'Hamlet' bears scarlet-red flowers, 'Oregon Rainbows' comes in pastel shades, and 'Pacino' is compact with yellow flowers.

ORIENTAL POPPY
Papaver orientale *pah-PAW-vehr or-ee-ehn-TAHL-ay*

Oriental poppy has papery flowers in vibrant orange-red hues to pastel pink, salmon, and white.

ZONES: 3–7
SIZE: 18–36"h × 24–36"w
TYPE: Perennial
FORM: Irregular
TEXTURE: Medium
GROWTH: Medium
LIGHT: Full sun
MOISTURE: Medium
SOIL: Fertile, well-drained
FEATURES: Flowers, foliage
USES: Border, naturalizing, container
FLOWERS: ■□■

SITING: Oriental poppy prefers full sun and deep, fertile, well-drained soil with a pH of 5.5–7.0. Protect papery flowers from strong winds. Plants prefer cool temperatures and dislike heat and humidity. Solitary, dashing red-orange flowers with black splashes in the center appear from late spring into summer. Plant in groups in borders or in containers or naturalize in a large, prepared area. Plants become dormant in summer and die back to the ground. Companions include 'Snowbank' white boltonia, bluebeard, and Russian sage.

CARE: Plant 24" apart in autumn or spring. Apply slow-release granular plant food at time of planting in spring. Apply 3" of vegetative mulch in summer and winter to reduce weed seed germination, retain soil moisture, and keep soil temperatures stable. Water deeply when the soil is dry.

PROPAGATION: Sprinkle seeds over the soil mix and leave exposed to light; do not cover. Thoroughly moisten and keep moist, not soggy, until seeds germinate. Germination occurs in 7–14 days at 65–75°F. Transplant 17–25 days after sowing. After transplanting, reduce temperature to 55°F. Divide in mid- to late summer while dormant and before new root growth starts.

PESTS AND DISEASES: Diseases include botrytis, powdery mildew, and root rot.

RELATED SPECIES: 'Allegro' has red-orange flowers with black at the base of the petals, 'Beauty of Livermere' bears red flowers up to 8" across stained black at the base, 'Black and White' has white flowers with a reddish-black stain at the base, 'Carnival' bears crinkly red-orange flowers stained white at the base, 'Cedric Morris' has crinkly pale pink flowers stained black at the base, 'Fatima' is compact with white flowers and pink edges and black-stained base, 'Harvest Moon' bears orange semidouble flowers, and 'May Queen' has nodding, double orange-red flowers.

1 Divide poppies after blooming when they are dormant.

2 Lift the entire plant from soil.

3 Split clump using a sharp spade.

4 Reset portions that contain healthy roots and shoots.

ROSE-SCENTED GERANIUM
Pelargonium graveolens pell-ar-GOHN-ee-uhm grahv-ee-OH-lehns

Rose-scented geranium's essential oils are used in perfumes.

ZONES: 9–10
SIZE: 18–24"h ×
12–24"w
TYPE: Perennial
FORM: Sprawling
TEXTURE: Medium
GROWTH: Medium
LIGHT: Full sun

MOISTURE: Medium
SOIL: Fertile,
well-drained
FEATURES: Flowers,
foliage
USES: Border,
container
FLOWERS: ■

SITING: Rose-scented geranium prefers full sun and fertile, well-drained soil with a pH of 5.5–7.3. Plants are commonly grown as annuals or tender perennials and moved indoors before frost. Tiny pink blooms appear in summer and complement the fragrant foliage. Good companions include fennel, lavender, and lemon thyme.

CARE: Plant 18" apart in late spring. Apply slow-release granular plant food at time of planting. Select one low in nitrogen to preserve fragrance. Water deeply when the soil is dry. Transplant into a container in late summer or early autumn to bring indoors, or treat as an annual in colder zones and remove once frost has killed the plant.

PROPAGATION: Take cuttings in summer. Cut nonwoody pieces that contain two healthy leaves and at least three nodes. Insert exposed nodes into rooting

hormone, shake off the excess, and insert stems into moist soil mix, keeping leaves above the soil level. Cover with plastic to raise humidity levels. Supply bottom heat and keep moist, not soggy, until root and top shoot growth is evident. Transplant the rooted cuttings.

PESTS AND DISEASES: Insect problems include aphids and spider mites. Diseases of geranium include botrytis, black leg, and Xanthomonas blight.

RELATED SPECIES: 'Lady Plymouth' has creamy-edged leaves, compact 'Little Pet' has rose-pink flowers, and 'Mint Rose' has white-rimmed leaves and a mint scent.

1 Take cuttings from nonwoody stems.

2 Dip end tip and exposed nodes in rooting hormone.

3 Stick cutting in soilless growing mix.

4 Cover cuttings with plastic to increase humidity.

ZONAL GERANIUM
Pelargonium ×hortorum pell-ar-GOHN-ee-uhm hor-TOR-uhm

Zonal geranium is the classic look in summer sun.

ZONES: 9–10
SIZE: 5–24"h ×
6–12"w
TYPE: Perennial
FORM: Upright
TEXTURE: Medium
GROWTH: Fast
LIGHT: Full sun

MOISTURE: Medium
SOIL: Fertile,
well-drained
FEATURES: Flowers,
foliage
USES: Bedding,
container
FLOWERS: ■□■■

SITING: Zonal geranium prefers full sun and fertile, well-drained soil with a pH of 5.5–7.0. In hot climates plants may benefit from afternoon shade. Mass for bedding or use in containers. Container companions include alyssum and rosemary.

CARE: Plant 6–24" apart in late spring. Apply slow-release granular plant food at time of planting. Water deeply when the soil is dry. Deadhead spent blooms to encourage reblooming; blooms snap off easily. Dig plants in early autumn and pot up to bring indoors; or leave until disfigured by frost, then discard. Indoors, shear back foliage by one-third in winter. Rootstocks may be hung in a cool spot indoors in the dark through winter, and planted back outdoors in spring. Plants may also be grown as annuals.

PROPAGATION:
Germination occurs in 7–10 days at 70–75°F. Transplant 10–15 days after sowing. After transplanting, reduce temperature to 60–65°F. Take cuttings in summer. Cut nonwoody pieces that contain two healthy leaves and at least three nodes. Insert

exposed nodes into rooting hormone, shake off excess, and insert into moist soil mix, keeping leaves above soil level. Cover with plastic to raise humidity levels. Supply bottom heat and keep soil mix moist until new growth is evident, then transplant.

PESTS AND DISEASES: Insect pest problems include aphids and spider mites. Diseases of geranium include botrytis, black leg, and Xanthomonas blight.

RELATED SPECIES: Trailing ivy geranium (*P. peltatum*) is well suited to container plantings or trailing over walls.

Zonal geranium's faded flowers may be snapped off by hand to stimulate reblooming.

Ivy geranium cascades nicely from containers.

BEARD-TONGUE

Penstemon barbatus *PEHN-stehm-uhn bar-BAY-tuhs*

Beard tongue, also known as beardlip penstemon or penstemon, attracts butterflies with its tubular flowers.

ZONES: 4–9
SIZE: 18–24"h × 12–24"w
TYPE: Perennial
FORM: Upright
TEXTURE: Medium
GROWTH: Medium
LIGHT: Full sun to partial shade

MOISTURE: Medium
SOIL: Fertile, well-drained
FEATURES: Flowers
USES: Border, container
FLOWERS: ■□■■

SITING: Beard-tongue prefers full sun or bright afternoon shade and fertile soil with a pH of 5.5–7.0. Plants tolerate heat and humidity. Well-drained soil in summer and winter is essential. Panicles of tubular red flowers with a yellow beard appear from late spring to early summer in the South and into early autumn in cooler regions. Flowers attract butterflies and are excellent fresh cut. Place in odd-number groups in borders or add freely to containers. The relative narrowness of the plant makes it ideal for container plantings.

Deadhead penstemon to stimulate reblooming.

Good companions include scaevola, 'Pink Mist' pincushion flower, and 'Burgundy Giant' purple fountain grass.
CARE: Plant 12–24" apart in spring or fall. Apply slow-release granular plant food at time of planting. Apply 3" of vegetative mulch around, but not touching, the plants in summer and winter. Water deeply when the soil is dry. Deadhead spent blooms to encourage reblooming. Older flower stalks fall and flop as they age. Plants also flop if they do not receive enough sun. Cut back in fall after frost disfigures foliage.
PROPAGATION: Sprinkle seeds over the growing medium and leave exposed to light; do not cover. Thoroughly moisten and keep moist, not soggy, until seeds germinate. Germination occurs in 7–10 days at 70°F. Transplant 25–28 days after sowing. After transplanting, reduce temperature to 55°F.
PESTS AND DISEASES: Diseases include powdery mildew, leaf spot, rust, and Southern blight.
RELATED SPECIES: 'Elfin Pink' reaches 12" high and has pink flowers, and 'Praecox Nanus Rondo' reaches 18" high.

SMOOTH WHITE PENSTEMON

Penstemon digitalis *PEHN-stehm-uhn dih-jih-TAHL-ihs*

'Husker Red' foliage is semievergreen in a shade of maroon. Smooth white penstemon is also known simply as penstemon.

ZONES: 2–8
SIZE: 24–48"h × 18"w
TYPE: Perennial
FORM: Upright
TEXTURE: Medium
GROWTH: Medium
LIGHT: Full sun to partial shade

MOISTURE: Medium
SOIL: Fertile, well-drained
FEATURES: Flowers, foliage
USES: Border, container
FLOWERS: □

SITING: Smooth white penstemon prefers full sun or bright afternoon shade and fertile soil with a pH of 5.5–7.0. Well-drained soil in summer and winter is essential. Plants tolerate high heat and humidity. Panicles of white tubular bell-shape flowers, sometimes marked with purple, appear from early to late summer. Flowers attract bees and butterflies and are excellent fresh cut. Place in groups in borders or use in containers. Good companions include 'Crimson Butterflies' gaura, 'Burgundy Giant' purple fountain grass, and 'Iceberg' rose.
CARE: Plant 18" apart in spring or autumn. Apply slow-release granular plant food at time of planting. To increase organic matter in the soil, add 1–2" of compost to the planting bed and till in to a depth of 12–15". Water deeply when the soil is dry. Apply 3" of vegetative mulch in summer and winter. Deadheading is essential to reblooming. Plants will fall and flop if they do not receive enough sun. Foliage is semievergreen, so leave plants erect for winter interest until frost disfigures foliage, then trim back.
PROPAGATION: Propagate cultivars by division or cuttings. Divide every 3 years in spring or fall to maintain vigor. Dig around the root clump and lift. Use a sharp spade to slice through the root system. Reset portions that contain healthy roots and top shoots. In summer, take cuttings from nonflowering stems. Cut pieces that contain two healthy leaves and at least three nodes. Dip exposed nodes into rooting hormone, shake off excess, and insert into moist soil mix, keeping leaves above the soil level.

Sprinkle seeds over the growing medium and leave exposed to light; do not cover. Thoroughly moisten and keep moist, not soggy, until seeds germinate. Germination occurs in 7–10 days at 70°F. Transplanting may begin 25–28 days after sowing. After transplanting, reduce temperature to 55°F.
PESTS AND DISEASES: Diseases include powdery mildew, leaf spot, rust, and Southern blight.
RELATED SPECIES: The cultivar 'Husker Red' was selected as the 1996 Perennial Plant of the Year by the Perennial Plant Association. Foliage is stained maroon, and flowers are tinted pink. Ornamental color may revert to green in the heat of the South. Cultivar 'Albus' bears white flowers, 'Nanus' is a dwarf form, and 'Woodville White' has white flowers.

EGYPTIAN STAR FLOWER

Pentas lanceolata PEHN-tuhs lahns-ee-oh-LAT-uh

Egyptian star flower loves the heat and produces clusters of star-shaped flowers.

ZONES: 9–11
SIZE: 1–6'h × 18–36"w
TYPE: Perennial
FORM: Rounded
TEXTURE: Medium
GROWTH: Fast
LIGHT: Full sun
MOISTURE: Medium

SOIL: Fertile, well-drained
FEATURES: Flowers, foliage
USES: Border, ground cover, container
FLOWERS: ■ ■ ■ □ ■

SITING: Egyptian star flower prefers full sun and fertile, well-drained soil with a pH of 5.5–7.0. Plants are usually grown as annuals. Clusters of star-shape flowers in bright pink, red, lavender, purple, blue, or white appear from spring to autumn. Place in groups in borders, mass as an annual ground cover, or use in containers. Good companions include 'Snowbank' white boltonia, 'Kobold' blazing star, and false indigo.

CARE: Plant 18–36" apart in late spring. Apply slow-release granular plant food at time of planting. Apply 3" of vegetative mulch in summer. Water deeply when the soil is dry. Plants withstand heavy pruning, but flower production will suffer. Remove plants just before first frost or right afterward when frost disfigures the foliage.

PROPAGATION: In summer take cuttings from nonflowering stems. Cut pieces that contain at least two healthy leaves and three nodes. Dip exposed nodes into rooting hormone, shake off excess, and insert into moist growing medium, keeping leaves well above the soil level.

Sprinkle seeds over the soil mix and leave exposed to light; do not cover. Germination occurs in 5–12 days at 72°F. Transplanting may begin 20–28 days after sowing. After transplanting, reduce temperature to 65°F.

PESTS AND DISEASES: Plants are relatively pest free when cultural requirements (sun, soil, planting depth, moisture) are met.

RELATED SPECIES: The cultivar 'Avalanche' has white flowers and white-stained leaves, 'Kermesina' has bright rose flowers with a violet throat, and 'Quartiniana' has rosey-pink flowers.

RUSSIAN SAGE

Perovskia atriplicifolia per-OV-skee-uh ah-trih-plihs-ih-FOL-ee-uh

Russian sage is a low-maintenance perennial with a long bloom cycle.

ZONES: 3–9
SIZE: 4'h × 4'w
TYPE: Perennial
FORM: Irregular
TEXTURE: Fine
GROWTH: Medium
LIGHT: Full sun
MOISTURE: Medium

SOIL: Moderately fertile, well-drained
FEATURES: Flowers, foliage
USES: Border, container
FLOWERS: ■

SITING: Russian sage prefers full sun and moderately fertile, well-drained soil with a pH of 5.5–7.3. It is heat and drought tolerant and pest resistant. Lavender flowers appear from summer into autumn. Fragrant foliage is silver-green and finely cut. Flowers attract bees and butterflies. Plant in borders, use in place of traditional woody shrubs, or use in large container plantings. Good companions include 'Kobold' blazing star, purple coneflower, and 'Snowbank' white boltonia.

CARE: Plant 24–36" apart in spring or fall. Apply with slow-release granular plant food at time of planting. Water only when the soil is dry 2–3" below the surface. Apply mulch in summer and winter. Plants are self-cleaning, so deadheading is not necessary. Plants may be rejuvenated by pruning. To rejuvenate, trim woody stems back almost to the ground once buds appear on the stems in spring. If left unpruned they become unkempt.

PROPAGATION: Plants may be layered in the landscape. Select a stem close to the ground, remove leaves to expose one or more nodes, and pin nodes directly to the soil. Cover the area with mulch. After roots form, cut the stem to separate it from the parent plant, leaving some top growth attached to new roots. New shoots that appear near the parent plant may be dug and transplanted. In spring take cuttings from new growth. Cut pieces that contain at least two healthy leaves and three nodes. Dip exposed nodes into rooting hormone, shake off excess, and insert into moist growing medium, keeping leaves well above the soil level. Supply bottom heat and keep moist, not soggy, until root and top shoot growth is evident, usually in 2–3 weeks, then transplant. To enhance humidity, cover with plastic, keeping it above the leaves.

PESTS AND DISEASES: Plants are relatively pest free.

RELATED SPECIES: 'Blue Mist' flowers early and has light blue flowers. 'Blue Spire' bears finely cut leaves and lavender-blue flowers.

To layer Russian sage, pin a shoot to the ground and cover it with mulch.

After roots develop, dig the new plant and transplant it.

PETUNIA
Petunia ×hybrida peh-TOO-nyuh HIH-brid-uh

Petunias produce nonstop summer color in the container or landscape.

ZONES: NA
SIZE: 6–15"h × 6–36"w
TYPE: Annual
FORM: Mounded
TEXTURE: Medium
GROWTH: Medium
LIGHT: Full sun to part shade

MOISTURE: Medium
SOIL: Moderately fertile, well-drained
FEATURES: Flowers
USES: Bedding, container
FLOWERS: ■ ■ □ ■ ■ ■ ■

SITING: Petunia prefers full sun and moderately fertile, well-drained soil with a pH of 5.5–7.0. Showy flowers appear in summer in reds, pinks, yellows, purples, and white. Good container companions include alyssum, dwarf fountain grass, fan flower, and lemon thyme.

CARE: When used as bedding plants, place 12–18" apart in late spring. Feed with slow-release granular plant food at time of planting or begin using water-soluble plant food 3 weeks after planting. Follow label directions for amount and frequency. Apply mulch in summer. Water deeply when the soil is dry. Shear plants back by one-third after first flush of flowers to encourage compact growth. Remove plants just before first frost or right afterward.

Old cultivars of petunias require shearing back after first flowering to encourage bushy compact growth; newer types don't.

PROPAGATION: Sprinkle seeds over the growing medium and leave exposed to light; do not cover. Thoroughly moisten and keep moist, not soggy, until seeds germinate. Germination occurs in 10–12 days at 75–80°F. Transplant 15–20 days after sowing. Reduce the temperature to 60°F after transplanting.

PESTS AND DISEASES: Diseases include tobacco mosaic virus, impatiens necrotic spot virus, botrytis, and bacterial soft rot.

RELATED SPECIES: Wave and Easy Wave Series petunias are spreading types in a broad range of colors that begin to flower quickly and perform well all season long. Double forms are also available. Explorer Series is another spreading type, and Opera Series is a creeping type. Cascadia Series petunias have a trailing habit with medium-sized flowers. Petitunia Series has a trailing habit with numerous smaller blooms. Avalanche Series is a trailer with full-size flowers. A petunia relative *Calibrachoa* is a trailing plant often grown in hanging baskets. It comes in a broad array of colors. Colorburst Series, Celebration Series, and Calimor® are some popular types.

GARDEN PHLOX
Phlox paniculata FLAHKS pahn-ik-yew-LAH-tuh

Garden phlox blooms are excellent fresh cut and attract bees and butterflies.

ZONES: 3–8
SIZE: 4'h × 2–3'w
TYPE: Perennial
FORM: Upright
TEXTURE: Medium
GROWTH: Fast
LIGHT: Full sun, partial shade

MOISTURE: Medium to high
SOIL: Fertile, moist, well-drained
FEATURES: Flowers, foliage
USES: Border, container
FLOWERS: □ ■ ■ ■ ■

SITING: Garden phlox prefers full sun or light afternoon shade and fertile, well-drained, moist soil with a pH of 5.5–7.0. Good air circulation is essential to discourage powdery mildew. Clusters of white, lavender, pink, rose, and blue flowers abound from summer to early autumn. Flowers are sometimes scented, attract bees and butterflies, and are excellent fresh cut. Good companions include 'Carefree Wonder' and 'Bonica' roses, and daylily cultivars.

CARE: Plant mildew-resistant cultivars 24–36" apart in spring or fall. Apply slow-release granular plant food at time of planting. Apply 3" of vegetative mulch in summer and winter. Water deeply when the soil is dry. Deadhead spent blooms to encourage reblooming and prevent self-seeding. Cut to the ground in fall after frost disfigures the foliage.

PROPAGATION: Divide every 3 years in spring or fall to maintain plant vigor.

PESTS AND DISEASES: Powdery mildew does not need moist air to thrive. It flourishes in dry weather.

Select mildew-resistant cultivars and place plants where there is plenty of air circulation among them. Keep soil moist but not soggy. Overhead irrigation tends to spread disease, so install drip systems when possible.

RELATED SPECIES: Mildew-resistant cultivars: 'David' has white flowers, 'Katherine' has lavender flowers, 'Little Boy' bears two-toned mauve and white flowers, 'Blue Paradise' bears purple-blue flowers, 'Eva Cullem' has pink flowers with red centers, and 'Robert Poore' has purple flowers.

Plant in groups for best effect.

Deadhead faded flowers to stimulate reblooming.

CREEPING PHLOX

Phlox stolonifera *FLAHKS stob-lubn-IHF-er-ub*

Creeping phlox is an ideal ground cover for partial shade.

ZONES: 2–8
SIZE: 6"h × 12"w
TYPE: Perennial
FORM: Spreading
TEXTURE: Medium
GROWTH: Medium
LIGHT: Partial shade
MOISTURE: Medium

SOIL: Fertile, moist, well-drained
FEATURES: Flowers, foliage
USES: Woodland, ground cover
FLOWERS: ■ ■ □

SITING: Creeping phlox prefers partial shade with protection from the afternoon sun and fertile, well-drained soil with a pH of 5.5–6.5. Lavender to purple flowers appear in spring. Leaves are dark green. Place in groups in woodland gardens or use as ground cover among trees and shrubs. Good companions include 'Pictum' Japanese painted fern, 'Elegans' Siebold hosta, and 'Mrs. Moon' lungwort.

CARE: Plant 6–12" apart in spring or fall. Apply slow-release granular plant food at time of planting. Apply 3" of vegetative mulch in summer and winter to reduce weed seed germination, hold moisture in the soil, and as it decomposes it will add organic matter to the soil. Maintain moist, not soggy, soil. Water new transplants daily; otherwise, water deeply only when the soil feels almost dry 2" below the surface. If using an irrigation system, maintain deep, infrequent waterings and

avoid delivering a light sprinkle every day. Organic matter in the soil and mulch on the soil surface help reduce watering frequency because they help the soil retain moisture. Shear plants back after flowering to encourage compact growth.

PROPAGATION: Divide in spring or fall. Dig around the root clump and lift. Use a sharp spade to slice through the root system. Reset portions that contain healthy roots and top shoots, then water and mulch. Discard any pieces that do not contain both healthy roots and top shoots.

PESTS AND DISEASES: Spider mites and powdery mildew are problems.

RELATED SPECIES: 'Ariane' bears white flowers with a yellow center, 'Home Fires' bears pink flowers, 'Pink Ridge' has pale pink flowers, and 'Violet Vere' has violet flowers. Woodland phlox *(P. divaricata)* is a native plant hardy in Zones 4–8 bearing purple, pink or white blooms in spring.

MOSS PHLOX

Phlox subulata *FLAHKS subb-yew-LAT-ub*

Moss phlox brightens up the landscape in early summer.

ZONES: 2–8
SIZE: 6"h × 24"w
TYPE: Perennial
FORM: Spreading
TEXTURE: Medium
GROWTH: Fast
LIGHT: Full sun, partial shade

MOISTURE: Medium
SOIL: Fertile, well-drained
FEATURES: Flowers, foliage
USES: Ground cover
FLOWERS: ■ ■ □ ■

SITING: Moss phlox prefers full sun or dappled shade in the afternoon and fertile, well-drained soil with a pH of 5.5–7.5. Flowers appear from late spring to early summer. Evergreen foliage is bright green and hugs the ground. Lilies such as 'Ariadne,' 'Casa Blanca,' and 'Journey's End' grow through moss phlox foliage and bloom later in the season, making them good companions for moss phlox.

CARE: Plant 24" apart in spring. Apply slow-release granular plant food at time

of planting. Maintain moist, not soggy, soil. When the soil feels almost dry 2" below the surface, water deeply. Shear back after flowering to promote compact form. Foliage is evergreen, so there is no need to trim back in autumn unless it is disfigured by frost.

PROPAGATION: Layering in the landscape is the easiest form of propagation. Select a stem close to the ground and remove leaves to expose one or more nodes; pin nodes directly to the soil and cover with mulch. After roots form, cut the stem from the parent plant, leaving some top growth

attached to the new plant. Gently dig the new plant and replant, water, and mulch.

PESTS AND DISEASES: Spider mites are occasional pests.

RELATED SPECIES: The cultivar 'Apple Blossom' has lilac blooms with a purple center, 'Candy Stripe' bears white and pink flowers, 'Emerald Blue' has light blue flowers, 'Emerald Pink' has pink flowers, 'Fort Hill' has deep pink flowers, 'Red Wings' has bright red flowers with a darker center, and 'White Delight' has white flowers and light green leaves.

1

After bloom shear back moss phlox.

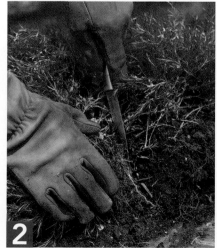

2

Divide moss phlox in spring or fall.

OBEDIENT PLANT

Physostegia virginiana *feye-soh-STEE-jee-uh vehr-jihn-ee-AY-nuh*

Obedient plant has moveable flowers that remain in position where they are placed.

ZONES: 3–8
SIZE: 4'h × 2'w
TYPE: Perennial
FORM: Upright
TEXTURE: Medium
GROWTH: Fast
LIGHT: Full sun to partial shade
MOISTURE: Medium

SOIL: Moderately fertile, moist, well-drained
FEATURES: Flowers, foliage
USES: Border, container
FLOWERS: ■□■

SITING: Obedient plant prefers morning sun and afternoon shade and moderately fertile, well-drained, moist soil with a pH of 5.5–7.0. If the soil is too fertile, plants may become invasive. Two-lipped purple, pink, or white flowers appear from midsummer to early autumn. Move the flowers on the stalk, and they obediently stay where placed. Plant in groups in borders or use in container plantings. Good companions for obedient plant include purple coneflower, 'Veitch's Blue' globe thistle, and hollyhock mallow.

CARE: Plant 18–24" apart in spring. Apply slow-release granular plant food at time of planting. Apply mulch in summer and

Pinch back obedient plant early in the season to promote compact, full growth.

winter. Water deeply when the soil is dry. Staking is not normally necessary when cultural requirements are met. If soil is too rich, excessive nitrogen is applied, or there is too little sun, foliage may become floppy. Trim back in fall once frost withers the foliage.

PROPAGATION: In moderately fertile soil, plants may be divided every 3 years to control growth. In rich soils division is needed sooner to maintain vigor and control growth. Dig around the rhizomes and lift. Use a sharp spade to slice through the root system. Reset portions that contain healthy roots and top shoots. Discard any pieces that do not contain both healthy roots and top shoots. Water deeply and apply 3" of vegetative mulch around, but not touching, the plants.

PESTS AND DISEASES: Plants are relatively pest free when cultural requirements (sun, soil, planting depth, moisture) are met.

RELATED SPECIES: The cultivar 'Alba' bears white flowers, 'Bouquet Rose' has pink flowers, 'Galadriel' has pale pink flowers and is dwarf, 'Morden Beauty' has pink flowers and willowlike leaves, 'Summer Snow' has white flowers, 'Variegata' has cream-rimmed leaves, and 'Vivid' bears deep vibrant pink flowers.

SMALL SOLOMON'S SEAL

Polygonatum biflorum *puhl-ihg-ih-NAY-tum bye-FLOR-um*

Small Solomon's seal has attractive flowers, stems and leaves, and berries.

ZONES: 3–9
SIZE: 36"h × 24"w
TYPE: Perennial
FORM: Upright
TEXTURE: Medium
GROWTH: Slow
LIGHT: Partial to full shade
MOISTURE: Medium

SOIL: Fertile, moist, well-drained
FEATURES: Foliage, flowers, fruit
USES: Border, woodland, container
FLOWERS: □
FALL COLOR: ■

SITING: Small Solomon's seal prefers full to partial shade, shelter from the afternoon sun, and fertile, well-drained, moist soil with a pH of 5.5–7.0. Small greenish-white flowers dangle from the leaf axils from late spring until midsummer. Dark black berries follow the flowers. Place in groups in woodland gardens, shade borders, or a mixed container planting. Good garden companions include 'Pictum' or 'Silver Falls' Japanese painted fern, 'Hillside Black Beauty' snakeroot, and 'Gold Standard' or 'Red October' hosta.

CARE: Plant 12–24" apart in spring or autumn in fertile soil high in organic matter. To increase organic matter, add 1–2" of compost to the planting bed and till in to a depth of 12–15". Apply slow-release granular plant food at time of planting or begin using water-soluble plant food 3 weeks after planting in spring. Cease feeding 6–8 weeks prior to first frost date. Maintain moist, not soggy, soil. When the soil feels almost dry 2" below the surface, water deeply. If using an irrigation system, maintain deep, infrequent waterings and avoid delivering a light sprinkle every day. Organic matter in the soil and mulch on the soil surface help retain soil moisture. Trim back in fall once frost withers the foliage.

PROPAGATION: Divide in spring or fall. Dig around the root clump and lift. Use a sharp spade to slice through the root system. Reset portions that contain healthy roots and top shoots. Discard any pieces that do not contain both roots and top shoots. Water deeply and apply 3" of vegetative mulch around, but not touching, the plants.

PESTS AND DISEASES: Plants are relatively pest free when cultural requirements (sun, soil, planting depth, moisture) are met.

RELATED SPECIES: Fragrant Solomon's seal (*P. odoratum*) has arching stems that reach 3' high and 2' wide. It bears pendant green-edged white flowers in late spring and early summer followed by black berries. Variegated forms are available. The cultivar 'Flore Pleno' bears double flowers, 'Gilt Edge' has gold-rimmed leaves, 'Grace Barker' bears striped creamy-white and green leaves, and 'Variegatum' has red stems early on and white-edge leaves.

CHRISTMAS FERN

Polystichum acrostichoides *pahl-ih-STIK-um ak-roh-stih-KOY-deez*

Christmas fern is a low-maintenance, hardy evergreen fern.

ZONES: 3–8
SIZE: 18"h × 36"w
TYPE: Perennial
FORM: Irregular
TEXTURE: Medium
GROWTH: Medium
LIGHT: Partial to full shade

MOISTURE: Medium
SOIL: Fertile, moist, well-drained
FEATURES: Foliage
USES: Border, woodland, container

SITING: Christmas fern prefers partial to full shade and fertile, moist, well-drained soil with a pH of 5.5–7.0. This evergreen low-maintenance fern has fronds that are narrow, lanceshaped, and deep green. Place in odd-numbered groups in woodland gardens, shade borders, or containers. Good companions include 'Frances Williams' hosta, goatsbeard, and dwarf Chinese astilbe.

CARE: Plant 24–36" apart in spring or autumn. Apply slow-release granular plant food at time of planting or begin using water-soluble plant food 3 weeks after planting in spring. Follow label directions for amount and frequency. Cease feeding 4–6 weeks prior to first frost date. Apply 3" of vegetative mulch in summer and winter to reduce weed seed germination, retain soil moisture, and keep soil temperatures stable. Water deeply when the soil is dry. Trim back damaged and dead fronds in early spring before new ones emerge.

PROPAGATION: Divide in spring. Dig around the rhizomes and lift. Use a sharp spade to slice through the root system. Reset portions that contain healthy roots and top shoots. Discard any pieces that do not contain both healthy roots and top shoots. Water deeply and apply 3" of vegetative mulch around, but not touching, the plants.

PESTS AND DISEASES: Plants are relatively pest free when their cultural requirements are met.

RELATED SPECIES: Hardy shield fern (*P. aculeatum*) is a European native hardy in Zones 3–6. It grows to 2' tall. Western sword fern (*P. munitum*) is hardy in Zones 3–8 and grows to 3'. Hedge fern (*P. setiferum*) grows 2–4' tall in Zones 6–9.

MOSS ROSE

Portulaca grandiflora *port-yoo-LAH-kuh grand-ih-FLOR-uh*

Moss rose provides nonstop color all summer long in hot, sunny, dry areas. It is also known as portulaca or rose moss.

ZONES: NA
SIZE: 6–8"h × 6–8"w
TYPE: Annual
FORM: Spreading
TEXTURE: Fine
GROWTH: Fast
LIGHT: Full sun
MOISTURE: Medium

SOIL: Moderately fertile, well-drained
FEATURES: Flowers, foliage
USES: Border, bedding, container
FLOWERS: ■☐■■ ■

SITING: Moss rose prefers full sun and moderately fertile, well-drained, even sandy soil with a pH of 6.5–7.5. Plants are relatively drought tolerant once established. Single and double bright rose, red, yellow, or white, sometimes striped, flowers appear in summer and open fully only in bright light. Red stems and succulent bright green leaves are additional assets. Place in odd-number groups in borders as ground cover, mass as bedding plants, or place in containers and allow stems to cascade over the sides. Good companions include heart-leaf bergenia, Russian sage, and 'Vivid' obedient plant.

CARE: Plant 6–8" apart in late spring. Apply slow-release granular plant food at time of planting. Plants that receive an abundance of water and high-nitrogen food may produce lush leaves yet few or no flowers. Provide new transplants with ample water; otherwise, water deeply only when the soil is dry 2–3" below the surface. Apply 2–3" of vegetative mulch around the plants in summer to reduce weed seed germination, hold moisture in the soil, and, as it decomposes, add organic matter to the soil. Deadhead spent blooms to encourage reblooming and prevent self-seeding. Remove plants just before first frost or right afterward. Cover bare soil with 3" of vegetative mulch during winter to preserve the topsoil.

PROPAGATION: Sprinkle seeds over the growing medium and leave uncovered, exposed to light. Thoroughly moisten and keep moist, not soggy, until seeds germinate. Germination occurs in 7–10 days at 75–80°F. Transplant 35–40 days after sowing. After transplanting, reduce the temperature to 65°F.

PESTS AND DISEASES: Diseases include black stem rot and white rust.

RELATED SPECIES: 'Afternoon Delight' is dwarf with large, double flowers in pink, white, orange, and red; 'Aztec Double' bears double red and gold flowers; Cloudbeater Hybrids have double red, gold, apricot, pink, and white flowers; Sundance Hybrids are semitrailing and bear large, semidouble or double flowers; Sundial Series cultivars have double flowers that open in lower light; and 'Swanlake' bears double white flowers.

Feed moss rose regularly with Miracle-Gro plant food to promote lush growth and prolific bloom.

POLYANTHUS PRIMROSE
Primula ×polyantha *PRIHM-yoo-luh pah-lee-ANN-thuh*

Polyanthus primrose flowers and leaves are attractive additions to moist gardens.

ZONES: 5–8
SIZE: 6–12"h × 8–12"w
TYPE: Perennial
FORM: Rounded
TEXTURE: Medium
GROWTH: Medium
LIGHT: Full sun to partial shade
MOISTURE: Medium to high

SOIL: Moderately fertile to fertile, well-drained
FEATURES: Flowers, foliage
USES: Border, woodland, container
FLOWERS: ■□■■ ■■

SITING: Polyanthus primrose prefers light shade in the afternoon and moderately fertile or fertile, well-drained soil with a pH of 5.5–7.0 Plants tolerate full sun if the soil is consistently moist (but not soggy). Bright pink, red, purple, yellow, or white flowers usually have a yellow center and appear in late spring or early summer. Rosettes of evergreen or semievergreen deep green leaves are heavily veined. Polyanthus primroses are old-fashioned favorites, comforting and nostalgic, often used in bouquets. Place in odd-numbered groups in woodland gardens, shade borders, or containers. Good companions include European wild ginger, 'Pictum' Japanese painted fern, and Lenten rose.

CARE: Plant 8–12" apart in spring or autumn. Apply slow-release granular plant food at time of planting. Follow label directions for amount and frequency. Cease feeding 6–8 weeks prior to first frost date. Apply 3" of vegetative mulch in summer and winter to reduce weed seed germination, retain soil moisture, and keep soil temperatures stable. Water deeply when the soil is dry. Remove damaged or brown leaves in spring before new ones appear.

PROPAGATION: Divide in spring right after flowering or in early autumn. Dig around the root clump and lift. Use a sharp spade to slice through the root system. Reset portions that contain healthy roots and top shoots. Discard any pieces that do not contain both healthy roots and top shoots. Water deeply and apply 3" of vegetative mulch around, but not touching, the plants. To start indoors, sprinkle seeds over the growing medium and leave uncovered, exposed to light. Thoroughly moisten and keep moist, not soggy, until seeds germinate. Germination occurs in 21–28 days at 60–65°F. Transplant in 40–45 days. After transplanting, reduce temperature to 55°F. If temperatures are too warm, flower stalks may be short and hidden in the foliage.

PESTS AND DISEASES: Diseases include botrytis, root rot, rust, and leaf spot. Occasional pests include slugs, aphids, and spider mites.

RELATED SPECIES: Polyanthus primroses are complex hybrids of common cowslip (*P. veris*), English primrose (see below), and Julian primrose (*P. juliae*). All require moist soil and prefer cool temperatures.

ENGLISH PRIMROSE
Primula vulgaris *PRIHM-yoo-luh vuhl-GAR-ihs*

English primrose blooms, in bright colors, are delightful in spring.

ZONES: 4–8
SIZE: 8–10"h × 15"w
TYPE: Perennial
FORM: Rounded
TEXTURE: Medium
GROWTH: Medium
LIGHT: Partial shade
MOISTURE: Medium to high

SOIL: Fertile, moist, well-drained
FEATURES: Flowers, foliage
USES: Border, woodland, container
FLOWERS: ■■□ ■■

SITING: English primrose prefers partial shade and fertile, well-drained soil with a pH of 5.5–7.0. Plants tolerate full sun, even southern heat, if the soil is consistently moist and deep and contains ample organic matter. Clusters of fragrant flowers appear in late spring or early summer. Cultivars are shades of white, yellow, pink, purple, and red. Rosettes of evergreen or semievergreen leaves are heavily veined and are bright glossy green. Plant in the old-fashioned cottage garden, the shade border, at the feet of shrubs, or in a container. Place in odd-number groups for best effect. Good companions for English primrose include peony, false indigo, and heart-leaf bergenia.

CARE: Plant 12–15" apart in spring or autumn. Apply slow-release granular plant food in spring. Follow label directions for amount and frequency. Water deeply when the soil is dry. Apply 3" of vegetative mulch in summer and winter to reduce weed seed germination, retain soil moisture, and keep soil temperatures stable. Remove damaged or brown leaves in spring before new ones emerge.

PROPAGATION: Divide right after flowering. Dig around the root clump and lift. Use a sharp spade to slice through the root system. Reset portions that contain healthy roots and top shoots. Discard any pieces that do not contain both healthy roots and top shoots. Water deeply and apply 3" of vegetative mulch around, but not touching, the plants.

PESTS AND DISEASES: Slugs and snails are common pests. Diseases include botrytis, root rot, rust, and leaf spot.

RELATED SPECIES: The cultivar 'Cottage White' has double white flowers on long stalks; 'Double Sulphur' bears double yellow flowers; 'Jack-in-the-Green' has pale yellow flowers and a green ruff; 'Marie Crousse' bears large, double violet flowers marked with white; and 'Miss Indigo' has double purple flowers rimmed in white. English primrose is one of the parents in the hybrid species polyanthus primrose (*P. ×polyantha*, see above). Other European native primroses include common cowslip (*P. veris*) and auricula primrose (*P. auricula*) with yellow or red flowers with yellow centers, for Zones 2–8. The drumstick primrose (*P. denticulata*) bears purple or white globelike heads on plants 12" tall. It is hardy in Zones 4–8. Japanese primrose (*P. japonica*) is a Candelabra type for Zones 5–7. The name derives from the whorls of flowers stacked on each flowering stem.

BETHLEHEM SAGE
Pulmonaria saccharata *pul-mohn-AR-ee-uh sahk-uh-RAH-tuh*

Bethlehem sage has violet flowers and attractive silver-splashed leaves. It is also known as lungwort or pulmonaria.

ZONES: 3–8
SIZE: 15"h × 24"w
TYPE: Perennial
FORM: Spreading
TEXTURE: Medium
GROWTH: Slow
LIGHT: Partial to full shade
MOISTURE: Medium

SOIL: Fertile, moist, well-drained
FEATURES: Flowers, foliage
USES: Border, woodland, container
FLOWERS: ■□■
FALL COLOR: ■

SITING: Bethlehem sage prefers partial to full shade and fertile, well-drained, moist soil with a pH of 5.5–7.0. Plants do not tolerate wet soil. Funnel-shaped flowers in shades of violet and sometimes white appear from early spring through early summer. Evergreen leaves are silver splotched and occasionally dusted in silver. Place in groups at the front of shade borders, in woodland gardens, or in containers. Good companions include 'Frances Williams' hosta, 'Elegans' Siebold hosta, heart-leaf brunnera, and fringe-leaf bleeeding heart.

CARE: Plant 15–18" apart in spring or autumn. Apply slow-release granular plant

Plant Bethlehem sage in partial or full shade and provide it with adequate moisture.

food. Apply 3" of organic mulch around the plants in summer and winter. Water deeply when the soil is dry. Remove brown or damaged foliage in early spring before new growth appears. Cut it back after flowering if foliage looks tattered.

PROPAGATION: Divide after flowering or in autumn every 3 years to maintain vigor. Dig around the root clump and lift. Use a sharp spade to slice through the root system. The larger the portion, the larger the resulting plant during the first year. Smaller pieces may take 2–3 years to reach mature size and bloom. Reset portions that contain healthy roots and top shoots.

PESTS AND DISEASES: Plants are relatively pest free when cultural requirements (sun, soil, planting depth, moisture) are met. Slugs and powdery mildew are occasional problems on Bethlehem sage.

RELATED SPECIES: The cultivar 'Alba' has large white flowers and silver-splashed leaves; 'Argentea' has silver-dusted leaves; 'Janet Fisk' bears pink flowers that turn blue and has silver-spotted leaves; and 'Mrs. Moon' has pink buds that open to blue flowers and heavily silver-splashed leaves.

RODGERSIA
Rodgersia pinnata *rohd-JEHR-zee-uh pihn-AY-tuh*

Rodgersia has star-shaped flowers in mid- to late summer. It is also known as featherleaf rodgersia or Roger's flower.

ZONES: 4–7
SIZE: 4'h × 3'w
TYPE: Perennial
FORM: Rounded
TEXTURE: Coarse
GROWTH: Medium
LIGHT: Partial shade to full sun

MOISTURE: Medium
SOIL: Fertile, well-drained
FEATURES: Flowers, foliage
USES: Border, woodland, wetland
FLOWERS: ■□

SITING: Rodgersia tolerates partial shade to full sun and prefers fertile, well-drained, moist soil with a pH of 5.5–7.0. Plants in full sun require consistently moist soil; partial shade locations may have drier soils. Panicles of star-shaped pink, reddish, or occasionally white flowers appear from mid- to late summer. Place in groups in the border or naturalize along the edge of a woodland. Good companions include hybrid anemone, 'The Rocket' ligularia, and royal fern.

CARE: Plant 24–36" apart in spring or autumn. Apply slow-release granular plant food. When the soil feels dry 2" below the surface, water deeply. Apply 3" of

Plants in full sun require more frequent waterings than plants in part shade.

vegetative mulch in summer and winter to reduce weed seed germination, retain soil moisture, and keep soil temperatures stable. Deadhead spent blooms to encourage reblooming. Prune back in fall once frost withers the foliage.

PROPAGATION: Divide in spring. Dig around the root clump and lift. Use a sharp spade to slice through the root system. Reset portions that contain healthy roots and top shoots. Water deeply and apply 3" of organic mulch around, but not touching, the plants.

PESTS AND DISEASES: Plants are relatively pest free when cultural requirements (sun, soil, planting depth, moisture) are met. Slugs are occasional problems.

RELATED SPECIES: The cultivar 'Alba' bears white flowers; 'Elegans' has pink-stained cream flowers; 'Rosea' bears rose flowers; 'Rubra' has deep red flowers; and 'Superba' has bronze-stained young leaves and bright pink flowers. Roger's flower (*R. aescufolia*) reaches 3–6' tall and bears star-shaped white or pink flowers in midsummer. Leaves grow up to 10" long and are deeply veined; leaves and stalks are red stained.

BLACK-EYED SUSAN

Rudbeckia fulgida *rud-BEHK-ee-uh FUHL-jih-duh*

Black-eyed Susan flowers attract butterflies and are excellent fresh cut flowers. The plant is also known as orange coneflower.

ZONES: 4–9
SIZE: 36"h × 18"w
TYPE: Perennial
FORM: Upright
TEXTURE: Medium
GROWTH: Medium
LIGHT: Full sun
MOISTURE: Medium
SOIL: Moderately fertile, well-drained
FEATURES: Flowers, foliage
USES: Border, container
FLOWERS: ■

SITING: Black-eyed Susan prefers full sun and moderately fertile, well-drained soil with a pH of 5.5–7.0. Daisylike yellow flowers with a mahogany brown disk appear from late summer through

midautumn. Plants are welcome additions to full-sun perennial borders and containers. Flowers attract butterflies and bees and are excellent fresh cut. Place in groups for best effect. Good companions include 'Snowbank' white boltonia, purple coneflower, and 'Autumn Joy' sedum.

CARE: Plant 18–24" apart in spring or autumn. Apply slow-release granular plant

Remove faded flower stalks of black-eyed Susan to encourage reblooming.

food at time of planting. Water deeply when the soil is dry. If soil is too rich, excessive nitrogen is applied, or there is too little sun, foliage may become floppy. Staking is not normally necessary when cultural requirements are met. Apply 3" of vegetative mulch in summer and winter. Deadhead spent blooms to encourage reblooming. Prune back in fall once frost withers the foliage.

PROPAGATION: Divide in spring or autumn every 3 years to maintain vigor. Dig around the root clump and lift. Use a sharp spade to slice through the root system. Reset portions that contain healthy roots and top shoots. Discard any pieces that do not contain both healthy roots and top shoots. Water deeply and apply 3" of organic mulch around the plants.

PESTS AND DISEASES: Slugs, powdery mildew, and rust are occasional pests.

RELATED SPECIES: *R. fulgida* var. *deamii* reaches 24" high, is relatively drought tolerant, and produces many flowers over an extended time. Var. *sullivantii* 'Goldsturm' reaches 24" high, is compact, bears large golden-yellow flowers, and is low maintenance.

GLORIOSA DAISY

Rudbeckia hirta *rud-BEHK-ee-uh HER-tuh*

Gloriosa daisy self-seeds well in the garden.

ZONES: 4–9
SIZE: 12–36"h × 18"w
TYPE: Perennial
FORM: Upright
TEXTURE: Medium
GROWTH: Medium
LIGHT: Full sun
MOISTURE: Medium
SOIL: Moderately fertile, well-drained
FEATURES: Flowers, foliage
USES: Border, naturalizing, container
FLOWERS: ■ ■

SITING: Gloriosa daisy prefers full sun and fertile, well-drained soil with a pH of 5.5–7.0. Plants are short-lived perennials commonly grown an annuals. Daisylike yellow flowers with a mahogany disk appear from summer to early autumn.

Flowers attract butterflies and are excellent fresh cut. Plants self-seed and perform well in sunny wildflower gardens, borders, and container plantings. Good companions for gloriosa daisy include 'Snowbank' white boltonia, tall cosmos, and 'Rotfuchs' spike speedwell.

CARE: Plant 18" apart in late spring. Apply slow-release granular plant food at time of

Transplant self-sown seedlings of gloriosa daisy to a new location where you would like the plants to grow.

planting. Water deeply when the soil is dry. If soil is too rich, excessive nitrogen is applied, or there is too little sun, foliage may become floppy. Apply 3" of vegetative mulch in summer. Deadhead spent blooms to encourage reblooming. Remove plants just before the first frost or right afterward.

PROPAGATION: Sprinkle seed over the growing medium and cover or leave uncovered. Thoroughly moisten and keep moist, not soggy, until seeds germinate. Germination occurs in 5–10 days at 70°F. Transplant 20–28 days after sowing. After transplanting, reduce temperature to 50°F.

PESTS AND DISEASES: Slugs, powdery mildew, and rust are occasional problems.

RELATED SPECIES: The cultivar 'Bambi' reaches 12" high and bears multicolored flowers of yellow, brown, and bronze; 'Goldilocks' reaches 24" high and has double and semidouble yellow-orange flowers; 'Irish Eyes' reaches 24" high and bears bright yellow flowers with a green disk; 'Marmalade' reaches 18", is compact, and has deep yellow flowers; 'Rustic Dwarfs' reach 24" high and has brownish, yellow and bicolored flowers; and 'Superba' has yellow and maroon flowers.

MEALY-CUP SAGE

Salvia farinacea SAHL-vee-uh far-ih-NAY-see-uh

Mealy-cup sage produces spikes of purple blossoms in summer.

ZONES: 8–10
SIZE: 18–24"h × 12"w
TYPE: Perennial
FORM: Upright
TEXTURE: Fine
GROWTH: Fast
LIGHT: Full sun

MOISTURE: Medium
SOIL: Moderately fertile, well-drained
FEATURES: Flowers, foliage
USES: Border, container
FLOWERS: ■□

SITING: Mealy-cup sage prefers full sun and moderately fertile, well-drained soil with a pH of 5.5–7.0. Plants are commonly grown as annuals. Spikes of two-lipped purple flowers appear from summer though autumn. Hairy white stems bear glossy medium green leaves. Cultivars have a tidy appearance and an abundance of blooms. Plant in odd-numbered groups in borders, mass as an annual ground cover, or place in container plantings. Good companions include gulf muhly, silver sage, and 'Silver Carpet' lamb's-ears.

CARE: Plant 6–12" apart in late spring. Apply slow-release granular plant food at time of planting, or begin using water-soluble plant food 3 weeks after planting. Follow label directions for amount and frequency. Apply 3" of vegetative mulch in summer to reduce weed seed germination, hold moisture in the soil, and as it decomposes, add organic matter to the soil. Water deeply when the soil is dry. Deadhead spent blooms to encourage reblooming. Remove plants after the first frost when foliage is disfigured. Cover bare soil with 3" of vegetative mulch during winter to preserve topsoil.

PROPAGATION: Sprinkle seeds over the growing medium and leave uncovered, exposed to light. Thoroughly moisten and keep moist, not soggy, until seeds germinate. Germination occurs in 12–15 days at 75–78°F. Transplant 14–21 days after sowing. Reduce the temperature to 60°F after transplanting.

PESTS AND DISEASES: Diseases include powdery mildew, rust, stem rot, and fungal leaf spots.

RELATED SPECIES: The cultivar 'Alba' has white flowers, 'Blue Bedder' is compact and bears deep blue flowers, 'Rhea' is compact with vibrant deep blue flowers, 'Silver' bears silvery-white flowers, 'Strata' has blue flowers with a white calyx, and 'Victoria' bears many deep blue flowers. Scarlet sage (*S. splendens*) is a perennial commonly grown as an annual and reaches 10–15" high. Plants produce spikes of tubular red flowers throughout the summer. Cultivars come in red, blue, orange, pink, mauve, and white.

Scarlet sage (*Salvia splendens*) bears blooms in red-hot colors all summer long.

Some cultivars of scarlet sage bear colorful bracts of pink, purple, or white instead of the more common red form.

PERENNIAL SALVIA

Salvia ×superba SAHL-vee-uh soo-PEHR-buh

Perennial salvia, also known as hybrid sage, produces attractive purple blooms.

ZONES: 5–9
SIZE: 24–36"h × 18–24"w
TYPE: Perennial
FORM: Upright
TEXTURE: Medium
GROWTH: Medium
LIGHT: Full sun
MOISTURE: Medium
SOIL: Moderately fertile, well-drained
FEATURES: Flowers, foliage
USES: Border, container
FLOWERS: ■

SITING: Perennial salvia prefers full sun and moderately fertile, well-drained soil with a pH of 5.5–7.0. Spikes of violet or purple flowers appear from midsummer though early autumn. Plant in groups in borders or place in container plantings. Good companions include baby's breath, gulf muhly, and 'Rotfuchs' spike speedwell.

CARE: Plant 18" apart in spring or fall. Apply slow-release granular plant food in spring. Cease feeding 6–8 weeks prior to first frost date. Apply 3" of vegetative mulch in summer and winter to reduce weed seed germination, hold moisture in the soil, and as it decomposes, add organic

Deadhead spent flowers to encourage reblooming.

matter to the soil. Water deeply when the soil is dry. Deadhead spent blooms to encourage reblooming. Shear back after flowering to encourage another flush of flowers. Prune back in fall once frost withers the foliage.

PROPAGATION: Divide in spring every 3 years to maintain vigor. Dig around the root clump and lift. Use a sharp spade to slice through the root system. Reset portions that contain healthy roots and top shoots. Discard any pieces that do not contain both healthy roots and top shoots. Water deeply and apply 3" of organic mulch around the plants.

PESTS AND DISEASES: Diseases include powdery mildew, rust, stem rot, and fungal leaf spot.

RELATED SPECIES: Common sage (*S. officinalis*) has several cultivars, hardy to Zones 7 and 8, that enhance the perennial border or container: 'Aurea' reaches 12" high and bears golden-yellow leaves; 'Berggarten' is compact, reaches 24" high, and has pebbly green leaves; 'Icterina' has variegated green-and-gold leaves; 'Purpurescens' has greenish-red leaves; and 'Tricolor' has blue-green leaves stained cream and pink.

LAVENDER COTTON

Santolina chamaecyparissus san-tuh-LEE-nah kam-uh-SIP-uh-rih-suhs

Silvery foliage and button-shaped yellow flowers are the main attractions of lavender cotton in the perennial border or container.

ZONES: 6–9
SIZE: 24"h × 36"w
TYPE: Perennial
FORM: Upright
TEXTURE: Fine
GROWTH: Medium
LIGHT: Full sun
MOISTURE: Medium
SOIL: Moderately fertile, well-drained
FEATURES: Flowers, foliage
USES: Border, container
FLOWERS: ■

SITING: Lavender cotton prefers full sun and moderately fertile, well-drained soil with a pH of 5.5–7.0. Plants are subshrubs

and develop a woody base. Buttonlike golden-yellow flowers to ½" across appear in mid- and late summer. Silver-green leaves are evergreen and aromatic. Place in odd-numbered groups in borders, or use in container plantings. Good companions include 'Silver Mound' artemesia, silver sage, and 'Silver Carpet' lamb's-ears; or *Liatris spicata* 'Snow Queen,' 'David' garden phlox, and 'Iceberg' rose.

CARE: Plant 18–24" apart in spring or autumn. Apply slow-release granular plant food. Cease feeding 6–8 weeks prior to first frost date. Apply 3" of vegetative mulch in summer to reduce weed seed germination, retain soil moisture, and keep soil temperatures stable. Deadhead spent blooms to encourage reblooming. Water deeply when the soil is dry.

PROPAGATION: Seed-grown plants flower during the second year of growth. Sprinkle seeds over the growing medium and leave uncovered, exposed to light, or cover lightly. Thoroughly moisten and keep moist, not soggy, until seeds germinate. Germination occurs in 5–10 days at 72°F.

Transplant 18–25 days after sowing. After transplanting, reduce temperature to 62°F. In summer take cuttings from new growth. Cut pieces that contain at least two or three healthy leaves and three nodes. Dip exposed nodes into rooting hormone, shake off excess, and insert into moist soil mix, keeping leaves well above the soil level. Supply bottom heat and keep moist, not soggy, until root and top shoot growth is evident, usually in 2–3 weeks, then transplant. To enhance humidity, cover with plastic and hold it above the leaves.

PESTS AND DISEASES: Plants are relatively pest free when cultural requirements (sun, soil, planting depth, moisture) are met.

RELATED SPECIES: Green lavender cotton (*S. rosmarinifolia* syn. *S. virens*) reaches 24" high and is winter hardy in Zones 6–9. Plants are heat tolerant and pest resistant. Buttonlike bright or pale yellow flowers appear atop slender stems in mid- and late summer. The finely textured foliage is fragrant. Plants are neat and attractive in and out of bloom.

CREEPING ZINNIA
Sanvitalia procumbens *san-vih-TAHL-yuh pro-KUHM-bens*

Creeping zinnia flowers well in heat, humidity, and drought.

ZONES: NA
SIZE: 8–10"h × 18"w
TYPE: Annual
FORM: Spreading
TEXTURE: Fine
GROWTH: Fast
LIGHT: Full sun
MOISTURE: Medium

SOIL: Moderately fertile, well-drained
FEATURES: Flowers, foliage
USES: Border, ground cover, container
FLOWERS: ■■□

SITING: Creeping zinnia prefers full sun and moderately fertile, well-drained soil with a pH of 5.5–7.0. Plants are tough and durable, tolerating heat, drought, and humidity. Creeping stems bear zinnialike single bright yellow flowers with a dark chocolate disk in summer. Leaves are tiny, oval, and medium green. Use as a ground cover in a sunny border or allow to cascade from container plantings. Good container companions include flowering kale, 'Moonbeam' threadleaf coreopsis, and 'Purpurascens' sage.

CARE: Plant 12–18" apart in late spring. Apply slow-release granular plant food at time of planting or begin using water-soluble plant food 3 weeks after planting. Follow label directions for amount and frequency. Water deeply when the soil is dry. Apply 3" of vegetative mulch in summer to reduce weed seed germination, retain soil moisture, and keep soil cool. Deadhead spent blooms to encourage reblooming. Remove plants just before first frost or right afterward when foliage is disfigured. Cover bare soil with 3" of vegetative mulch during winter to preserve topsoil.

PROPAGATION: Sprinkle seeds over the growing medium and cover lightly. Thoroughly moisten and keep moist, not soggy, until seeds germinate. Germination occurs in 7–10 days at 70°F. Transplant 12–15 days after sowing. Reduce the temperature to 60°F after transplanting.

PESTS AND DISEASES: Plants are relatively pest free when cultural requirements (sun, soil, planting depth, moisture) are met.

RELATED SPECIES: The cultivar 'Gold Braid' is dwarf with double gold flowers and a brown disk, 'Golden Carpet' is dwarf with orange-tinted flowers and a black disk, 'Mandarin Orange' is dwarf with vibrant orange flowers and a black disk, and 'Yellow Carpet' is dwarf with small single pale yellow flowers and a black disk.

SOAPWORT
Saponaria ocymoides *sap-oh-NAR-ee-uh os-ih-MOY-deez*

Soapwort or rock soapwort spreads fast and has pink flowers in late spring and summer.

ZONES: 3–8
SIZE: 4"h × 18"w
TYPE: Perennial
FORM: Spreading
TEXTURE: Medium
GROWTH: Fast
LIGHT: Full sun
MOISTURE: Medium

SOIL: Moderately fertile, well-drained
FEATURES: Flowers, foliage
USES: Border, ground cover, container
FLOWERS: ■□

SITING: Soapwort prefers full sun and moderately fertile, well-drained soil with a pH of 5.5–7.0. Certain cultivars have a compact, neat habit, whereas the species tends to grow with great vigor and exuberance. Plants hug the ground and produce a profusion of five-petal bright pink flowers in late spring and summer. Leaves are bright green and hairy. Place in groups in borders to serve as ground cover to other perennials or use to spill over the edge of containers. Good companions include white gaura, 'Bruno' Helen's flower, and rosemary lavender cotton (*Santolina rosmarinifolia*).

CARE: Plant 12–24" apart in late spring. Apply slow-release granular plant food at time of planting. Cease feeding 6–8 weeks prior to first frost date. Soapwort plants may overwhelm their neighbors if the soil is too fertile. Apply 3" of vegetative mulch in summer and winter to reduce weed seed germination, retain soil moisture, and keep soil temperatures stable. Water deeply when the soil is dry. Shear back after first flowering to encourage compact habit. Deadhead spent blooms to encourage reblooming. Plants freely self-seed in the landscape. Prune back in fall once frost withers the foliage.

PROPAGATION: In moderately fertile soil plants may be divided in spring or autumn every 3 years to maintain vigor. In rich soils division is needed sooner to maintain vigor and control growth.

PESTS AND DISEASES: Plants are relatively pest free when cultural requirements (sun, soil, planting depth, moisture) are met.

RELATED SPECIES: The cultivar 'Alba' bears white flowers and grows more slowly than the species, 'Bressingham' has bright pink flowers and compact growth, 'Rubra Compacta' has deep red flowers and is compact, and 'Versicolor' bears rose flowers that open white.

Shear soapwort back after first flowering is complete to encourage rebloom.

Plants 2–4 weeks after being sheared exhibit attractive, compact regrowth.

SCABIOUS
Scabiosa columbaria *skab-ee-O-suh kohl-uhm-BAR-ee-uh*

Scabious is a low-maintenance perennial with long-season blooms. It is also known as pincushion flower or scabiosa.

ZONES: 5–8
SIZE: 24"h × 30"w
TYPE: Perennial
FORM: Rounded
TEXTURE: Fine
GROWTH: Medium
LIGHT: Full sun
MOISTURE: Medium

SOIL: Moderately fertile, well-drained
FEATURES: Flowers, foliage
USES: Border, container
FLOWERS: ■■

SITING: Scabious prefers full sun and moderately fertile, well-drained soil with a pH of 6.5–7.5. Each wiry stem bears a violet-blue flower that resembles a pincushion from summer into early autumn. Plants are heat tolerant and pest resistant. They bloom on and off all winter in the South. Plant in odd-numbered groups in borders or use in container plantings. Good companions include 'Taplow Blue' globe thistle, white gaura, 'Kobold' blazing star, and 'Alba Meidiland' rose.

CARE: Plant 18–24" apart in spring or autumn. Apply slow-release granular plant

Deadhead scabious to reduce self-seeding and to encourage reblooming.

food in spring. Cease feeding 6–8 weeks prior to first frost date. Apply 3" of vegetative mulch in summer and winter to reduce weed seed germination, retain soil moisture, and keep soil temperatures stable. Water deeply when the soil is dry. Deadhead spent blooms to encourage reblooming. Plants lightly self-seed in the landscape. Prune back in fall once frost withers the foliage or leave erect in warmer zones for winter viewing and occasional flowering.

PROPAGATION: In moderately fertile soil plants may be divided in spring every 3 years to maintain vigor. Dig around the root clump and lift. Use a sharp spade to slice through the root system. Reset portions that contain healthy roots and top shoots. Discard any pieces that do not contain both healthy roots and top shoots. Water deeply and apply 3" of organic mulch around the plants.

PESTS AND DISEASES: Plants are relatively pest free when cultural requirements (sun, soil, planting depth, moisture) are met.

RELATED SPECIES: The cultivar 'Butterfly Blue' has purplish-blue flowers in midsummer, and 'Pink Mist' bears purplish-pink flowers in midsummer.

FAN FLOWER
Scaevola aemula *skuh-VOL-uh AY-myoo-luh*

Fan flower is a superb landscape plant for warm climates. It is also known as scaevola.

ZONES: NA
SIZE: 6–18"h × 18"w
TYPE: Annual
FORM: Spreading
TEXTURE: Fine
GROWTH: Medium
LIGHT: Full sun to partial shade

MOISTURE: Medium
SOIL: Moderately fertile, moist, well-drained
FEATURES: Flowers, foliage
USES: Border, container
FLOWERS: ■□

SITING: Fan flower prefers full sun or light afternoon shade and moderately fertile, well-drained, moist soil with a pH of 5.5–7.0. Plants are usually grown as annuals. Purplish-blue flowers appear in summer. Leaves are evergreen and spoon shaped. Plants are excellent annual ground cover in perennial or shrub borders and add spillover charm to containers. Plant in odd-numbered groups for best effect. Companions include 'Purpureum' purple fountain grass, 'Andenken an Friedrich Hahn' beard tongue, and 'Miss Willmott' pincushion flower.

Pinch fan flower in spring to promote branching and compact habit.

CARE: Plant 12–18" apart in late spring. Apply slow-release granular plant food at time of planting. Apply vegetative mulch in summer. Water deeply when the soil is dry. Trim back new growth by one-third in late spring to encourage branching. Deadhead spent blooms to encourage reblooming. Remove plants just before first frost or right afterward when foliage is disfigured. Cover bare soil with 3" of vegetative mulch during winter to preserve topsoil.

PROPAGATION: In spring take cuttings from new growth. Cut pieces that contain at least two healthy leaves and three nodes. Dip exposed nodes into rooting hormone, shake off excess, and insert into moist growing medium, keeping leaves well above the soil level. Supply bottom heat and keep moist, not soggy, until root and top shoot growth is evident, usually in 2–3 weeks, then transplant. To enhance humidity, cover with plastic and hold it above the leaves.

PESTS AND DISEASES: Plants are relatively pest free when cultural requirements are met. Spider mites are an occasional problem during hot, dry periods.

GOLDMOSS STONECROP

Sedum acre SEE-duhm AY-kehr

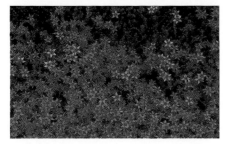

Goldmoss stonecrop, also known as sedum, is a fast-spreading ground cover with star-shaped yellow flowers.

ZONES: 3–9
SIZE: 24"h × 24"w
TYPE: Perennial
FORM: Spreading
TEXTURE: Fine
GROWTH: Fast
LIGHT: Full sun
MOISTURE: Medium to low

SOIL: Moderately fertile, well-drained
FEATURES: Flowers, foliage
USES: Border, ground cover, container
FLOWERS: ■

SITING: Goldmoss stonecrop prefers full sun and moderately fertile, well-drained soil with a pH of 6.5–7.3. Plants are invasive in fertile conditions but may be slowed slightly by providing light afternoon shade. They are also drought tolerant once established. Flat-topped clusters of tiny, star shaped yellowish-green flowers appear in summer. Use as a ground cover in rock gardens or as spillover plants in containers. Good companions include rue, rosemary lavender cotton, and 'Autumn Joy' sedum.

CARE: Plant 18–24" apart in spring or fall. Apply slow-release granular plant food in spring. Water only when the soil is dry 2–3" below the surface.

PROPAGATION: In summer take cuttings from new growth. Cut pieces that contain at least two or three healthy leaves and

1 Take cuttings of sedum in summer.

2 Stick cuttings into growing medium.

three nodes. Plant directly in the garden where new plants are desired. Seed germination occurs in 7–14 days when daytime temperatures are 85°F and nighttime temperatures are 70°F. Transplant 20–30 days after sowing seed. After transplanting, reduce temperature to 60°F.

PESTS AND DISEASES: Plants are relatively pest free except for slugs and snails.

RELATED SPECIES: The cultivar 'Aureum' has variegated yellow leaves, 'Elegans' has silver-striped leaf tips, and 'Minor' is only 1" high. Two-row stonecrop (*S. spurium*) cultivars are popular, vigorous ground covers that reach 4" high: 'Atropurpureum' has burgundy leaves and rose-red flowers, 'Bronze Carpet' has bronze-stained leaves and pink flowers, 'Erdblut' has crimson-tipped green leaves and red flowers, 'Fuldaglut' has bronze-stained leaves and maroon flowers, 'Golden Carpet' has light green leaves and yellow flowers, 'Red Carpet' has red-stained leaves and red flowers, 'Schorbuser Blut' ('Dragon's Blood') leaves age to burgundy and flowers are dark pink, and 'Tricolor' has cream-, green-, and pink-splashed leaves and pink flowers.

AUTUMN JOY SEDUM

Sedum × 'Autumn Joy' (*Hylotelephium* × 'Herbstfreude') SEE-duhm (high-loh-tel-EE-fee-um)

Mulch enhances 'Autumn Joy' sedum, a superb low-maintenance perennial.

ZONES: 3–10
SIZE: 24"h × 24"w
TYPE: Perennial
FORM: Upright
TEXTURE: Medium
GROWTH: Medium
LIGHT: Full sun
MOISTURE: Medium

SOIL: Moderately fertile, well-drained
FEATURES: Flowers, foliage
USES: Border, container
FLOWERS: ■

SITING: Autumn Joy sedum prefers full sun and moderately fertile, well-drained soil with a pH of 6.5–7.3. Flowers first turn pink in mid- to late summer, then rose-red, then deep brown-burgundy in late autumn. Flowers attract bees and butterflies. Good companions include purple coneflower, 'Shenandoah' switchgrass, fountain grass, and 'Color Guard' yucca.

CARE: Plant 18–24" apart in spring or fall. Apply slow-release granular plant food in spring. Apply 3" of vegetative mulch in

Autumn Joy sedum attracts butterflies late in the season when it is in bloom.

summer and winter. Water deeply when the soil is dry. In moderately fertile soil plants must be divided every 3 years to maintain form and vigor. In rich soils division is needed sooner. It is required when stems emerging in spring flop to the ground. Lack of sun also causes foliar flopping. Prune back in fall or leave erect for winter viewing.

PROPAGATION: Dig around the root clump and lift. Use a sharp spade to slice through the root system. The larger the portion, the larger the resulting plant during the first year. Smaller pieces may take 2–3 years to reach mature size and bloom. Reset portions that contain healthy roots and top shoots. Discard the center portion if it is dead. Water deeply and apply 3" of vegetative mulch around, but not touching, the plants.

PESTS AND DISEASES: Plants are relatively pest free when cultural requirements (sun, soil, planting depth, moisture) are met.

RELATED SPECIES: *S.* 'Ruby Glow' reaches 12" high and 18" wide and has red stems, bronze-stained deciduous green leaves, and ruby-red flowers from midsummer to early fall.

DUSTY MILLER

Senecio cineraria *sebn-EE-see-ob sibn-er-AR-ee-ub*

Dusty miller provides delightful silver foliage that complements pink or purple annuals and perennials.

ZONES: 8–10
SIZE: 12–24"h × 12–24"w
TYPE: Perennial
FORM: Rounded
TEXTURE: Medium
GROWTH: Medium
LIGHT: Full sun
MOISTURE: Medium

SOIL: Moderately fertile, well-drained
FEATURES: Flowers, foliage
USES: Border, ground cover, container
FLOWERS: ■

SITING: Dusty miller prefers full sun and moderately fertile, well-drained soil with a pH of 5.5–7.0. Yellow flowers appear during the second year of growth but are rarely seen because the plants are usually grown as annuals. Place in groups among brightly colored plants; use in moon gardens, where silver and white foliage is attractive when viewed by moonlight; mass as a ground cover; or plant in containers. Good companions include cockscomb, torch lily, and 'Vivid' obedient plant.
CARE: Plant 6–12" apart in late spring. Apply slow-release granular plant food at

Plant dusty miller between brightly colored annuals or perennials to soften their effect.

time of planting. Apply 3" of vegetative mulch in summer to reduce weed seed germination, hold moisture in the soil, and as it decomposes, add organic matter to the soil. Water deeply when the soil is dry. Remove plants just before first frost or right afterward when foliage is disfigured. Cover bare soil with 3" of vegetative mulch during winter to preserve topsoil.
PROPAGATION: Sprinkle seeds over the growing medium and leave exposed to light; do not cover. Thoroughly moisten and keep moist, not soggy, until seeds germinate. Germination occurs in 10–15 days at 72°F. Transplant in 20–25 days. After transplanting, reduce the temperature to 62°F.
PESTS AND DISEASES: Rust is common.
RELATED SPECIES: The cultivar 'Alice' has deeply cut silver-white-stained foliage, 'Cirrus' has rounded bright silver leaves and is dwarf, 'New Look' has lobed pure white leaves, 'Silverdust' has lacy silver-dusted leaves, 'Silver Filigree' has gray leaves, 'Silver Queen' is compact and has silvery-white leaves, and 'White Diamond' has silver-gray leaves.

NARROW-LEAF BLUE-EYED GRASS

Sisyrinchium angustifolium *sis-ib-RINK-ee-ubm an-gust-ib-FOHL-ee-ubm*

Narrow-leaf blue-eyed grass shows delicate blue blossoms in spring.

ZONES: 5–8
SIZE: 18–22"h × 6–12"w
TYPE: Perennial
FORM: Upright
TEXTURE: Fine
GROWTH: Medium
LIGHT: Full sun

MOISTURE: Medium
SOIL: Moderately fertile, well-drained
FEATURES: Flowers, foliage
USES: Border, container
FLOWERS: ■

SITING: Narrow-leaf blue-eyed grass prefers full sun and moderately fertile, well-drained soil with a pH of 6.5–7.3. In early spring in the South and late spring in the North, deep blue flowers with a yellow throat appear. Lance-shape, grasslike deep-green leaves are semievergreen. Flowers appear and disappear quickly but are considered worthy of viewing, even for a short time. Plants self-seed freely. Place in odd-numbered groups in borders or rock

Feed narrow-leaf blue-eyed grass with a water-soluble plant food.

gardens, in containers, or among spring-flowering bulbs. Good companions include sea pink, Johnny-jump-up, and pansy cultivars.
CARE: Plant 6–12" apart in spring or autumn. Apply slow-release granular plant food in spring or feed through the summer with a water-soluble plant food. Apply 3" of vegetative mulch in summer and winter to reduce weed seed germination, retain soil moisture, and keep soil temperatures stable. Water deeply when the soil is dry. Plants are extremely low maintenance and durable when their cultural preferences (soil, sun, planting depth, moisture) are met. Plants self-seed in the landscape.
PROPAGATION: Lift self-sown seedlings and reset in spring or autumn. Divide in spring. Dig around the clump of bulbs and lift. Use a sharp spade to slice through the root system. Reset portions that contain healthy roots and top shoots. Discard any pieces that do not contain both healthy bulbs and top shoots. Water deeply and apply 3" of vegetative mulch around, but not touching, the plants.
PESTS AND DISEASES: Plants are relatively pest free.

FALSE SOLOMON'S SEAL

Smilacena racemosa smil-uh-SEE-nuh ray-seh-MOH-sub

False Solomon's seal has attractive flowers, berries, and foliage. It is also known as Solomon's plume.

ZONES: 3–8
SIZE: 24–36"h × 24"w
TYPE: Perennial
FORM: Spreading
TEXTURE: Medium
GROWTH: Slow
LIGHT: Partial to full shade
MOISTURE: Medium

SOIL: Moderately fertile, moist, well-drained
FEATURES: Flowers, foliage, berries
USES: Border, woodland, container
FLOWERS: □
FALL COLOR: ■

SITING: False Solomon's seal prefers partial to full shade and moderately fertile, humus-rich, moist, well-drained soil with a pH of 5.5–7.0. Panicles of fragrant creamy-white-tinged-green flowers appear in mid- and late spring. Green berries follow the flowers and turn red, sometimes splashed with purple. Berries attract wildlife. Zigzagging stems bear narrow, pointed, medium green leaves, up to 6" long, that turn an attractive yellow in autumn. Place in groups in shade borders or woodland gardens, or arching lines to container plantings. Good companions include 'Pictum' Japanese painted fern, heart-leaf brunnera, 'Alba' bleeding heart, and Lenten rose.

CARE: Plant 12–24" apart in spring or autumn. Apply slow-release plant food, such as Miracle-Gro Shake 'n Feed All Purpose, in spring. Follow label directions for amount and frequency. Apply 3" of vegetative mulch in summer and winter to reduce weed seed germination, hold moisture in the soil, and add organic matter to the soil as it decomposes. Water deeply when the soil is dry. Plants take a full season or two to recover after root disturbance, so move and divide only when necessary.

PROPAGATION: Divide in spring or autumn. To root in soil, dig around the rhizomes and lift. Use a sharp spade to slice through the root system. Reset portions that contain healthy roots and top shoots. Discard any pieces that do not contain both healthy roots and top shoots. Water deeply and apply 3" of vegetative mulch around, but not touching, the plants.

PESTS AND DISEASES: Plants are relatively pest free when cultural requirements (sun, soil, planting depth, moisture) are met.

RELATED SPECIES: Starflower (*S. stellata*) bears white flowers followed by black berries. It grows 8–24" tall in Zones 3–7.

COLEUS

Solenostemon scuttellarioides **hybrids** sob-len-AH-steb-mun skoo-teh-lahr-OY-deez

Coleus foliage comes in many interesting color combinations.

ZONE: NA
SIZE: 6–36"h × 12–36"w
TYPE: Annual
FORM: Upright
TEXTURE: Medium
GROWTH: Fast
LIGHT: Full sun, partial shade

MOISTURE: Medium to high
SOIL: Fertile, moist, well-drained
FEATURES: Foliage
USES: Border, bedding, container
FLOWERS: ■□

SITING: Newer coleus cultivars prefer full sun or partial shade and fertile, well-drained, moist soil, with a pH of 5.5–7.0. Plants are evergreen perennials commonly grown as annuals. Colorful foliage thrives in bright shade. Flowers appear during summer but are considered inconsequential and are usually removed. Use as an annual ground cover for a tapestry effect or in containers. Good companions include *Bergenia cordifolia* 'Purpurea', *Heuchera micrantha* var. *diversifolia* 'Palace Purple', and hosta 'Gold Standard'.

CARE: Plant 12–24" apart in late spring. Apply slow-release granular plant food at time of planting. Apply 3" of vegetative mulch in summer. When the soil feels dry 2" below the surface, water deeply. Remove plants just before first frost or right afterward when foliage is disfigured.

PROPAGATION: Seed germination occurs in 10–15 days at 72°F. Transplant 20–25 days after sowing. After transplanting, reduce temperature to 65–70°F. In summer take cuttings from new growth. Cut pieces that contain at least two to four healthy leaves and three nodes. Root cuttings in water or soil. Dip exposed nodes into rooting hormone, shake off excess, and insert into moist soil mix, keeping leaves well above the soil level.

PESTS AND DISEASES: Slugs and leaf spots are common.

RELATED SPECIES: Bellevue Hybrid Blend leaves are splashed with pink, red, ivory, and green; Dragon Series leaves are splashed with purple, black, and red, rimmed with gold; Old Lace Mixed leaves are white, lilac, and salmon, with a rose center and yellow rim; and 'Striped Rainbow' leaves are heart shaped and striped red, maroon, yellow, and green.

Remove developing flower stalks to focus attention on the foliage.

Cut shoot tips for propagating new plants.

Root coleus cuttings in soilless growing mix or in water.

GOLDENROD
Solidago hybrids *sohl-ih-DAY-goh*

Beautiful goldenrod flowers appear in mid- to late summer.

ZONES: 3–9
SIZE: 36"h × 18–24"w
TYPE: Perennial
FORM: Upright
TEXTURE: Medium
GROWTH: Fast
LIGHT: Full sun
MOISTURE: Medium to low

SOIL: Moderately fertile, well-drained
FEATURES: Flowers, foliage
USES: Border, naturalizing, container
FLOWERS: ■

SITING: Goldenrod prefers moderately fertile, well-drained, even sandy soil and full sun. The preferred pH range is 5.5–7.0. Cultivars are usually well behaved and stay within bounds. Plumelike panicles of tiny golden-yellow flowers appear in mid- and late summer. Flowers attract bees and butterflies. Plant in groups in perennial borders, naturalize along a fence, or use in mixed container plantings. Good companions include 'Snowbank' white boltonia, 'Bruno' Helen's flower, and 'Sky Racer' purple moor grass.

CARE: Plant 18–24" apart in spring or fall. Apply slow-release granular plant food in spring. Water deeply when the soil is dry. Plants self-seed; seedlings may not be as desirable as the parent plant. Prevent self-seeding by removing faded flowers before seeds fall to the ground. Prune back in fall once frost withers the foliage or leave erect in warmer zones for winter viewing.

PROPAGATION: Divide in spring or autumn at least every 3 years to maintain vigor and control growth. Dig around the root clump and lift.

PESTS AND DISEASES: Plants are relatively pest free when cultural requirements (sun, soil, planting depth, moisture) are met.

RELATED SPECIES: Dwarf cultivars include 'Golden Baby', 'Golden Dwarf', and 'Queenie' with variegated green and gold leaves; 'Laurin' with light gold flowers; 'Golden Gate', a semi-dwarf with deep golden flowers; and 'Praecox', which flowers early. 'Crown of Rays' grows to 24" and begins blooming in mid-summer. Taller cultivars include 'Leraft', with bright yellow flowers; 'Ledsham' and 'Lemore', with paler yellow flowers; and 'Loddon Gold', with deep gold flowers. *S. sphacelata* 'Golden Fleece' tolerates considerable shade and grows to only 18" tall and tolerates dry soils well.

LAMB'S-EARS
Stachys byzantina *STAK-iss biz-uhn-TEE-nuh*

Lamb's-ears has velvety soft leaves.

ZONES: 3–8
SIZE: 18"h × 24"w
TYPE: Perennial
FORM: Spreading
TEXTURE: Medium
GROWTH: Fast
LIGHT: Full sun
MOISTURE: Medium

SOIL: Moderately fertile, well-drained
FEATURES: Flowers, foliage
USES: Border, container, ground cover
FLOWERS: ■

SITING: Lamb's-ears prefers full sun and moderately fertile, well-drained soil with a pH of 5.5–7.0. Plants are susceptible to disease in high humidity. Spikes of woolly pink flowers appear from early summer into early autumn. Soft velvety foliage is silvery green. Flowers attract butterflies and bees. Place in groups in perennial borders, use as a ground cover, or in container plantings. Good companions include 'David' garden phlox, 'The Fairy' rose, 'Freckles' violet, and Johnny-jump-up.

CARE: Plant 18–24" apart in spring or fall. Apply slow-release granular plant food in spring. Cease feeding 6–8 weeks prior to first frost date. Water deeply when the soil is dry. Groom regularly to remove brown or diseased leaves from the thick mat; cultivars rarely require foliage grooming. Deadhead spent blooms. Prune back in fall once frost withers the foliage.

PROPAGATION: Divide in spring or autumn at least every 3 years to maintain vigor and control growth. Discard any nonbearing center portions. Sprinkle seeds over the growing medium and leave exposed to light; do not cover. Thoroughly moisten and keep moist, not soggy, until seeds germinate. Germination occurs in 10–15 days at 70°F. Transplant in 20–25 days after sowing. Reduce the temperature to 60°F after transplanting. Plants grown from seed produce flowers during the second season.

PESTS AND DISEASES: Powdery mildew is the main pest. Select mildew-resistant cultivars and provide adequate air circulation and spacing.

RELATED SPECIES: *S. byzantina* 'Silver Carpet' is nonflowering, low maintenance, and tidier than the species. The cultivar 'Big Ears' has large silver-green leaves; 'Cotton Ball' has clusters of modified flowers along the stem that resemble cotton balls; 'Margery Fish' has mauve flowers; 'Primrose Heron' has yellow-green leaves; and 'Striped Phantom' has cream-stripe leaves and striped flower bracts.

1 Dig the root ball of lamb's-ears to divide it.

2 Pull or cut the clump apart.

3 Reset pieces that have healthy roots and shoots.

AFRICAN MARIGOLD
Tagetes erecta *tuh-JEE-teez eh-REHK-tuh*

African marigolds have large flowers and may grow tall. They are also known as Aztec marigolds.

ZONES: NA
SIZE: 12–32"h × 12–18"w
TYPE: Annual
FORM: Upright
TEXTURE: Medium
GROWTH: Medium
LIGHT: Full sun

MOISTURE: Medium
SOIL: Moderately fertile, well-drained
FEATURES: Flowers, foliage
USES: Border, bedding, container
FLOWERS: ■ ■ ■ □

SITING: African marigold prefers full sun and moderately fertile, well-drained soil with a pH of 5.5–7.0. Plants are relatively drought tolerant once established. Large, vibrant, double orange or yellow flowers, up to 5" across, appear from late spring through late summer. Fragrant foliage is deeply dissected and toothed. Place in groups in borders, mass as bedding plants, or add to container plantings. Good companions include snapdragon, flowering kale, and dusty miller.

CARE: Plant 10–15" apart in late spring. Apply slow-release granular plant food at time of planting, or begin using water-soluble plant food 3 weeks after planting. Follow label directions for amount and frequency. Apply 3" of vegetative mulch in summer to reduce weed seed germination, hold moisture in the soil, and as it decomposes, add organic matter to the soil. Water deeply when the soil is dry. Rainfall and overhead irrigation may damage heavy dense flower heads. Drip irrigation is preferred when available. Deadhead spent or damaged blooms to encourage reblooming. Remove plants by frost or after foliage is disfigured. Cover bare soil with 3" of vegetative mulch during winter to preserve topsoil.

PROPAGATION: Sprinkle seeds over the growing medium and leave exposed to light or cover lightly. Thoroughly moisten and keep moist, not soggy, until seeds germinate. Germination occurs in 7 days at 72–75°F. Transplant 10–15 days after sowing. After transplanting, reduce temperature to 65°F.

PESTS AND DISEASES: Diseases include botrytis and powdery mildew.

RELATED SPECIES: French marigold (*T. patula*) reaches 6–12" high and bears single or double flowers up to 2" across in single or multicolors including yellow, orange, and red-brown.

French marigolds are shorter and have smaller flowers than African marigolds.

1 Sprinkle seeds into a seed tray filled with Miracle-Gro soilless mix.

2 Newly emerged marigold seedlings will soon be ready to transplant.

3 Transplant marigold seedlings into cell packs or individual pots.

WALL GERMANDER
Teucrium chamaedrys TOO-kree-uhm kam-EH-drihs

Wall germander, also known as germander blooms with attractive purple flowers.

ZONES: 5–9
SIZE: 12–20"h × 18"w
TYPE: Perennial
FORM: Upright
TEXTURE: Fine
GROWTH: Medium
LIGHT: Full sun

MOISTURE: Medium
SOIL: Moderately fertile, well-drained
FEATURES: Flowers, foliage
USES: Border, knot, container
FLOWERS: ■

SITING: Wall germander prefers full sun and moderately fertile, well-drained soil with a pH of 6.5–7.5. The evergreen foliage may be sheared into a miniature hedge. Flowers attract butterflies and bees. Plants are ideal for knot gardens, in borders, or in containers. Good companions are lavender, rosemary, lavender cotton *(Santolina rosmarinifolia)*, and creeping zinnia.

CARE: Plant 12–18" apart in spring or autumn. Apply slow-release granular plant food in spring. Cease feeding 6–8 weeks prior to first frost date. Apply 3" of vegetative mulch in summer and winter.

Germander is an excellent edging plant in a knot garden. It can be pruned and shaped to a tight form.

Water deeply when the soil is dry. Shear back low in spring to maintain a compact habit.

PROPAGATION: Divide in spring or autumn. Dig around the root clump and lift. Use a sharp spade to slice through the root system. Reset portions that contain healthy roots and top shoots. In summer take cuttings from new growth. Cut pieces that contain at least two or three healthy leaves and three nodes. Root cuttings in water or soil. To root in soil, dip exposed nodes into rooting hormone, shake off excess, and insert into moist soil mix, keeping leaves well above the soil level. Supply bottom heat and keep moist, not soggy, until root and top shoot growth is evident, usually in 2–3 weeks, then transplant. To enhance humidity, cover flat with plastic and hold it above the leaves.

PESTS AND DISEASES: Plants are relatively pest free when cultural requirements (sun, soil, planting depth, moisture) are met.

COLUMBINE MEADOW RUE
Thalictrum aquilegifolium thuh-LIHK-trum ahk-wih-lee-jee-FOH-lee-uhm

Columbine meadow-rue is fine-textured and graceful both in and out of bloom.

ZONES: 4–9
SIZE: 36"h × 18"w
TYPE: Perennial
FORM: Upright
TEXTURE: Fine
GROWTH: Medium
LIGHT: Partial shade
MOISTURE: Medium

SOIL: Fertile, moist, well-drained
FEATURES: Flowers, foliage
USES: Border, woodland, container
FLOWERS: ■□■

SITING: Columbine meadow rue prefers partial shade and fertile, well-drained, moist soil with a pH of 5.5–7.0. Greenish-white sepals surround showy bright pink, purple, or white stamens in early summer. Blue-green foliage appears delicate and graceful. Place in odd-number groups in brightly shaded borders, woodland gardens, or in containers. Good companions include McKenna hybrids columbine, goatsbeard, and foxglove.

CARE: Plant 18" apart in spring or autumn in fertile soil having high organic matter content. To increase organic matter, add 1–2" inches of compost to the top of the entire planting bed. Till in to a depth of 12–15". Apply slow-release granular plant food at the time of planting. Apply 3" of vegetative mulch in summer and winter to reduce weed seed germination, retain soil moisture, and keep soil temperatures stable. Water deeply when the soil feels dry 2" below the surface. Prune back in fall once frost withers the foliage.

PROPAGATION: Plants self-seed in the landscape and may be dug and transplanted. Sprinkle seeds over the growing medium and leave exposed to light; do not cover. Thoroughly moisten and keep moist, not soggy, until seeds germinate. Germination occurs in 5–10 days at 70°F. Transplant in 15–25 days after sowing. After transplanting, reduce temperature to 60°F.

PESTS AND DISEASES: Plants are relatively pest free when cultural requirements are met. Rust and powdery mildew are occasional diseases.

RELATED SPECIES: 'Atropurpureum' has dark purple stamens, 'Aurantiacum' has orange-stained stamens, 'Purpureum' has purple stamens, 'Roseum' has pink stamens, 'Thundercloud' has deep purple stamens, and 'White Cloud' has yellow-rimmed white stamens. 'Lavender Mist' *(T. rochebrunianum)* reaches 60" high and 18" wide. Loose panicles of white, sometimes lavender, flowers appear in summer.

SOUTHERN LUPINE
Thermopsis villosa *ther-MAHP-sihs vil-OH-suh*

Southern lupine is long-lived and attracts butterflies when in bloom. It is also known as Carolina lupine or false lupine.

ZONES: 3–9
SIZE: 3–5'h × 24"w
TYPE: Perennial
FORM: Upright
TEXTURE: Medium
GROWTH: Medium
LIGHT: Full sun to partial shade

MOISTURE: Medium
SOIL: Fertile, well-drained
FEATURES: Flowers, foliage
USES: Border, woodland, container
FLOWERS: ■

SITING: Southern lupine prefers full sun (part shade in warmer regions) and fertile, well-drained soil with a pH of 5.5–7.0. Racemes of pealike bright yellow flowers appear in late spring and early summer. Leaves are blue-green and divided into three leaflets, lightly hairy underneath. Plants are long-lived and resent root disturbance. Flowers attract bees and butterflies. Place in odd-numbered groups in perennial borders, cottage gardens, or lightly shaded woodland gardens, or use in containers for early-season color. Good companions include 'Morning Light' maiden grass, Oriental poppy, and 'Aurantiacum' columbine meadow rue.

Place a support over southern lupine in partial shade to prevent plants from toppling over.

CARE: Plant 18–24" apart in spring or fall. Apply slow-release granular plant food at time of planting. Cease feeding 6–8 weeks prior to first frost date. Apply 3" of vegetative mulch in summer and winter. Water deeply when the soil is dry. In partial shade, plants may require staking. Prune back in fall once frost withers the foliage.

PROPAGATION: Divide in spring or autumn; plants take several seasons to grow at a normal pace. Dig around the root clump and lift. Use a sharp spade to slice through the root system. Reset portions that contain healthy roots and top shoots. Discard any pieces that do not contain both healthy roots and top shoots. Water deeply and apply 3" of vegetative mulch around, but not touching, the plants. Fresh seed is essential to germination. Sow seeds in spring or early summer and maintain 50–55°F temperatures until germination occurs. Transplant seedlings directly to their landscape site as early as possible.

PESTS AND DISEASES: Powdery mildew is a problem.

BLACK-EYED SUSAN VINE
Thunbergia alata *Thuhn-BEHR-jee-uh ah-LAY-tuh*

Black-eyed Susan vine climbs on trellises or arbors up to 8' in height.

ZONES: NA
SIZE: 5–8'h × 6–12"
TYPE: Annual
FORM: Upright
TEXTURE: Medium
GROWTH: Fast
LIGHT: Full sun
MOISTURE: Medium

SOIL: Fertile, moist, well-drained
FEATURES: Flowers, foliage
USES: Trellis, container
FLOWERS: ■■□

SITING: Black-eyed Susan vine prefers full sun and fertile, well-drained, moist soil with a pH of 5.5–7.0. These perennial climbing plants are usually grown as annuals. Five-petaled tubular yellow, orange, or occasionally white flowers appear from summer through autumn. The flower center is sometimes mahogany brown. Leaves are almost triangular, toothed, and medium green. Plants require support and may be used on low trellises or arbors, in container plantings, or at the sunny base of a tree. Good container companions include 'Moonbeam' threadleaf coreopsis, 'Purpureum' purple fountain grass, and 'White Bedder' beard tongue.

CARE: Plant 12–24" apart in late spring. Apply slow-release granular plant food at time of planting. Apply 3" of vegetative mulch in summer. Maintain moist, not soggy, soil. When the soil feels almost dry 2" below the surface, water deeply. If using an irrigation system, maintain deep, infrequent waterings and avoid delivering a light sprinkle every day. Organic matter in the soil and mulch on the soil surface help reduce watering frequency. Remove plants just before first frost or right afterward when foliage is disfigured. Cover bare soil with 3" of vegetative mulch during winter to preserve topsoil.

PROPAGATION: Sprinkle seeds over the growing medium and cover lightly. Thoroughly moisten and keep moist, not soggy, until seeds germinate. Germination occurs in 6–12 days at 75°F. Transplant 15–20 days after sowing. After transplanting, reduce temperature to 60°F.

PESTS AND DISEASES: Plants are relatively pest free when cultural requirements (sun, soil, planting depth, moisture) are met.

RELATED SPECIES: The cultivar 'Alba' has white flowers, 'Aurantiaca' bears orange or yellow flowers with a dark throat, 'Bakeri' has white flowers, and Suzie hybrids bear orange, yellow, or white flowers with a dark throat.

LEMON THYME
Thymus ×citriodorus   TIME-ubs siht-ree-oh-DOR-ubs

Lemon thyme is a fragrant ground cover or container plant for full sun.

ZONES: 4–9
SIZE: 12"h × 12"w
TYPE: Perennial
FORM: Rounded
TEXTURE: Fine
GROWTH: Medium
LIGHT: Full sun
MOISTURE: Medium

SOIL: Moderately fertile, well-drained
FEATURES: Flowers, foliage
USES: Border, ground cover, container
FLOWERS: ■

SITING: Lemon thyme prefers full sun and moderately fertile, well-drained soil with a pH of 6.5–7.5. Plants are woody subshrubs with tiny, evergreen, lemon-scented leaves. Lavender-pink flowers appear in summer. Leaves have culinary value and may be used fresh or dried. Use as a ground cover in borders or as a spillover plant in containers. Summer container companions include pink coreopsis, 'Moonbeam' threadleaf coreopsis, 'Purpureum' fennel, and lavender.

CARE: Plant 6–12" apart in spring or fall. Apply slow-release granular plant food in spring at time of planting. Cease feeding 6–8 weeks prior to first frost date. Shear back hard in early spring; trim back lightly after flowering to promote compact habit. Scent is strongest when plants are grown in moderately fertile soil. For culinary use trim one-third of the leaf branch at a time. Water deeply when the soil is dry.

PROPAGATION: Plants naturally layer in the landscape. Pin a branch to the ground so that nodes connect with soil. Cover with mulch. Check periodically for root growth; when roots have formed, snip the branch from the parent plant, leaving some green top growth to accompany the new root system. In early summer, take cuttings from new growth. Cut pieces that contain at least two or three healthy leaves and three nodes. Dip exposed nodes into rooting hormone, shake off excess, and insert into moist soil mix, keeping leaves well above the soil level.

PESTS AND DISEASES: Plants are relatively pest free when cultural requirements are met.

RELATED SPECIES: 'Anderson's Gold' hugs the ground and has golden leaves; 'Archer's Gold' has bright yellow leaves; 'Argenteus' has silver leaves; 'Argenteus Variegatus' bears green leaves rimmed in silver; 'Aureus' has green leaves splashed with gold that often revert to solid green; 'Doone Valley' is prostrate with green leaves splashed with gold and stained red in winter; and 'Silver Queen' bears silver-marbled leaves.

Plant lemon thyme in a container garden to trail over the edge.

SPIDERWORT
Tradescantia virginiana   trahd-ehs-KAHN-tee-uh vehr-jihn-ee-AY-nuh

Spiderwort flowers have three petals and perform best in lean soils.

ZONES: 4–9
SIZE: 18–24"h × 18–24"w
TYPE: Perennial
FORM: Spreading
TEXTURE: Medium
GROWTH: Medium
LIGHT: Full sun to partial shade

MOISTURE: Medium
SOIL: Moderately fertile, moist, well-drained
FEATURES: Flowers, foliage
USES: Border, container
FLOWERS: ■ ■ ■ □

SITING: Spiderwort prefers full sun or light shade during the afternoon and moderately fertile, well-drained, moist soil with a pH of 5.5–7.0. Flowers appear in shades of blue, purple, pink, or white from early summer to early autumn. Flower production is higher in full sun than in partial shade. Place in groups in informal borders, cottage gardens, or bright woodland gardens, or use in container plantings. Good companions include 'Ice Queen' torch lily, 'Kobold' blazing star, and 'Yankee Lady' Rugosa rose.

CARE: Plant 18–24" apart in spring or fall. Apply slow-release granular plant food in spring at time of planting. Plants flop or fall apart if the soil is rich and plant food is high in nitrogen. Apply 3" of vegetative mulch in spring and fall. Maintain moist soil. After the first flush of flowers, feed again and shear back plant to promote compact habit and encourage more flower production. Spiderwort is self-cleaning and does not need regular deadheading to appear attractive, though deadheading is recommended if self-sown plants are not desired in the landscape.

PROPAGATION: Divide in spring or autumn at least every 3 years to maintain vigor. In late spring or early summer, before full bloom, take cuttings from new growth. Cut pieces that contain at least two or three healthy leaves and three nodes. Root cuttings in water or soil. Seed germination occurs in 7–14 days at 72°F. Transplant 20–30 days after sowing. Reduce the temperature to 62°F after transplanting.

PESTS AND DISEASES: Viruses are occasional problems.

RELATED SPECIES: The cultivar 'Alba' bears white flowers; 'Blue Stone' has blue flowers; 'Caerulea Plena' bears double blue flowers; 'Innocence' bears clear white flowers; 'Iris Pritchard' bears white flowers stained pale blue; 'Isis' has deep blue flowers; 'Karminglut' has red flowers, 'Osprey' bears white flowers; 'Purewell Giant' has purplish-pink flowers; 'Snowcap' bears extra large white flowers; and 'Zwanenburg Blue' has deep blue flowers.

Cut back spiderwort after first bloom to encourage compact growth and rebloom.

TOAD LILY
Tricyrtis hirta   *try-SER-tuhs HER-tuh*

Toad lily has exotic flowers that resemble those of an orchid.

ZONES: 5–9
SIZE: 36'h × 24"w
TYPE: Perennial
FORM: Upright
TEXTURE: Medium
GROWTH: Medium
LIGHT: Partial to full shade

MOISTURE: Medium
SOIL: Fertile, moist, well-drained
FEATURES: Flowers, foliage
USES: Border, woodland, container
FLOWERS: ☐ ▧

SITING: Toad lily prefers partial to full shade and fertile, well-drained, moist soil with a pH of 5.5–6.5. Curious funnel-shaped white flowers with purple specks appear in late summer. Leaves are lance shape, pale green, and very hairy. Plants are attractive to connoisseur gardeners who collect the unusual. Place in odd-number groups in shaded borders or woodland gardens, or use in containers. Good companions for toad lily include lady's mantle, heart-leaf brunnera, and 'Elegans' Siebold hosta or 'Gold Standard' hosta.

CARE: Plant 12–24" apart in spring or autumn in fertile soil high in organic matter. To increase organic matter, add 1–2" of compost, peat moss, or bagged humus to the planting bed, then till in to a depth of 12–15". Apply slow-release granular plant food. Cease feeding 6–8 weeks prior to first frost date. Apply 3" of vegetative mulch in summer and winter to reduce weed seed germination, retain soil moisture, and keep soil temperatures stable. Water deeply when the soil feels dry 2" below the surface. Prune back in fall once frost withers the foliage.

PROPAGATION: Divide in early spring while plants are dormant. Plants self-seed in the landscape.

PESTS AND DISEASES: Plants are relatively pest free when cultural requirements (sun, soil, planting depth, moisture) are met. Snails and slugs may be pests.

RELATED SPECIES: 'Alba' has white flowers; 'Miyazaki' bears white flowers spotted with lilac; 'Miyazaki Gold' has leaves edged in gold; and 'White Towers' has white flowers in the leaf axils. Formosa toad lily (*T. formosana*) is hardy in Zones 4–9 and reaches 36" high and 18" wide. Attractive unusual star-shaped pinkish-purple or white flowers appear in late summer. Lightly hairy stems and glossy deep green leaves, sometimes spotted with purple, create interest. The cultivar 'Amethystina' bears amethyst blue and white flowers speckled in yellow and maroon.

Mulch toad lily to keep the surrounding soil moist and reduce weeds.

GREAT WHITE TRILLIUM
Trillium grandiflorum   *TRIL-ee-uhm grand-ih-FLOR-uhm*

Trillium offers spectacular foliage, flowers, and berries for the shade garden. Toad trillium bears maroon flowers.

ZONES: 3–8
SIZE: 18"h × 12"w
TYPE: Perennial
FORM: Upright
TEXTURE: Medium
GROWTH: Slow
LIGHT: Partial to full shade
MOISTURE: Medium

SOIL: Fertile, moist, well-drained
FEATURES: Flowers, foliage, berries
USES: Border, woodland, ground cover
FLOWERS: ☐ ▧

SITING: Great white trillium prefers partial to full shade and fertile, well-drained, moist soil with a pH of 5.5–7.0. Pure white flowers with three wavy petals and green sepals appear in midspring. Flowers often age to pink and are followed by white berries. Leaves are deep green and oval or rounded. Plants are classic woodland beauties that add grace to any shaded location that meets their cultural preferences (soil, sun, moisture, planting depth). Place plants in odd-numbered groups in the foreground of shaded borders or woodland gardens, or mass as ground cover at the feet of evergreen trees and shrubs. Woodland shade companions include 'Pictum' Japanese painted fern, Kousa dogwood, and Lenten rose.

CARE: Plant 6–12" apart in spring or autumn. Apply slow-release granular plant food in spring. Apply 2–3" of organic mulch in spring and winter; as it decomposes, it adds organic matter to the soil. Maintain moist, not soggy, soil. When the soil feels almost dry 2" below the surface, water deeply. If using an irrigation system, maintain deep, infrequent waterings and avoid delivering a light sprinkle every day. Organic matter in the soil and mulch on the soil surface will help reduce watering frequency. Plants often die back to the ground by midsummer, especially if they are dry. Purchase great white trillium from a reputable nursery. Avoid digging wild plants from the woods; they are slow growing, taking 5–7 years to flower and produce seed, and do not transplant easily. Container-grown plants transplant successfully.

PROPAGATION: Let seeds self-sow in the landscape whenever possible; it may take two seasons for leaves to develop and up to 7 years for flowering and seed development. Dig plantlets in spring and reset in shaded, fertile soil; water and mulch. Divide after flowering, in early summer. Plants may take 2 years before resuming normal growth patterns.

PESTS AND DISEASES: Fungal spot, rust, and smut are occasional diseases.

RELATED SPECIES: Toad trillium (*T. sessile*) reaches 12" high in late spring and bears maroon flowers above deep green leaves splashed with maroon, cream, and light green.

TULIP
Tulipa hybrids *TOO-lip-uh*

Tulips in bloom announce the arrival of springtime to the landscape.

ZONES: 3–8
SIZE: 12–30"h × 8"w
TYPE: Perennial
FORM: Upright
TEXTURE: Medium
GROWTH: Medium
LIGHT: Full sun, partial shade
MOISTURE: Medium

SOIL: Fertile, well-drained
FEATURES: Flowers, foliage
USES: Border, mass, container
FLOWERS: ■ ■ ■ □ ■ ■

SITING: Tulips prefer fertile, well-drained soil with a pH of 5.5–7.0. They prefer full sun in Zones 3–6 and partial shade in warmer zones. Most tulips are grown as annuals or short-lived perennials. Flowers appear in early, mid-, or late spring, depending on species and cultivar, in cheerful crayon colors of red, yellow, pink, white, orange, and purple. Select tulips based on hardiness zone ratings; they require cold treatment to properly flower and thrive. Plants are reliably hardy in Zones 3–6. In Zones 7 and 8 plants are more sensitive and need afternoon shade. In Zones 9 and 10 plants may be grown as annuals. Tulips are classified according to their flowering characteristics. Groups include single early, double early, triumph, Darwin hybrid, single late, lily-flowered, fringed, viridiflora, parrot, Rembrandt, double late, Kaufmanniana, Fosteriana, Gregii, and miscellaneous. Place tulips in large swaths in herbaceous borders, mass as bedding plants or ground cover, or place in containers. Annual companions to help cloak the necessary foliage dieback process include snapdragon, pot marigold, or pansy.

CARE: In autumn plant tulips 3–6" apart and two to three times deeper than their diameter. In Zones 9 and 10, precool bulbs for 8–10 weeks at 40°F before planting outdoors in early winter. Add bonemeal to the soil at planting time. Follow label directions for application amount. Apply slow-release plant food, such as Miracle-Gro Shake 'n Feed All Purpose, in spring or, if growing bulbs as perennials, begin using water-soluble plant food every week

for 3–4 weeks as flowering ends and foliage dies back. Follow label directions for application amount. Water deeply when the soil is dry. Deadheading flowers will promote perennial bulb development. Allow foliage to die back naturally so bulbs store enough energy to produce flowers the following season. Do not braid foliage or fold and wrap it with rubber bands as these practices will limit the amount of light reaching the foliage. The result will be poor bloom the following spring. Add 1" of vegetative mulch to planting beds. Keep soil moist during the growing season; allow it to dry somewhat in summer to coincide with the bulbs' dormancy.

PROPAGATION: After flowering, when leaves fade, lift clumps and separate bulbs. Replant, water, and mulch.

PESTS AND DISEASES: Root rot and bulb rot are common in soggy soils.

RELATED SPECIES: Late tulip (*T. tarda*) reaches 4–6" high and bears small, star-shaped white flowers with yellow centers in midspring. Lady tulip (*T. clusiana*) grows to 10" tall and has pink and white blooms. *T. c.* var. *chrysantha* has yellow

Late tulip (*T. tarda*) stays small and blooms earlier than most hybrid tulips.

flowers with purplish stripes. *T. praestans* produces clusters of red-orange flowers early in the season on plants 12" tall. 'Fusilier' is a common cultivar. *T. bakeri* 'Lilac Wonder' has pink to lilac blooms.

1 Dig the planting hole for tulips to a depth 2–3 times their diameter.

2 Mix bonemeal thoroughly into the soil before planting to get the phosphorus to the root zone.

3 Scatter bulbs in the hole, and space them 3–6 inches apart.

4 Cover bulbs with soil, water in, and wait for the show to begin next spring.

VERBENA
Verbena ×hybrida ver-BEE-nuh HYE-brihd-uh

Bedding verbena provides nonstop summer color in full sun.

ZONES: NA
SIZE: 12–18"h × 12–24"w
TYPE: Annual
FORM: Spreading or upright
TEXTURE: Medium
GROWTH: Medium
LIGHT: Full sun

MOISTURE: Medium
SOIL: Moderately fertile, well-drained
FEATURES: Flowers, foliage
USES: Border, bedding, container
FLOWERS: ■■■□□

SITING: Bedding verbena prefers full sun and moderately fertile, well-drained soil

with a pH of 5.5–7.0. Plants are usually grown as annuals. Clusters of tiny flowers in popsicle shades of red, white, pink, and purple, often with a white or yellow eye, appear from summer to early autumn. Plants may be upright or spreading, depending on cultivar. Deep to medium green leaves are hairy, rough, and toothed. Mass as bedding plants, use in odd-number groups in full-sun borders, or use in container plantings. Good garden companions include 'Iceberg' rose, nettle-leaf mullein, and *Verbena corymbosa*.

CARE: Plant 12–24" apart in late spring. Apply slow-release granular plant food at time of planting, or begin using water-soluble plant food 3 weeks after planting. Follow label directions for amount and frequency. Apply 3" of vegetative mulch in summer to reduce weed seed germination, hold moisture in the soil, and as it decomposes, add organic matter to the soil. Water deeply when the soil is dry. Deadhead spent blooms to encourage reblooming. When grown as an annual,

remove plants just before first frost or right afterward when foliage is disfigured. Cover bare soil with 3" of vegetative mulch during winter to preserve topsoil.

PROPAGATION: Chill seed for 7 days before sowing. Sprinkle seeds over the growing medium and cover lightly. Thoroughly moisten and keep moist, not soggy, until seeds germinate. Germination occurs in 10–20 days at 75–80°F. Transplant 20–30 days after sowing. Reduce the temperature to 60°F after transplanting.

PESTS AND DISEASES: Diseases include powdery mildew and rust. Insect pests include aphids, spider mites, and whitefly.

RELATED SPECIES: The cultivar 'Amethyst' has small blue flowers with white eyes; 'Blue Knight' bears lilac flowers; 'Cardinal' has red flowers; 'Carousel' has purple-and-white-striped flowers; 'Imagination' has deep violet-blue flowers; and 'Peaches and Cream' has flowers in shades of peach, pink, and orange.

AUSTRIAN SPEEDWELL
Veronica austriaca ssp. *teucrium* vuh-RAHN-ih-kuh aw-stree-AY-kuh TOO-kree-uhm

Austrian speedwell has gentian blue flowers in early or midsummer. It is also known as veronica.

ZONES: 4–8
SIZE: 24–36"h × 24"w
TYPE: Perennial
FORM: Spreading
TEXTURE: Medium
GROWTH: Medium
LIGHT: Full sun

MOISTURE: Medium
SOIL: Moderately fertile, well-drained
FEATURES: Flowers, foliage
USES: Border, container
FLOWERS: ■■■□□

SITING: Austrian speedwell prefers full sun (light afternoon shade in the warmer zones) and moderately fertile, well-drained soil with a pH of 5.5–7.0. Erect spikes of deep blue flowers appear in early summer in the South, midsummer in cooler zones. Place plants in groups in borders or use in containers. Companions include 'Caesar's

Brother' Siberian iris, 'Silver Carpet' lamb's-ears, and 'White Icicle' spike speedwell.

CARE: Plant 18" apart in spring or fall. Apply slow-release granular plant food in spring. Water deeply when the soil is dry. Apply 3" of vegetative mulch in spring and winter. Mulch in wintertime to help keep soil temperatures from fluctuating. Soils that freeze and quickly thaw may damage root systems as they contract and expand. Sometimes plants are heaved out of the ground and perish due to physical damage, desiccation, or cold temperatures. Mulch reduces the chances of heaving. Deadhead spent blooms to encourage

Harebell speedwell is low growing and has purplish blue flowers in early summer.

reblooming. Shear back hard after flowering to promote compact, attractive foliage. Prune back in fall once frost withers the foliage.

PROPAGATION: Divide in spring or fall. Dig around the root clump and lift. Use a sharp spade to slice through the root system. Reset portions that contain healthy roots and top shoots.

PESTS AND DISEASES: Diseases include powdery mildew, downy mildew, and rust. Wet soils promote root rot.

RELATED SPECIES: The cultivar 'Blue Fountain' bears bright blue flowers in summer; 'Crater Lake Blue' plants form neat mounds and bear cobalt-blue flowers in early summe;, 'Kapitan' has gentian-blue flowers; and 'Shirley Blue' has bright blue flowers. Harebell speedwell (*V. prostrata*) is winter hardy in Zones 5–8. Plants reach 6" high. Spikelike racemes of deep blue flowers appear in early summer. The cultivar *V. prostrata* 'Alba' has white flowers; 'Heavenly Blue' bears purplish-blue flowers in spring; 'Loddon Blue' has bright blue flowers; 'Mrs. Holt' bears pale pink flowers; 'Rosea' has pale pink flowers; 'Silver Queen' bears silvery-blue flowers; and 'Trehane' has violet-blue flowers and golden-tinted leaves.

SPIKE SPEEDWELL
Veronica spicata *vuh-RAHN-ih-kuh spih-KAH-tuh*

Spike speedwell's flowers appear all summer long and attract butterflies. It is also known as Veronica.

ZONES: 3–8
SIZE: 12–24"h × 18"w
TYPE: Perennial
FORM: Upright
TEXTURE: Medium
GROWTH: Medium
LIGHT: Full sun

MOISTURE: Medium
SOIL: Moderately fertile, well-drained
FEATURES: Flowers, foliage
USES: Border, container
FLOWERS: ■■□

SITING: Spike speedwell prefers full sun and moderately fertile, well-drained soil with a pH of 5.5–7.0. Erect spires of star-shaped blue flowers appear from early to late summer. Flowers attract butterflies and bees. Place in groups in perennial borders, or use in containers. Good companions for spike speedwell include 'Shenandoah' switch grass, fountain grass, and white Culver's root.

CARE: Plant 15–18" apart in spring or autumn. Apply slow-release granular plant food in spring. Apply mulch in summer and winter. Water deeply when the soil is dry. Deadhead spent blooms to encourage reblooming. Prune back in fall once frost withers the foliage.

Cut back spike speedwell after first flush of bloom to promote compact growth and reblooming.

PROPAGATION: Reproduce cultivars through division; reproduce the species by seed or division. Divide in spring or autumn. Dig around the root clump and lift. Use a sharp spade to slice through the root system. Reset portions that contain healthy roots and top shoots. Seed germination occurs in 7–14 days at 65–75°F. Transplant 15–25 days after sowing. Reduce the temperature to 55°F after transplanting.

PESTS AND DISEASES: Plants are relatively pest free when cultural requirements (sun, soil, planting depth, moisture) are met. Root rot may occur in wet soils.

RELATED SPECIES: The cultivar 'Alba' has white flowers; 'Blue Fox' bears deep blue flowers; 'Caerula' has sky-blue flowers; 'Erica' bears pink flowers; 'Heidekind' has deep red flowers and silvery-gray leaves; 'Icicle' bears white flowers; 'Minuet' reaches 10" high and has pink flowers in late spring and silvery-gray leaves; 'Rosea' bears pale pink flowers; and 'Rotfuchs' ('Red Fox') is compact with deep pink flowers. 'Sunny Border Blue' is a low-maintenance optimum performer that reaches 18" high and 12–15" wide and bears violet-blue flowers all summer long.

CULVER'S ROOT
Veronicastrum virginicum *vuh-rahn-ih-KAST-ruhm ver-JIN-ih-kum*

Culver's root produces slender, branched flower spikes in midsummer.

ZONES: 3–8
SIZE: 6'h × 18"w
TYPE: Perennial
FORM: Upright
TEXTURE: Medium
GROWTH: Medium
LIGHT: Full sun
MOISTURE: Medium

SOIL: Moderately fertile, moist, well-drained
FEATURES: Flowers, foliage
USES: Border, container
FLOWERS: □■■

SITING: Culver's root prefers full sun and moderately fertile, well-drained, moist soil with a pH of 5.5–7.0. Slender, erect spikes of white, pink, or purplish-blue flowers appear from midsummer to early autumn. Good companions for Culver's root include 'Bressingham Glow' Japanese anemone, 'Veitch's Blue' globe thistle, and 'Rotfuchs' spike speedwell.

CARE: Plant 15–18" apart in spring or fall. Apply slow-release granular plant food in spring. Water deeply when the soil is dry. If the soil is too rich, excessive nitrogen is applied, or there is too little sun, foliage may become floppy. If grown in partial shade, support may be needed. Maintain moist soil. Apply 3" of vegetative mulch in summer and winter to reduce weed seed germination, hold moisture in the soil, and add organic matter to the soil as it decomposes. Prune back in fall once frost withers the foliage or leave erect in warmer zones for winter viewing.

Set up supports for Culver's root to grow through. Because it is quite tall, support is often needed.

PROPAGATION: Divide in spring or fall. Dig around the root clump and lift. Use a sharp spade to slice through the root system. Reset portions that contain healthy roots and top shoots. Discard any pieces that do not contain both healthy roots and top shoots. Water deeply and apply 3" of vegetative mulch around, but not touching, the plants. Plants may take up to 3 years to resume normal growth patterns.

PESTS AND DISEASES: Occasional diseases include powdery mildew, downy mildew, and leaf spot.

RELATED SPECIES: *V. virginicum* f. *album* bears white flowers. The variety *rosea* has pale pink blooms.

LARGE PERIWINKLE
Vinca major VING-kuh MAY-jur

Large periwinkle is often used in container gardens as an annual due to lack of winter hardiness in colder zones.

ZONES: 6–9
SIZE: 12–18"h × 24"w
TYPE: Perennial
FORM: Spreading
TEXTURE: Medium
GROWTH: Medium
LIGHT: Full sun to partial shade

MOISTURE: Medium to high
SOIL: Moderately fertile, well-drained
FEATURES: Flowers, foliage
USES: Ground cover, woodland, container
FLOWERS: ■□ ■
FALL COLOR: ■

SITING: Large periwinkle prefers partial shade and moderately fertile, well-drained soil with a pH of 5.5–7.3. This evergreen, woody, low-growing plant bears violet-blue flowers from midspring to autumn. It is an ideal ground cover in bright woodlands or as a spillover plant in a mixed container. Container companions include 'Bicolor' Cupid's dart, 'Sour Grapes' beard-tongue, and 'Victoria' mealycup sage.

CARE: Plant 12–24" apart in spring or fall. Apply slow-release granular plant food

Plant large periwinkle in a pot to trail over and soften the edges of the container.

in spring. Maintain moist soil. Shear back hard in spring to keep plants tidy.

PROPAGATION: Plants naturally layer in the landscape. Pin a branch to the ground so that nodes contact the soil. Cover with mulch. Check periodically for root growth; when roots have formed, snip the branch from the parent plant, leaving some green top growth to accompany the new root system. Gently remove the new plant and reset. Divide in spring or autumn. Dig around the root clump and lift. Use a sharp spade to slice through the root system. Reset portions that contain healthy roots and top shoots. Discard any pieces that do not contain both healthy roots and top shoots. Water deeply and apply 3" of vegetative mulch around, but not touching, the plants.

PESTS AND DISEASES: Leaf spot is a common disease. Scale and leafhoppers are insect pests.

RELATED SPECIES: The cultivar 'Jason Hill' has dark green leaves and deep violet flowers; 'Maculata' bears variegated yellow-and-green leaves and pale blue flowers; and 'Variegata' has yellow-white margins on dark green leaves and white flowers.

PERIWINKLE
Vinca minor VING-kuh MYE-nur

Periwinkle is a superb evergreen ground cover for shade.

ZONES: 4–9
SIZE: 6"h × 24"w
TYPE: Perennial
FORM: Spreading
TEXTURE: Fine
GROWTH: Medium
LIGHT: Partial to full shade
MOISTURE: Medium

SOIL: Moderately fertile, well-drained
FEATURES: Flowers, foliage
USES: Ground cover, container
FLOWERS: ■ ■□

SITING: Periwinkle prefers partial to full shade and moderately fertile, well-drained soil with a pH of 5.5–7.0. Full sun may be tolerated in moist soil. Provide plants with shelter from strong, drying winds. Trailing stems with small, dark, evergreen leaves form an attractive ground cover. Blue flowers appear in spring and bloom lightly on and off all season long. Place at the feet of irrigated woody trees. Good companions to interplant in the ground cover for added texture and depth include fringed bleeding heart, 'Alba' bleeding heart, and 'Frances Williams' hosta.

CARE: Plant 12–24" apart in spring or fall. The closer the spacing, the faster the ground will be covered. Apply slow-release granular plant food in spring. Cease feeding 6–8 weeks prior to first frost date. If plants are competing with tree roots, water and feed regularly. Apply vegetative mulch in summer and winter. Water deeply when the soil is dry. Too much sun and dry soil conditions may result in yellowing or crispy brown leaves in summer.

PROPAGATION: Plants naturally layer in the landscape. Pin a branch to the ground so that nodes contact the soil. Node sites will produce roots if cultural conditions (moisture and soil) are met. Cover with mulch and check periodically for root growth; when roots have formed, snip the branch from the parent plant, leaving some green top growth to accompany the new root system. Gently remove the new plant; reset, water, and mulch. Divide in spring or autumn. Dig around the root clump and lift. Use a sharp spade to slice through the root system. Reset portions that contain healthy roots and top shoots. Discard any pieces that do not contain both healthy roots and top shoots. Water deeply and apply 3" of vegetative mulch around, but not touching, the plants.

PESTS AND DISEASES: Leaf spot is a common disease pest. Scale and leafhoppers are insect pests.

RELATED SPECIES: 'Alba Variegata' has white flowers and yellow-edged leaves; 'Argenteovariegata' bears pale blue flowers and creamy white-marked leaves; 'Atropurpurea' has burgundy flowers and deep green leaves; 'Bowles's Variety' bears large violet flowers and deep green leaves; 'Gertrude Jekyll' bears white flowers and deep green leaves; and 'Multiplex' has double burgundy flowers.

SWEET VIOLET

Viola odorata vye-OH-luh oh-duh-RAHT-uh

Sweet violet offers simple beauty to the spring and fall landscape.

ZONES: 5–8
SIZE: 4–8"h × 15"w
TYPE: Perennial
FORM: Upright
TEXTURE: Medium
GROWTH: Medium
LIGHT: Partial shade to full sun
MOISTURE: Medium

SOIL: Fertile, moist, well-drained
FEATURES: Flowers, foliage
USES: Border, woodland, container
FLOWERS: ■□

SITING: Sweet violet prefers light afternoon shade and fertile, moist, well-drained soil with a pH of 5.5–7.0. Plants tolerate full sun if the soil is consistently moist. Fragrant flowers in violet-blue and occasionally white appear in spring in cooler zones and in autumn, winter, and spring in southern zones. Bright green leaves are heart-shaped or rounded, toothed, and semievergreen. Flowers are excellent fresh cut or press dried. Good companions include bleeding heart, sweet woodruff, and Lenten rose.

CARE: Plant 8–12" apart in late spring. Apply slow-release granular plant food at time of planting. Apply vegetative mulch around, but not touching, the plants in

Press sweet violet and Johnny-jump-up blossoms in a book until dry. Place a marker in the page to find the flowers later.

summer and winter to protect roots from summer heat and winter cold. Maintain moist soil. Deadhead spent blooms to encourage reblooming. Leave flowers to fade on plant if self-seeding is desired. Prune back in fall once frost withers the foliage, or leave erect in warmer zones for winter viewing and occasional flowering.

PROPAGATION: Divide in spring or autumn. Dig around the root clump and lift. Use a sharp spade to slice through the root system. Reset portions that contain healthy roots and top shoots.

PESTS AND DISEASES: Diseases include botrytis, powdery mildew, downy mildew, rust, and root rot. Slugs and snails are occasional pests.

RELATED SPECIES: The cultivar 'Queen Charlotte' bears dark violet flowers; 'Royal Robe' has deep violet flowers; and 'White Czar' bears large white flowers lightly stained purple in the center. Johnny-jump-up (*V. tricolor*) is an old-fashioned plant with nostalgic charm. Plants are short lived and often grown as annuals. Flowers have royal purple petals above and lavender, white, and yellow petals below. Plants self-seed freely.

PANSY

Viola ×wittrockiana vye-OH-luh wit-rahk-ee-AY-nuh

Pansy flowers perform best in the cooler weather of spring and fall.

ZONES: 5–8
SIZE: 6–10"h × 6–12"w
TYPE: Perennial
FORM: Irregular
TEXTURE: Medium
GROWTH: Medium
LIGHT: Full sun to partial shade

MOISTURE: Medium
SOIL: Fertile, moist, well-drained
FEATURES: Flowers, foliage
USES: Border, bedding, container
FLOWERS: ■□■■ ■■

SITING: Pansy prefers full sun and fertile, well-drained, moist soil with a pH of 5.5–7.0. Plants are usually grown as cool-season annuals. Flowers are borne in a wide selection of colors, in solids or bicolors. Good companions include 'Purpureum' fennel, 'Tuscan Blue' rosemary, and lemon thyme.

CARE: Plant 6–12" apart in midspring or early autumn. Apply slow-release granular plant food at time of planting. Water deeply when the soil is dry. Deadhead spent blooms to encourage reblooming. When temperatures warm into the high 70s, replace with warm-season annuals.

PROPAGATION: Sprinkle seeds over the growing medium and cover lightly. Thoroughly moisten and keep moist, not soggy, until seeds germinate. Germination occurs in 7–14 days at 65–75°F. Transplant 15–25 days after sowing. After transplanting, reduce temperature to 55°F.

PESTS AND DISEASES: Diseases include powdery mildew, downy mildew, botrytis, rust, and root rot. Slugs and snails are occasional pests.

1 **Replace heat-loving annuals in a container planting with pansies in the fall.**

2 **Add fresh Miracle-Gro planting mix to the container.**

3 **The finished planting will brighten autumn days.**

ADAM'S NEEDLE

Yucca filamentosa *YUK-uh fil-uh-men-TOH-suh*

Adam's needle, also known as yucca, is spectacular in bloom.

ZONES: 5–10
SIZE: 3–6'h × 5'w
TYPE: Perennial
FORM: Rounded
TEXTURE: Coarse
GROWTH: Slow
LIGHT: Full sun
MOISTURE: Medium to low

SOIL: Moderately fertile, well-drained
FEATURES: Flowers, foliage
USES: Border, container
FLOWERS: □

SITING: Adam's needle prefers full sun and moderately fertile, well-drained soil with a pH of 5.5–7.3. Plants tolerate heat, humidity, and drought once established. Panicles of nodding creamy-white flowers up to 6' tall appear in mid- to late summer. Evergreen leaves are in stiff rosettes. Place in groups in the center of the sunny perennial border. Plants dislike root disturbance. Good companions include 'Bicolor' Cupid's dart, 'Sky Racer' purple moor grass, and 'Icicle' spike speedwell.

CARE: Plant 3–4' apart in spring or autumn. Apply slow-release granular plant food in

Cut back the faded flower stalk of Adam's needle after it has finished blooming.

spring. Apply 3" of vegetative mulch in summer and winter to reduce weed seed germination, hold moisture in the soil, and add organic matter to the soil as it decomposes. Give transplants ample water; otherwise, water only when the soil is dry 2–3" below the surface. Deadhead spent blooms to encourage reblooming.

PROPAGATION: In spring remove offsets from the base of the parent plant and reset; then water and mulch.

PESTS AND DISEASES: Plants are relatively pest free when cultural requirements (sun, soil, planting depth, moisture) are met. Scale insects may be occasional pests.

RELATED SPECIES: 'Bright Edge' has gold-rimmed leaves; 'Bright Eye' leaves have bright yellow margins; 'Rosenglocken' bears pink-stained flowers; 'Schneetanne' has yellow-stained white flowers; and 'Variegata' leaves have white margins that turn pink.

BEDDING ZINNIA

Zinnia elegans *ZIN-ee-uh EL-eh-gehnz*

Bedding zinnia cultivars offer many bright colors to choose from.

ZONES: NA
SIZE: 12–36"h × 12"w
TYPE: Annual
FORM: Upright
TEXTURE: Medium
GROWTH: Medium
LIGHT: Full sun
MOISTURE: Medium

SOIL: Fertile, well-drained
FEATURES: Flowers, foliage
USES: Border, bedding, container
FLOWERS: □ ■ ■ ■ ■ ■

SITING: Bedding zinnia prefers full sun and fertile, well-drained soil with a pH of 5.5–7.0. Good air circulation is essential. The species has daisylike purple flowers; cultivars come in shades of orange, yellow, red, pink, and white in summer. Locate plants in the middle or back of the border because the foliage may become disfigured by disease in summer. Flowers are ideal for cutting. Good garden companions include 'Moonbeam' threadleaf coreopsis, chartreuse-leaved cultivars of sweet potato, and 'Purpureum' purple fountain grass.

Narrow-leaf zinnia is a marvelous annual ground cover for full sun.

CARE: Plant 8–12" apart in late spring in well-drained soil. Spacing should promote good air circulation to reduce powdery mildew. Apply slow-release granular plant food at time of planting. Apply 3" of vegetative mulch in summer. Water deeply when the soil is dry. Deadhead spent blooms to encourage reblooming. Remove diseased foliage from plants rather than allowing leaves to fall to the ground. Remove plants after the first fall freeze.

PROPAGATION: Sprinkle seeds over the growing medium and cover. Keep moist, not soggy, until seeds germinate in 4–7 days at 70°F. Transplant 10–15 days after sowing. After transplanting, reduce temperature to 65°F. Zinnias may also be sown directly in place in the garden after frost damage has passed and soil is warm.

PESTS AND DISEASES: Diseases include powdery mildew, bacterial wilt, Southern blight, stem rot, and bacterial and fungal spot.

RELATED SPECIES: Narrowleaf zinnia (*Z. angustifolia* 'Orange Star') reaches 10" tall and is a superb annual ground cover. Tangerine flowers appear in summer. Plants are mildew resistant.

INDEX

*Note: Page references in bold type refer to Encyclopedia entries. Page references in italic type refer to additional photographs, illustrations, and information in captions. Plants are listed under their common names.

RESOURCES FOR PLANTS & SEEDS

PERENNIAL PLANTS

Bluestone Perennials, Inc.
7211 Middle Ridge Rd.
Madison, OH 44057-3096
800/852-5243
www.bluestoneperennials.com
Mail-order and Internet source of
perennials and shrubs

High Country Gardens
2902 Rufina St.
Santa Fe, NM 87505
800/925-9387
www.highcountrygardens.com
Mail-order and Internet source
specializing in drought-tolerant plants

Jackson & Perkins
1 Rose Ln.
Medford, OR 97501
800/292-4769
www.jacksonandperkins.com
Mail-order and Internet source of
perennials, roses, and Dutch bulbs

Joy Creek Nursery
20300 NW Watson Rd.
Scappoose, OR 97056
503/543-7474
www.joycreek.com
Mail-order and Internet source for
perennials of all kinds

Klehm's Song Sparrow Perennial Farm
13101 E. Rye Rd.
Avalon, WI 53505
800/553-3715
www.songsparrow.com
Mail-order and Internet source of
peonies, hemerocallis, hosta, and
newer perennials

Paradise Garden
474 Clotts Rd.
Columbus, OH 43230
614/893-0896
www.paradisegarden.com
Mail-order source of new and hard-to-
find daylilies, hostas, irises, peonies,
roses, grasses, perennials, and herbs

Perennial Pleasures Nursery
P.O. Box 147
63 Brickhouse Rd.
East Hardwick, VT 05836
802/472-3737
www.perennialpleasures.net
Mail-order and Internet source for old-
fashioned and heirloom perennials

Proven Winners
www.provenwinners.com
International marketing cooperative
dedicated to developing new hybrid
plants for the Proven Winner brand

Van Bourgondien
245 Route 109
P.O. Box 1000-MGA
Babylon, NY 11702-9004
800/622-9997
www.dutchbulbs.com
Mail-order and Internet source of more
than 1,000 varieties of perennials and
bulbs

Wayside Gardens
1 Garden Ln.
Hodges, SC 29695-0001
800/845-1124
www.waysidegardens.com
Mail-order and Internet source of
perennials, bulbs, shrubs, trees, and
gardening aids

White Flower Farm
P.O. Box 50
Litchfield, CT 06759-0050
800/503-9624
www.whiteflowerfarm.com
Mail-order and Internet source of
perennials, annuals, bulbs, and seeds

SEEDS

Ed Hume Seeds
P.O. Box 73160
Puyallup, WA 98373
Mail-order and Internet source of
flower and herb seeds for cool,
short-season climates

McKenzie Seed Co.
30 Ninth St.
Brandon, MB Canada R7A 6E1
204/571-7500
Mail-order and Internet source of
flower and vegetable seeds and
perennial plants; orders shipped only
to Canadian destinations

Park Seed
1 Parkton Ave.
Greenwood, SC 29647
800/213-0076
www.parkseed.com
Mail-order and Internet source of
flower seeds and plants, growing
supplies and equipment

Seeds of Change
P.O. Box 15700
Santa Fe, NM 87506
888/762-7333
www.seedsofchange.com
Mail-order and Internet source of
certified organic seeds, bulbs, and
plants

Select Seeds Company
180 Stickney Hill Rd.
Union, CT 06076-4617
860/684-9310
www.selectseeds.com
Mail-order and Internet source of
flower seeds and plants, specializing in
heirloom flowers

Stokes Seeds
P.O. Box 548
Buffalo, NY 14240-0548
800/396-9238
www.stokeseeds.com
Mail-order and Internet source of more
than 2,500 varieties of seeds for
flowers, herbs, and vegetables, and for
garden accessories

Thompson & Morgan Seedsmen, Inc.
P.O. Box 1308
Jackson, NJ 08527-0308
800/274-7333
www.thompson-morgan.com
Mail-order and Internet source of
flower and vegetable seeds,
specializing in rare and unusual seeds

Miracle-Gro® www.miracle-gro.com

For more information on how to garden successfuly, go to www.miracle-gro.com where you'll find:

- **Miracle-Gro Garden Helpline: 800/645-8166**
- **Email Reminder Service:** Free gardening tips and reminders sent to you via email.
- **Miracle-Gro Product Consumer Guide:** The latest information on all Miracle-Gro products, including plant foods, soil mixes, plants, and exciting new product lines from Miracle-Gro.
- **Garden Problem Solver:** Link into a comprehensive library of diagnostic tools and solutions for insect, disease, and weed problems.
- **Streaming How-to Videos:** Click into a library of more tham 50 quick gardening and lawn care video clips.

USDA PLANT HARDINESS ZONE MAP

This map of climate zones helps you select plants for your garden that will survive a typical winter in your region. The United States Department of Agriculture (USDA) developed the map, basing the zones on the lowest recorded temperatures across North America. Zone 1 is the coldest area and Zone 11 is the warmest area.

Plants are classified by the coldest temperature and zone they can endure. For example, plants hardy to Zone 6 survive where winter temperatures drop to –10°F. Those hardy to Zone 8 die long before it's that cold. These plants may grow in colder regions but must be replaced each year. Plants rated for a range of hardiness zones can usually survive winter in the coldest region as well as tolerate the summer heat of the warmest one.

To find your hardiness zone, note the approximate location of your community on the map, then match the color band marking that area to the key.

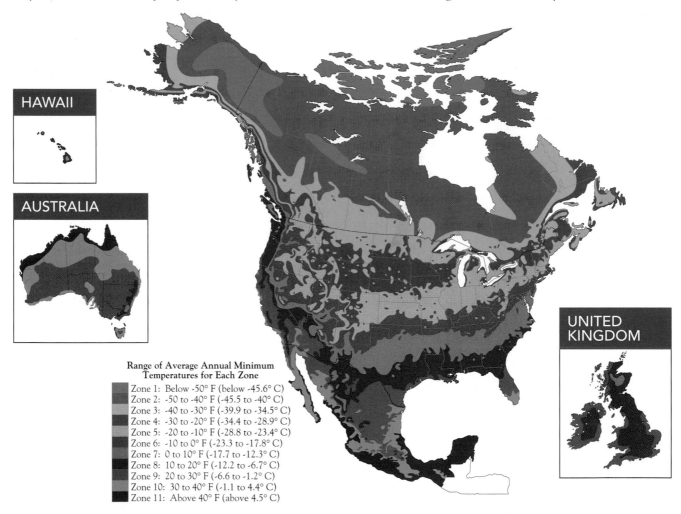

HAWAII

AUSTRALIA

UNITED KINGDOM

Range of Average Annual Minimum Temperatures for Each Zone

Zone 1: Below -50° F (below -45.6° C)
Zone 2: -50 to -40° F (-45.5 to -40° C)
Zone 3: -40 to -30° F (-39.9 to -34.5° C)
Zone 4: -30 to -20° F (-34.4 to -28.9° C)
Zone 5: -20 to -10° F (-28.8 to -23.4° C)
Zone 6: -10 to 0° F (-23.3 to -17.8° C)
Zone 7: 0 to 10° F (-17.7 to -12.3° C)
Zone 8: 10 to 20° F (-12.2 to -6.7° C)
Zone 9: 20 to 30° F (-6.6 to -1.2° C)
Zone 10: 30 to 40° F (-1.1 to 4.4° C)
Zone 11: Above 40° F (above 4.5° C)

METRIC CONVERSIONS

U.S. Units to Metric Equivalents			Metric Units to U.S. Equivalents		
To Convert From	Multiply By	To Get	To Convert From	Multiply By	To Get
Inches	25.4	Millimeters	Millimeters	0.0394	Inches
Inches	2.54	Centimeters	Centimeters	0.3937	Inches
Feet	30.48	Centimeters	Centimeters	0.0328	Feet
Feet	0.3048	Meters	Meters	3.2808	Feet
Yards	0.9144	Meters	Meters	1.0936	Yards

To convert from degrees Fahrenheit (F) to degrees Celsius (C), first subtract 32, then multiply by 5/9.

To convert from degrees Celsius to degrees Fahrenheit, multiply by 9/5, then add 32.